Closure

CLOSURE

*The Rush to End Grief
and What It Costs Us*

Nancy Berns

TEMPLE UNIVERSITY PRESS   PHILADELPHIA

TEMPLE UNIVERSITY PRESS
Philadelphia, Pennsylvania 19122
www.temple.edu/tempress

Library of Congress Cataloging-in-Publication Data

Berns, Nancy.
    Closure : the rush to end grief and what it costs us / Nancy Berns.
      p. cm.
    Includes bibliographical references and index.
    ISBN 978-1-4399-0576-0 (hardback)
    ISBN 978-1-4399-0577-7 (paperback)
    ISBN 978-1-4399-0578-4 (e-book)
    1. Loss (Psychology)   2. Grief.   3. Bereavement.   I. Title.
    BF575.D35B47 2011
    155.9'3—dc22

                                                        2011002611

Printed in the United States of America

2 4 6 8 9 7 5 3

For David and our beautiful children,
Zachariah, Lydia, and Chloe

Contents

Preface

My Own Tangled Story

I am not just a casual observer of closure, grief, or hope. To help you understand the lens through which I did this research, a glimpse at my own story is necessary. In 2001, our son was stillborn. Our world crashed around us and we were left picking up the pieces. During this traumatic time, many people reached out to us and offered kind words. I am deeply grateful for their support, especially those who continue to listen to me talk about my grief over ten years later.

There were other experiences, though, that left me lonely and disconnected from others. The most hurtful words said to me after our son died were: "Someday this will just be a memory." That was what I most feared. I wanted my child, not a memory. As time went on, I had more people either encouraging me to move on from grief or assuming I had already done so. The circle of people to whom I could talk about my grief grew smaller. Although I was not seeking an end to my grief, I felt the pressure from others to "move on." I did not think that people meant anything bad by assuming that it was time to move on from my grief. That is just what they thought was expected and what was best for me.

I had an academic interest in grief and closure before our son's death, but this experience gave me a personal reason for exploring narratives of grief, including the popular notion of closure. I am not personally seeking closure, but rather choose other language and perspectives for living with my grief. However, in doing this research and reading people's various understandings of closure, I can see why some think they need to find it.

I do not hate the word "closure," as some do. But I have a sense why others are angry when those around them tell them they need closure. They do not want a death or a separation to be the end of the story. They want love to continue. I get that. For me, I seek a way to still be a mother to my son who died. Many people want to know how to redefine relationships after their loved ones die. How does this fit in with talk about closure?

This book will expose the tangled web of closure talk. However, it is not just a personal story that unfolds. As a sociologist, I shed light on how closure has become a new emotion that people are seeking even when it is not at all clear what closure means or even if it exists. Closure has emerged as a new way of talking about grief and loss, which has led to new expectations for those who are grieving. Talk about closure has intensified with debates about whether the death of Osama bin Laden provided any closure to the attacks of September 11, 2001.

I wrote this book for many reasons. I empathize with people who are hurting and are seeking relief from their pain. I am wary of businesses and politicians who commonly, if not casually, promise closure as they sell products and agendas. And, importantly, I appreciate the power of hope, and fear the exploitation of that hope by people trying to make a profit or advance a political agenda. Also, I want to let people know that there are many ways to grieve and that healing does not necessarily require closure.

Words we choose to describe concepts are important. Semantics—the study of meaning and language—does matter. I want to help others recognize the costs and consequences that accompany the words we use to describe grief, justice, healing, and hope.

I do not intend to take away people's hope for healing by questioning the concept of closure. Instead, I hope to offer valuable insights into the tangled web of closure that might help us along our journeys of grief and loss when bad things happen.

Acknowledgments

Many years ago at a conference on restorative justice, I sat at a table with two mothers whose teenage daughters had been murdered by the girls' ex-boyfriends. Their stories provided a window to intense pain and heartache. I could see in their faces and hear in their words how much pain remained but also how much healing and hope survived. I was struck by how different their grieving journeys were even though they shared a similar tragedy. Hearing their stories planted a seed that grew into this book. I continue to be inspired by many people—strangers and friends—who are living with grief.

It is difficult to make progress on a book without people traveling beside you asking questions and providing critical insights. I thank those who read a draft of this book and gave valuable feedback, including Joel Best, Jennifer Dunn, Kathe Lowney, David Schweingruber, Don Schweingruber, Cat Siebel, and Amanda Sparkman. I am grateful that you believed enough in this project to give so much of your time. Thank you for your questions, critique, encouragement, witty remarks, and personal anecdotes. I enjoyed sharing this process with you.

I am also grateful to those who read earlier chapters or whose conversations helped spark an idea or build enthusiasm for the project, including Jennifer Eaton Bertagnolli, John Burney, Renee Cramer, Fred Haan, Elizabeth Jenner, David Maxwell, Jennifer McCrickerd, Brian Monahan, Kristin Niehof, Andrew Oftedal, Michael Radelet, Joseph Schneider, Stefan Timmermans, Fred Van Liew, and Dan West. A special thank you to Brooks

Douglass for taking the time to share with me more of his story, which is featured in chapter 7.

Another person who encouraged me and asked wonderful questions about my research on closure was Frank Schweingruber. Uncle Frank died before he could read the finished manuscript. Still, I can picture his inquisitive reactions and hear his enthusiasm.

While researching and writing this book, I have had the pleasure of teaching at Drake University. Thank you to my insightful and curious students who have frequently provided inspiration to develop these ideas. Specifically, I enjoyed working with three wonderful undergraduate research assistants. Thank you to Sarah Twinem Roeder, Gina Schlesselman, and Stephanie Garinger Woodson for conducting research that contributed to the material in this book. Thank you to the Humanities Center at Drake University for providing a research grant that gave me time to write. I also benefited greatly from the participation of those who came to my research talk for the Humanities Colloquium Series.

I thank Brian Donovan and Bill Staples for supporting my research on closure and the death penalty that resulted in a 2009 article in *The Sociological Quarterly* under their editorship ("Contesting the Victim Card: Closure Discourse and Emotion in Death Penalty Rhetoric").

I thank my editor at Temple University Press, Mick Gusinde-Duffy, for believing in this project and expressing enthusiasm for the book from the beginning of our first conversation in San Francisco. I appreciate your help in making this book happen and hope it has been a positive part of your own journey. Thank you also to Gary Kramer, Charles Ault, Ann-Marie Anderson, Irene Imperio Kull, and others at Temple University Press for the work involved in getting this book into print and to its readers. Thank you to Rebecca Logan and others at Newgen for managing the production process and to Fran Andersen for her caring work as copyeditor.

My journey in academia has been greatly enriched by the mentoring and friendship of Joel Best. His research and guidance have provided a significant influence on my own work. Thank you, Joel, for your enduring interest in this project. Although my research may not be on the "sunny side of the street," you certainly are.

On any life's journey, there are bumps along the way. Mine is no exception. Many people have provided support and encouragement in my life, which nurtured my ability to develop and finish this book. In particular, I thank Teresa Postma, Ron Stubbs Jr., and Tom and Deb Niehof for their willingness to enter some difficult emotional trenches with me. Teresa, I appreciate your support whether through words of encouragement, hope, or sarcasm. Like it or not, you are stuck with me as a friend. Ron, you wonderfully model the balm of listening and the power of compassion. Thank you for the solace, calm, and wisdom you bring to my life. Tom and Deb, you continue to remain on the front lines of my life sharing your love, support, and wise counsel. A debt of my gratitude belongs to you both.

Many others have provided support in important ways through the years that span the writing of this book. Thank you to the loving people at Trinity Christian Reformed Church in Ames, Iowa, for surrounding our family with kindness and prayer. To my sister Kathy, I wish I could have sat on your porch more often to write. Thank you for your continued support. I am also grateful to my parents, David and Sharon Berns, and my parents-in-law, Don and Nancy Schweingruber, for their unconditional enthusiasm for our family and research. I thank my sweet father-in-law, Don, for many conversations about illness, grief, and death that helped provide insights into these difficult worlds.

It is one thing to help an author during various phases of a book. It is quite another to have to live with one and learn how to support her in not just writing a book but every other aspect of life. I am fortunate that I have a loving family who do just that. To them, I owe my biggest thank you. This book would not have been possible without the unwavering support of my husband, David Schweingruber, who read numerous versions of the book and provided enthusiasm for my research all along the way. David, thank you for giving of your own time and energy to help me through all stages of this book and of life. I also thank my two amazing daughters, Lydia Grace and Chloe Joy, for their endearing encouragement for my writing and most of all for the love, laughter, joy, and beauty they bring into our lives. Lydia and Chloe, I want you to always know that being your mom is the most amazing opportunity I could ever have. For these reasons and more, I dedicate this book to David, Lydia, and Chloe. Finally, I offer this book as a loving tribute in memory of our son, Zachariah.

1. Seeking Closure

"Let me start with my tattoo, it's of two flowers on my back," said an anonymous woman as she explained the aftermath of a bad relationship. "The tattoo helped to give me closure on the emotional strain I had experienced."[1]

Another woman, whose husband had cheated on her, found closure to his affair only after he agreed to shave his head. Her psychiatrist recalled that his client was fortunate that her husband was willing to go through with this "closure ritual." As the psychiatrist stated, "In therapy we often suggest a small ritual to bring closure, such as writing letters to those they have an issue with and burying or burning them."[2]

Getting tattoos and shaving heads are not the only rituals suggested for closure after bad relationships. "Six Feet Isn't Deep Enough!" reads the plaque on an official Wedding Ring Coffin. Jill Testa, creator of the coffin, encourages people to "give a dead marriage its proper, final resting place. The Wedding Ring Coffin is the perfect gift for yourself or a loved one for bringing closure after a divorce. It's time to bury the past and move on to a new tomorrow."[3]

People in the death care business—whether for humans or for pets—also talk about closure.

Melissa Tomlinson works on dead people's hair for a living. She has been dressing the dead for over twelve years, time enough to change her perspective on death. "When I was younger, I thought of it as sort of morbid or scary. Now I look at it with a lot more compassion. I see the families, and I just try to give them a little closure. When the deceased appears peaceful and healthy, the family receives some closure."[4]

"Welcome to At Peace Pet Memorials," reads a website selling pet urns. "I don't know how to truly emphasize how important closure is. When my companion of 10 years 'Mr. Sibbs' passed away, I was not there. I paid a disposal fee and never saw him again. . . . I still to this day have nightmares that I left him somewhere and now I can't find him."[5]

How can one compare closure for affairs, divorce, death, and pet grief? And can tattoos, shaved heads, Wedding Ring Coffins, peaceful-looking deceased loved ones, and pet memorials all really bring closure? People ranging from psychiatrists, tattoo artists, and entrepreneurs to pet grief experts and death workers speak of closure as if everyone knows what it means. Yet it seems to have many different, if not contradictory, meanings.

From bad relationships to terrorist attacks, the concept of closure enters the cultural debate about how to respond when traumatic things happen. Schoolchildren are told to find closure after a shooting. A nation seeks closure after 9/11. Mourners search for closure after a funeral, and family members want it following a homicide. Families of missing persons search for closure, as do Katrina survivors and other victims of natural disasters. People are told to find closure after their pets die. Closure is also sought after divorces, bad dates, abortions, adoptions, and abusive experiences.

But what is closure? There is no agreed-upon answer. Closure has been described as justice, peace, healing, acceptance, forgiveness, moving on, resolution, answered questions, or revenge. And *how* are you supposed to find this closure? People try to find closure by planting trees, acquiring memorial tattoos, forgiving murderers, watching killers die, talking to offenders, writing letters, burning letters, burning wedding dresses, burying wedding rings, casting spells, taking trips to Hawaii, buying expensive pet urns, committing suicide, talking to dead people, reviewing autopsies, and planning funerals. And this is just a partial list.

Although there are numerous definitions and interpretations of closure that I will attempt to untangle in this book, closure usually relates to some type of ending. Closure typically implies that something is finished, ended, closed. Finally you can move on. Yet this dominant use of closure receives plenty of criticism. Although some who are grieving seek closure and others report finding it, a significant number of voices cry foul; they argue that closure does not exist and that it only promises false hope. Still, advice for finding closure thrives. Journalists, politicians, businesspeople, and other professionals use closure as a central theme in writing, politics, and sales. People offer others hope through the promise of closure, but can it be found?

It is exploited for political gain. It is sold for financial gain. It is used to counsel those who hurt, to help them through their grief. But is that what they need or even want?

This book explores how and why the idea of closure jumped from a relatively unknown research term to a new emotional state that people are seeking or telling others to find. I uncover the varied interpretations of closure and demonstrate how it became a political tool and a commodity used to sell products and services.

Closure has become a new emotion for explaining what we need after trauma and loss and how we should respond. When I argue that closure is a new emotion, I am not claiming that people are experiencing some feelings that were never felt before, such as the experience of grief lessening. I am arguing that there is a new way of thinking about and talking about emotions.[6]

Although humans' physiological emotional responses may be limited, the way we label emotional states and try to achieve (or not achieve) them changes. For instance, consider "self-esteem." Although people may have always had some level of regard for themselves, the idea of "self-esteem" is recent (and quite different from "pride," which was long considered sinful). Self-esteem became a goal for people to achieve for themselves and for others, especially children. It resulted in products, experts, curricula, and policy decisions. The creation of self-esteem had significant consequences.

Similarly, people have felt grief and may have wished that it would end, but "closure" is a new term and new way of thinking and acting on this grief. Our grandparents did not seek closure after the death of a loved one. Closure is a state that people want to bring about in themselves and in others. And, like "self-esteem," it has resulted in new products, rituals, experts, strategies, and ways of seeing the world. This is especially true in the funeral industry. Historically, funeral rituals had many purposes: comforting the grieving, caring for the body, preparing the departed for the next life, building solidarity among the survivors, sharing religious messages, and so on. The importance of these purposes varied culturally and historically. However, for the past two decades, funeral directors have emphasized the "need for closure" as a major purpose of funeral rituals. Although closure has become a form of common knowledge, there has been little critical insight into its consequences. Funeral homes would have you believe that closure will result from the products and services they provide, but there is no clear evidence that this is true.

To help explain the rise of closure and its impact on our social world, I build on research in the sociology of emotions and social constructionist studies of social problems. From the sociology of emotions, I borrow the understanding that society provides *feeling rules* and people are expected to change their emotions to fit these rules. Feeling rules are informal guidelines that tell us how we should react to certain situations.[7] Societies and institutions have different feeling rules, and these rules change, with consequences for the people who are expected to meet them. Furthermore, when one set of feeling rules becomes dominant in a culture, it makes it difficult for us to imagine other ways of handling a situation. Closure represents a new set of feeling rules and expectations for people.

From the social constructionist study of social problems, I use the idea that the way we name and describe experiences has consequences.[8] "Closure" is not some naturally occurring emotion that we can simply "find" with the right advice. Rather, closure is a made-up concept: a frame used to explain how we should respond to loss. The term "frame" has been adopted from the sociologist Erving Goffman to describe how people identify, interpret, understand, and label their experiences and to explain social problems.[9] We make something like closure "real" through social interactions. Any understanding we have of closure comes from how people have defined it through stories, arguments, court cases, and so on. This does not mean that the pain from loss is just imaginary, but how we interpret and respond to the loss is shaped by our social world, such as popular culture, life history, social norms, friends, and family.

Often, when a concept like closure becomes so popular in our culture, people assume it must exist. We do not examine how it emerged as a belief or what alternative views might be better in understanding our world. Using a sociological lens, this book will show how the meanings of closure have been constructed through social processes and how that affects us. Describing a set of emotional experiences as "closure" and creating a number of cultural narratives about it have implications for the way people experience grief, tell others how to grieve, sell and buy products, and make political arguments. Because the meaning of closure is shaped by the social context, we have a variety of contradictory interpretations of how to get closure. And these dominant arguments about loss marginalize alternative ways of thinking about grief.

In order to understand the history of the term "closure" as well as contemporary interpretations of it, I examined a wide range of documents, including newspaper and popular magazine articles, websites, research journal articles, court cases, autobiographies, and other books.[10] Since closure is used to talk about so many issues, my research covers topics from pet grief to terrorist attacks and people ranging from psychics to forensic pathologists. Throughout this book, some examples I share are funny and others are heartbreaking.

The Rise of Closure

Beginning in the 1990s, the concept of closure became more prevalent in popular media. On November 9, 1995, an episode of *Friends* featured Rachel on a date complaining about not getting over Ross. Her date tells her, "Look, I've been through a divorce; trust me, you're gonna be fine. You just can't see it now because you haven't had any closure." Rachel replies, "Yeah! Closure." She finds a cell phone and, drunk, leaves a slurred message on Ross's answering machine, including the line "I am over you. And that, my friend, is what they call closure." In 1997, Dr. Frasier Crane, the main character of the sitcom *Frasier*, also searched for closure after getting dumped. *Law & Order: Special Victims Unit* aired an episode called "Closure" in 2000, in which Detective Olivia Benson tells a rape victim that closure does not exist. Other television shows and movies featured closure in the cases of missing people, death of loved ones, recovery of dead bodies, revenge after a rape, and preparation for the end of the world.

Closure talk goes beyond sitcoms and crime shows. Tangled understandings of closure began showing up prominently in journalistic accounts of national tragedies in the 1990s. Contradictory claims about closure are interwoven in the painful stories surrounding these tragic cases.

On April 19, 1995, at 9:02 a.m., Timothy McVeigh bombed the Alfred P. Murrah Federal Building in Oklahoma City, killing 168 people and injuring more than 800—at that time the deadliest terrorist act on American soil. Nineteen of the victims were children from the day care center in the building. People who followed the media coverage of the tragedy may remember the poignant photograph of the firefighter holding a dying infant, bloodied and limp. Closure emerged as a political buzzword during McVeigh's trial and pending execution. For instance, in a discussion about moving the trial venue, Patti Hall, a survivor of the bombing, protested moving the trial out of Oklahoma, saying, "This was done to Oklahoma people and we should . . . be able to attend the trial and be there for closure."[11]

Four years and one day after the Oklahoma City bombing, on April 20, 1999, people watched in disbelief as Eric Harris and Dylan Klebold carried out what is now commonly known as the Columbine High School massacre at Columbine High School near Littleton, Colorado. They killed twelve students and one teacher before committing suicide. Four months later, Columbine High School reopened. Jennifer, a seventeen-year-old junior, said at the time, "Most people have already had some kind of closure at the school. We went back a couple of times for renovation, registration, to paint tiles. Now, we're just ready to move on."[12] Some of the parents of slain children disagreed. In December 1999, Brian Rohrbough, father of Daniel, one of the first students killed, told a reporter that "to say that we want to move on and put this behind us, that's not true." As the reporter interviewing Brian stated in his article, "For some of the families of the dead children of Columbine, the very idea of 'closure' is an insult and a hoax. There can never be closure for them."[13]

In the spring of 2001, attention shifted back to Oklahoma as Timothy McVeigh's case became a rallying cry for death penalty advocates and a high-profile forum for the discussion of whether families of victims should be allowed to view an execution. Closure was a central theme in media coverage of the case and a powerful rhetorical tool for politicians, prosecutors, and advocates pushing for the death penalty. Entertainment Network, Inc., an Internet company in Florida, unsuccessfully claimed that McVeigh's execution needed to be broadcast on the web in order to give the country closure.[14] Attorney General John Ashcroft used the closure argument in his decision to allow closed-circuit television of McVeigh's execution for the victims and their families. Ashcroft said that he hoped his closed-circuit television show would help Oklahoma City's bereaved "meet their need to close this chapter in their lives."[15]

Although more than 1,000 people were given the opportunity to view McVeigh's execution in June 2001, fewer than 300 did.[16] The day after McVeigh's execution, the front page of the *Hartford Courant* featured the following quotation from a family member: "It Still Hurts."[17] One family member told a reporter, "The only 'closure' I'm ever going to have is when they close the lid on my coffin."[18] Others were holding out hope. A brother of a victim said, "I expected more closure or relief. It really didn't provide as much as I thought it would but time will tell."[19]

The 9/11 terrorist attacks came only four months after McVeigh's execution. Within a few years of this tragedy, we heard claims that some people were achieving closure on 9/11.[20] However, others argued that there was no closure. On the sixth anniversary of the attacks, the *New York Times* published an article highlighting criticisms of former mayor Rudolph Giuliani's response to the people killed in the attacks. Sabrina Riversa, who was mourning a friend and firefighter killed on 9/11, blamed Giuliani for her lack of closure: "Because of Giuliani we never had closure. We never had closure because as soon as 9/11 happened he had all the remains shipped to Staten Island, in the dump, in the landfill. And we never had closure because of him."[21] Earlier that year, a firefighters' union also protested Giuliani's treatment of the missing bodies, saying that his "scoop-and-dump operation" to remove debris from Ground Zero did not protect the human remains.

"Mayor Giuliani's actions meant that fire fighters and citizens who perished would either remain buried at Ground Zero forever, with no closure for families, or be removed like garbage and deposited at the Fresh Kills Landfill."[22]

After the death of Osama bin Laden on May 1, 2011, people immediately debated whether we could finally have closure on the 9/11 attacks. Throughout the nation, headlines declared that his death did indeed mean closure: "Bin Laden's Death Brings Closure to Many," or "Families Find Closure in Bin Laden's Death." Strikingly, other headlines proclaimed the opposite—there is no closure: "Bin Laden's Death Does Not Bring Closure," or "For 9/11 Families, No Such Thing as Closure." Some argued that closure was possible after bin Laden's death because there was justice, the end of a chapter, or relief after a decade-long hunt for him. However, many people wanted others to know that closure incorrectly implies that the pain and grief has ended. In other cases, individuals claimed there is no closure because the war against terror will continue or because they were not able to see pictures of bin Laden's dead body. It was clear in reading the commentary on Osama bin Laden's death that even though people did not agree as to whether his death provided closure, most stories assumed closure was real and something people needed.

Unfortunately, 9/11 was not our last tragedy. Hurricane Katrina. A shooting at an Amish school in Pennsylvania. A shooting at Virginia Tech. Another killer at Northern Illinois University. Devastating tornadoes. The list goes on. In today's world, a tragedy does not happen without someone suggesting how people can find closure. Contradictory claims about closure are interwoven in the pain and grief surrounding these stories.

Obviously, we had national and personal tragedies in our world before the 1990s. However, no one called for closure after the Holocaust. Media coverage of John F. Kennedy's assassination did not focus on closure for the nation. (However, closure is discussed in *contemporary* media coverage of past tragedies such as the Holocaust and Kennedy's assassination.) Why, in today's world, do so many expect closure? And is it needed? Or possible? And from where did closure emerge?

Closure did not just spring up in journalism or television shows. We need to follow several threads in our culture to understand the rise of closure: research studies, political movements, court cases, shifts in popular culture, and the funeral industry's need to broaden its services. We turn first to various research studies that have focused on closure.

One of the earliest uses of the term "closure" was in Gestalt psychology. In 1923, Gestalt pioneer Max Wertheimer used the concept of closure to explain how our brains group objects together as a whole rather than as individual parts. A mind fills in missing information to complete an image. Another use of closure in Gestalt psychology argues that people have better memory of events or tasks that are unfinished or not closed.[23] Contemporary psychologists tend to view closure as a psychological concept that can be measured and correlated with its causes and effects. In the early 1990s, researchers in social psychology developed a scale that is supposed to measure one's "need for closure." According to this research, those who have a high need for closure prefer order, predictability, security, and decisiveness and are uncomfortable with ambiguity.[24] A decade later, in psychological studies about coping strategies following the September 11, 2001, attacks, closure is defined as the ability to put a trauma behind you and reach an even keel.[25]

Even within the discipline of psychology, we can see that closure has been defined differently over time. There is no natural or constant definition of the term. The concept shifts in meaning depending on the particular researcher studying it. We can see through a social constructionist lens that these processes introduce varied interpretations of closure.

Beyond psychological studies, there have been disparate uses of closure in disciplines such as sociology, philosophy, mathematics, and computer science.[26] However, there is no one definition of closure, and popular use of the term is quite different from the way it is used in scholarly studies. Closure went from a little-known research term to a popular concept in mass media.

Why did closure take off in our popular culture during the 1990s in spite of not being well defined or understood? To answer that question, we look to what happened culturally and politically in the previous three decades, which set the stage for closure's popularity. Victims' social movements; a rise in therapeutic language and goals; court decisions; and our cultural expectation for happy, inspiring, and quick resolutions have all contributed to the popularity of closure. We turn next to the world of crime victims and their advocates.

The crime victims' rights movement was part of the broader "victim movements" in the 1960s and 1970s that helped change the way we think about victimization and gave new language to frame personal problems.[27] Other movements central to this time and related to crime victims include feminism, civil rights, restorative justice, and law-and-order conservatism. These movements brought the role of victim front and center in U.S. culture and were instrumental in setting up scenarios and creating language that ushered in the political use of closure.

The crime victims' rights movement grew out of a mix of liberal and conservative ideologies in the 1960s and 1970s and led to more resources and rights for victims, including increased participation in the justice system.

Hundreds of organizations emerged out of the larger crime victims' rights movement. Groups such as Murder Victims' Families for Reconciliation (founded in 1976), Parents of Murdered Children (founded in 1978), and Mothers Against Drunk Driving (founded in 1980) significantly changed how we think about crime victims and their role in the criminal justice system. These groups vary in their focus and ideology. For example, Parents of Murdered Children advocates the death penalty, while Murder Victims' Families for Reconciliation opposes the death penalty. However, they all played an essential role in expanding the scope of victims to include family and friends of the direct crime victim. Perhaps most significantly in the case of homicide, families of the direct crime victim are now routinely seen as victims or co-victims. In 1982, Congress passed the Victim and Witness Protection Act, which included, among other things, victim restitution and the use of victim impact statements at sentencing in federal cases. Also in 1982, President Ronald Reagan created the President's Task Force on Victims of Crime to examine and recommend improvements in how the victims of crime are treated.

Over time, many advocates in these various movements adopted the concept of closure to help explain why victims needed particular resources or rights. Exactly *what* victims needed was debated. Some groups argued that closure would come through more punitive criminal justice policies, while other groups said closure would come through practices that emphasized healing. We see this exchange of closure politics most clearly in the death penalty debate, which is discussed in chapter 7.

But why closure? After all, "victims' rights" does not automatically translate into "closure." To better understand the appeal of closure, we turn to therapeutic movements in law and media.

In 1987, David Wexler and Bruce Winick introduced the concept of "therapeutic jurisprudence."[28] They used the term to argue for a perspective within law that is concerned with how laws, legal proceedings, and the people involved produce and experience both therapeutic and anti-therapeutic consequences. Therapeutic jurisprudence is interested in the impact of the law on emotions and psychological health. It encourages the use of law and legal processes as a means to heal people.

The U.S. Supreme Court has also brought together law and mental health. In *Payne v. Tennessee* (1991), the Court ruled that the Eighth Amendment does not prohibit a capital sentencing jury from considering victim impact evidence. In its decision, the Court offered several reasons why it reversed its earlier position, including a statement that fostered future use of closure rhetoric in crime politics. The Court argued that allowing victims to give their testimonies would help redress some of the harm caused by the crime. This decision signals a willingness for using victim impact information for therapeutic reasons and thus opening the door for other arguments calling for legal practices as means for victims to find healing—or "closure."

Victim impact statements, which are not limited to death penalty cases, acknowledge the importance of victims' families' emotions and have legitimated punishment for therapeutic reasons. Although not all victims support the death penalty or call for vengeance, victim impact statements have paved the way for the institutionalization of closure. The U.S. Supreme Court's *Payne* decision in particular gives legal support for legitimizing this new reason for punishment. The closure argument has allowed advocates of victims' rights more success in the justice system whereas expressions of other emotions such as grief, shame, and vengeance are usually not allowed in legal debates.[29]

Indeed, since the 1991 decision in *Payne*, closure has been referenced in numerous legal decisions. Jody Madeira, an advocate of therapeutic jurisprudence and professor of law, proposes that we view closure as a "strategic, sense-making process" that can be used in the legal system to help victims. She notes the increasing number of legal decisions referencing closure in cases of procedural concerns (preventing unjust delays in process), victim participation in legal proceedings, and therapeutic goals.[30] Following are some examples of such cases.

In 1994, the Arizona Supreme Court stated that "victims are entitled to closure."[31] In 1995, a Mississippi judge argued that accepting guilty pleas in murder cases in exchange for life imprisonment allows family members a "certain degree of closure."[32] A 2001 court decision in Hawaii ruled that a victim's family and friends are deprived of closure that comes from a conviction when the defendant commits suicide.[33] In the same year, a court decision in Tennessee argued that a defendant's refusal to say where a victim's body was located deprived the victim's family of closure. The defendant's "refusal to give closure to the victim's family" was cited as evidence of the "cold, heartless nature" of the defendant.[34] In a 2003 decision in Louisiana, a state court argued that finality of judgment is an important goal: "Those who have been victimized and the families of those who have been victimized desire closure, especially in a brutal and senseless crime against an innocent victim."[35] In Florida, a 2005 court decision stated that a defendant's confession provided closure to the victims' families.[36] In 2006, an Illinois court argued that one of the main reasons for the collection of DNA was to "bring closure to victims."[37]

Court decisions were not the only places where therapy for victims became the focus. In the 1960s and 1970s, a new "pop psychology" and self-help movement emerged that set guidelines for how to help your broken self heal after traumatic events.[38] Popular culture, including talk shows, movies, and television shows, also introduced formats and language that invited the use of closure talk. New forms of victimization and melodrama appeared on television talk shows, which became increasingly popular in the 1980s. Oprah Winfrey's "change your life TV" and the *Dr. Phil* show led the way in showing people how to "regain their power" and change their own lives.[39] This pop psychology helped shape the victim as someone who needed to be fixed. The self-help movement opened up new narratives for victimization, healing, and the central role of therapeutic stories.

Popular culture has a melodramatic focus on crime victims, revenge, and the need for therapeutic closure. Typically, crime stories are framed as a story about the victims' pain and suffering and revenge on the offender, thus offering closure to the victim. Television has fostered a model of criminal justice based on revenge and concern for victims. The connection between television and the victims' rights movement took off in 1983 when John Walsh became a spokesperson and helped create two docudramas about his son's disappearance as well as the television series *America's Most Wanted* in 1988. Walsh's format helped create a retributive perspective about crime as innocent victims versus evil offenders and the search for justice as defined through the lens of vengeance. Shows like *America's Most Wanted, COPS,* and a host of movies help to make this image popular. Preceding these shows were vigilante movies such as *Dirty Harry* (1971) and *Death Wish* (1974) that tapped into the audience's desire for revenge.

We see a similar storyline play out in court cases. Elayne Rapping argues that the format of death penalty hearings shocks people by showing the victims' horror story, enraging viewers, and offering moral closure "in which the highly personalized resolution of one person's experience of victimization, through the court's revenge on a single perpetrator, suggests, disingenuously, that the larger problem of social violence itself has somehow been solved."[40]

Social problems and court cases have become entertainment in the form of tabloid news and reality crime shows. Producers see victims, conflict, and emotion as key in getting people to watch their shows. Prosecutors and politicians see victims and emotion as crucial in winning cases. Grief, pain, and hope have increasingly become popular topics, and the concept of closure is a useful narrative for telling these stories.

The concept of closure has also benefited from a culture in which the focus on people's grief is common but mostly constrained by limited patience and expectations that the person will solve the problem within a brief amount of time, without much discussion of the actual pain, and with a relatively quick resolution so that bystanders can assume that the person is moving on.

We live in a society that is uneasy with pain. There are few storylines that allow us to sit with pain and grieve for very long, let alone for the rest of our lives. It is not surprising that journalists and television producers are also cautious about showing too much pain without a happy ending. Happy and inspiring endings are dominant themes in mass media that open the way for the concept of closure. An editor for *Good Housekeeping* told me that a positive resolution to any problem is an important part of good storytelling: "If you leave people unresolved and adrift, it is not going to give the reader the sense that she can also take charge in her life." Editors and producers believe that people need to be given hope that situations can change and that there will be a happy ending or they will not tune in for more. People do not like downers.[41] The concept of closure provides a perfect framework for telling stories about pain and grief while providing a reassuring ending.

But it is not just media editors and producers who like the concept of closure. To get a complete picture of why closure emerged so prominently in the 1990s, we need to look at what happened in the funeral industry prior to that time. Closure in the death care industry is the focus of chapter 4, so here I will just mention a shift in our culture that helped introduce closure into the funeral profession.

Again, we go back to the 1960s, when the funeral industry came under heavy attack from its critics. In the twentieth century, the number of funeral homes increased, and the funeral industry became the dominant way of caring for our dead. However, criticism of the funeral industry emerged with the profession and continues today. One of the most famous books criticizing the modern funeral industry was Jessica Mitford's *The American Way of Death*, published in 1963. Like many critics, Mitford focused largely on the economic side of the industry, accusing funeral homes of inflating prices and exploiting those who grieve. Her book was a best seller and got people talking. Funeral home directors had to go on the offense to justify their services. As part of this strategy, funeral directors began selling themselves as grief counselors in addition to their other services. Rather than just selling services for the dead, they billed themselves as helping the living. They added grief counseling services to their language and, in some cases, literally to the bill. Closure eventually became a neat package to explain those services.

Winding its way through different avenues such as politics, law, media, self-help, and the funeral industry, closure has emerged as a dominant—though not consistent—concept in our everyday talk about grief and loss. It has become a central part of sales talks in the funeral, grief, relationship advice, and memorialization industries. This marketing reinforces further the popular belief that closure exists and can be found. Closure has emerged as a "need" that people can fill through services such as funerals, psychic readings, private investigations, lawsuits, memorials, executions, divorce parties, private cremations, and autopsies. Although closure is not the only need that is used in selling these services and products, it has emerged as an important theme in advertising for these industries. Through all of this, some people believe that closure is an emotional state that exists and can be reached.

However, closure is not just a marketing device. Used to tell stories about an array of issues, including grief, victimization, the criminal justice system, capital punishment, abortion, terrorism, adoption, euthanasia, and school violence, closure has developed into a powerful political tool for talking about social problems.

Closure is entrenched in our popular culture not because it is a well-defined, understood concept that we *know* people need but rather because it is a useful way to tell stories for many people, including journalists, salespeople, politicians, and, sometimes, those who are hurting.

Perhaps you are thinking, so what if people are seeking closure? And more power to them if they can find it. What is the problem? And if businesses can sell products and services that help with closure, is that not a good thing? Similarly, you might argue that politicians ought to be helping crime victims find closure. Maybe you are even seeking closure yourself so you can move on from a traumatic event. Despite Americans' widespread acceptance and support for closure, the phenomenon is nevertheless accompanied by social and emotional risk. Furthermore, closure is not the only narrative for guiding us in our response to bad things. This book explores how our social world is shaped through the recent expectations that we need closure and raises concerns that accompany this cultural perspective. Significantly, we must uncover how closure talk shapes feeling rules for grief and loss.

There may be helpful things about some narratives for seeking closure. The concept of closure may help some people think about loss in their life, but the very same word enrages others. Whether you choose to dismiss closure or embrace it, the fact is that closure is changing our social world, and we need to understand how.

The Rest of the Story

Here is the plan for our exploration of closure. In chapters 2 and 3, we learn more about the many interpretations of closure, including those that deny its existence. Chapter 2 shows why closure is used to describe so many situations and seemingly contradictory emotions. In this chapter, we start to untangle the web by identifying six types of closure talk: closing a chapter, remembering, forgetting, getting even, knowing, and confessing or forgiving. We also begin to see that in spite of the range of interpretations, all six types imply that closure exists and encourage people to assume that finding closure is possible, good, desired, and necessary.

Chapter 3 examines the bereavement research that has helped shape popular notions that closure is needed for normal grieving. Then I identify two types of people who argue there is no closure. The Walking Wounded represent those who say they cannot find closure even though they want it, and Myth Slayers are those who say closure does not exist. These types of individuals help us think about feeling rules and the impact closure talk can have on emotions, grief, and relationships.

The next three chapters turn our attention to how closure is used in marketing campaigns to sell services and products. In chapter 4, we learn about the sales talks of those who are in the business of death, including funeral home directors, home funeral advocates, ash-handling businesses, and the pet grief industry. Competing groups shape feeling rules through their debates about what are "proper" and "dignified" ways to care for and remember our dead loved ones.

Chapter 5 explains the growing "assurance business" that taps into closure as knowledge. Lawyers, psychics, medical consultants, and forensic pathologists all use closure as part of their sales talks. Not only are these individuals and businesses selling answers, but they are creating worry as a way to generate more business.

In chapter 6, we learn how businesses sell mock vengeance and symbolic death as therapy that is supposed to provide closure after a bad relationship. To help grieve a relationship and find closure, you can now write relationship obituaries, buy Wedding Ring Coffins, symbolically bury your ex-partner, and plan end-of-a-relationship services and divorce ceremonies complete with divorce announcements, cake, and party gifts.

The next two chapters turn our attention to closure as a powerful political tool for talking about social problems. Chapter 7 invites us to consider the ongoing trauma and grief that family members of homicide victims face and the contradictory advice about closure offered from pro– and anti–death penalty advocates. Not only does the closure talk in death penalty debates affect feeling rules for grieving loved ones, but it also shapes our policies and public opinion about capital punishment.

Chapter 8 alerts us to the politics of mourning, sacred space, and public memory as we examine how closure plays a role in debates about roadside memorials and memorials for Columbine and 9/11, as well as politics in abortion. In the politics of mourning and public memory, there is a collision of competing definitions of closure and perspectives on how to find it. The main collision involves whether closure means forgetting (one gains closure when one stops thinking about the loss) or remembering (one achieves closure by finding ways to memorialize the loss). Other collisions involve *who* is worthy of remembrance and how much, if at all, public mourning should be regulated.

The concluding chapter focuses on how we might frame grief beyond closure. Why is the concept of closure a concern and how might we better navigate around the marketing and political rhetoric? How can we think about grief in ways that might give us hope without the pressure of finding closure?

Although I emphasize the need to pay attention to how closure is used in political and commercial rhetoric, it would be wrong to suggest that it is *only* politics and profit-driven marketing that drive the concept of closure. Hope also keeps people seeking closure: hope for healing and hope that the pain will lessen. Individuals and businesses compete to tell people how to find that healing. Although hope itself is not created by politics and marketing, the narratives for fulfilling hope are often influenced by these forces. And certainly those using the concept of closure to market products or push political agendas are targeting people's hope for healing.

The hope for a healed self after the devastation of tragedy and grief is poignant and common. Hope keeps people searching for help. Hope keeps people looking for answers in other people's stories and advice. Because people who grieve are often broken and hanging on to hope, it is important to examine grief narratives and the motivations behind those stories to help understand the implications they have on those who hurt. There are many ways to grieve, and there is hope for healing. Along the way, though, there are people trying to shape what you do in the midst of pain for a variety of reasons. Hope is a valuable resource and, unfortunately, used as a means for marketing products and ideas. We need to guard hope.

I invite readers to use the knowledge gained in this book to help understand experiences with loss. By recognizing the tangled web of closure and the reasons behind the rhetoric, we can help ourselves and others navigate the emotions and feeling rules that come with grief and loss.

2. Closure and Its Tangled Meanings

Two-year-old Caylee Anthony disappeared June 2008. Suspiciously, her mother waited a month before reporting her missing. The case became an international mystery receiving ongoing media coverage. Even before authorities found Caylee's remains, her mother was arrested. Closure is part of the story.

In December, Caylee's bones were found not far from her home, in a black bag, along with a Winnie the Pooh blanket and a pink backpack. After the discovery, Orange County sheriff Kevin Beary said, "I believe we can start putting some closure to those open wounds."[1] People from diverse places hoped for that closure. A posting on a website called Mom Logic read, "I'm saddened by the fact this could be Caylee, but am happy that if it is, she and the world who fell in love with her can have closure." Caylee's grandfather, however, does not think closure will come for him. He shares, "I don't think I'll ever have closure. At this point I'm just hoping to someday be able to accept that Caylee is gone."[2]

On February 10, 2009, around 1,200 people attended Caylee's public memorial in Orlando, Florida. Countless others watched via the Internet. Her uncle told the mourners, "If it is closure you seek, I hope you find it."[3] Apparently, that is exactly what bystander Carolyne needed, saying, "I want to put closure to this." That is why she drove to the church rather than watch the service on television. Eric and his girlfriend drove to Orlando from Tennessee to attend the memorial. He said that watching the case on TV every day made him feel a part of it. He, and others, wanted to see the ending.

People mourning for others whom they only know through the media are seeking closure. Others are tired of the coverage and want closure to the case so that they can stop hearing about it.

Onlookers—through the television lens—sought closure in Caylee's case. Family members talk about closure, but are not as sure it will be found.

Why did Caylee's case generate so much media attention? Why did so many people watch the reports, comment on blogs, talk about it with friends, and, for some, actually go to the memorial service? In the world of journalism and entertainment media, some stories elicit closure—the end of the story—after one news cycle while others turn into a series of stories. Strategies of closure and nonclosure are used in storytelling.

Journalists refer to three nonclosure devices that enhance a reader's involvement in a story and maintain long-term viewership: maintaining suspense, thickening the plot, and keeping the protagonist alive.[4] These nonclosure strategies turn some stories into serial narratives rather than short stories. Caylee's story naturally provided all of these devices. A little girl disappeared and for months no one knew where she was or even whether she was alive. Over time, details emerged raising suspicions about the mother. Caylee was the protagonist in the story—the main character. Once her remains were found, onlookers and media viewers began to find closure. Confirmation of her remains brought closure to some. Others found closure in the public memorial service. Some onlookers say that only answers and justice will bring closure.

For Caylee's family, closure looks different—if it is in the storyline at all. Her grandfather says there will be no closure. For those intimately involved, wrapping up the story after finding the body is not possible. The end of the story has not arrived—nor do they necessarily want it to come. Many want to keep Caylee, the main character, alive in memory and conversations.

What advice are people given when bad things happen? Are they told to treat it like a short story or an end of the chapter? "Finish this part of your life and move on with a different story." Or are they encouraged to live that part of their life in additional, but redefined, ways that reflect continued bonds; the story continues even if it goes in a different direction? Does the death of a loved one mean "the end" or "to be continued"? What about a divorce? Or when a pet dies? What kinds of narratives do people want when they face trauma? What would you want?

With Caylee's case, we can see that strangers, who were following the story through the media, were more likely to view closure as closing a chapter or answering questions. Once they knew that Caylee was dead and were reasonably sure who did it, they believed closure was reachable. They are seeing "the end" of the story. Family members are more likely to have additional questions (e.g., could Caylee's mom really have done this?) and also have a fear of forgetting Caylee. They are working on continuing the story of Caylee's life, not ending it. They want to remember, not forget. And it is possible that some of Caylee's family members want revenge while others seek forgiveness. Each of these responses might be an attempt at closure. Yet others may not believe in closure or want it.

It should now be obvious that closure is used to discuss a broad range of topics, often in contradictory ways. It is no wonder, then, that there is confusion about the concept. Not only are different types of issues at play in closure talk but a wide variety of people use the concept, each of whom tries to influence how you think about grieving: salespeople, politicians, friends, journalists, onlookers, and counselors. The story of Caylee Anthony illustrates how multiple interpretations of closure by different types of people are all at play in understanding a particular situation.

Closure involves a tangled story of experiences and emotions. The concept of closure has gained widespread use, but those who use it do not mean the same thing by it. People define the concept in so many ways, and apply it in so many varied contexts, that it is hard to summarize what is meant by the word. Some people become angry about the idea of closure and what it seems to imply about grief and losing loved ones. Other people do not believe that closure even exists, and among those who do, there is no consensus about how it can be achieved. In a 2001 column for the *National Post*, Robert Fulford insightfully highlights a problem with the use of closure. "Every era brings popular words that no one quite understands, or—worse—everyone understands differently. Closure has been such a word for 10 or 15 years."[5] Let's take a closer look at why this word is so confusing.

What Is Closure?

In the age of Internet access, many people search the web for information. A search for definitions of closure raises enough variety to realize there is no consensus. Now granted, the word closure refers to a multitude of things, including computer programming, mathematics, Ziploc bags, medical practice, roadblocks, business closings, clothing elements, Gestalt psychology, and parliamentary procedures. More recent subtypes of closure also appear. There is spiritual closure, cognitive closure, and conceptual closure. One can also seek psychological closure, which is not to be confused with psychic closure. We are also told we need emotional closure, symbolic closure, political closure, and life closure. The broad concept of closure I am discussing here is the type that people use to refer to the end to a traumatic event or an emotional process. I am not discussing computer programming, zippers, surgical procedures, or roadblocks.

Although the word "closure" has been in dictionaries for a long time, the use of closure as a popular psychological concept connected to grieving is relatively recent.[6] The 1999 edition of the *Cambridge Dictionary of American English* included a new definition for closure: "the satisfying feeling that something bad or shocking has finally ended." Its example: "Only the recovery of the bodies of the victims of the crash would bring closure to their families." An editor from the *Cambridge Dictionary* told me that "the meaning had become relatively frequent, especially in newspaper articles, by the late 1990s, and the evidence in our corpus of American English showed it merited inclusion." *Collins English Dictionary* added what it called a new "U.S." definition for closure in 2000: "a) a resolution of a significant event or relationship in a person's life, or b) the sense of contentment experienced after such a resolution."[7] In 2003, *Merriam-Webster's Dictionary* added a seventh definition for closure: "an often comforting or satisfying sense of finality: (victims needing *closure*)."[8]

People have space to freely and publicly define their own view of closure since there are multiple Internet sites that invite personal definitions. One of those sites, Answerbag, asks, "What is your personal definition of closure?"[9] Here are a few answers:

> The acceptance that I have done all I can in a situation. The understanding that there are things I cannot control or change.

> To be able to forgive, and have forgiveness of why there needed to be closure. For then and only then can you have true closure.

> When I can finally put something behind me and move on. It doesn't mean that I don't feel anything regarding whatever it is anymore, but I've accepted what happened and don't "stew" over it.

> Finding out why [a particular circumstance happened], thoroughly comprehending that answer, and then consciously choosing to move forward.

> Closure to me, is that you close that chapter of your life, and start anew, with what you have.

Definitions of closure also get shaped through psychological research. Psychologists attempt to measure high and low rates of closure among individuals.

For instance, in one study, people who can talk about something that happened, and not become emotional while discussing it, might be labeled as having closure. When people think of an event frequently, they are described as having less closure.[10] Researchers in social psychology developed a scale that is supposed to measure one's "need for closure," which is defined as "a desire for a stable, solid knowledge in order to avoid uncertainty, and as a desire for a firm answer to a question and an aversion toward ambiguity."[11] Furthermore, people with a high need for closure are labeled as closed-minded.[12] They are said to engage in social stereotyping more often and desire simplistic answers that most often reflect the status quo. Researchers claim that a high need for closure is associated with right-wing politics, support for the death penalty and a strong military, authoritarianism, and religious conservatism.[13]

In yet a different interpretation, psychological studies about coping strategies following the September 11, 2001, attacks define closure as the ability to not think as much about the trauma.[14] Other psychologists have defined closure as individuals' ability to tell a story with evidence of coherent resolution.[15] In a 2009 study about 9/11 and psychological well-being, researchers tried to determine who had closure. The scale for measuring closure was based on a person's self-described rating of having achieved closure in a way that he or she was not stuck in the consequences of the traumatic experience. High scores of closure are described as those narratives "reflecting a sense of closure, a capacity to experience positive emotion, and a lack of unresolved issues and emotions." One example of how researchers measured closure was whether individuals used past-tense verbs or present-tense verbs. The researchers argued that those who use past-tense verbs to describe an event have more closure.

Researchers provided the following example of a response that was rated as the highest score of closure ("very resolved"): "It was a strange day. I don't usually watch TV news but I did that morning while talking with my husband on the phone. . . . At no point did I ever feel unsafe and since the attacks I have unwavering faith in our nation's security." A second example was given that represented the lowest rating of closure ("very unresolved"): "Living in Oklahoma City at the time of the Murrah Building bombing, it was hard not to loose [sic] control of my emotions; the Murrah Building was so small compared to the [World Trade Center]. The loss of life that took place before my eyes (via TV) is something I will never forget and it still brings in a sinking sad scared feeling. . . . I don't think I will get over this for a while."[16]

What is interesting about these studies is that while the researchers are trying to measure whether or not people *have* closure, they fail to consider whether or not closure even *exists*. They use generalized definitions of closure but do not take into consideration the multiple interpretations people have of the concept. Even if we assume closure exists, think about how difficult it is not only to define but also to measure this emotional state. Examining whether or not one uses past-tense verbs is not a rigorous way to measure closure. This research on closure fails to take into account both the various interpretations of closure and the diverse types of situations and individuals involved in closure talk.

Other psychiatrists, psychologists, and grief counselors say that closure is a troubling myth. For example, psychiatrists Frank Ochberg and Gordon Livingston both reject the idea that closure exists. Similarly, grief expert Kenneth Doka also denies the notion of closure. However, they still provide hope for healing by using different language and concepts. We will learn more about those who say there is no closure in the next chapter.

Closure means many different things to people. It has no one set definition or usage. Although it is used in legal contexts, there is no official legal definition of closure. And it is used in some psychological settings, but again, the definitions vary. Even though multiple definitions of closure exist, a dominant use of it has emerged as reflected in popular culture and in dictionary definitions. The most common understanding of closure implies a "satisfying end" to something. A sense of finality.

A satisfying sense of finality? If you get stuck on the word "satisfying," you are not alone. Common definitions in dictionaries and psychological research include the concept of a satisfying conclusion as a part of closure. It is not hard to see why others bristle at the idea that there can be anything satisfying regarding death or the end of other painful relationships.

Why are there contradictory meanings about closure and so many different suggestions for how to find it? And why do some people hate the word? Closure talk is tangled, in part, because people apply it to a wide variety of situations. In addition to the various definitions of closure and the diverse range of issues connected to it, there are also different types of emotions that people are trying to manage. Closure is used in two seemingly contradictory ways. Sometimes people use it to refer to something they want to end. Other times people use it to refer to something they want to keep. To help us start unraveling the tangled web of closure, I distinguish six types of closure.

How to Dissect Closure Talk—Nomenclosure

Did you have one of those chemistry classes in school where you had to memorize chemical nomenclature—the language of chemistry? If you want to understand chemistry, you need to know the terms and language used to describe compounds. Every discipline has its own set of nomenclature.

When discussing complicated issues, it can be helpful to have a system of naming different things in order to provide a shared language—a nomenclature. Or in this case—we might speak of a *nomenclosure*—a system for describing different types of closure.

To give us language that will help in untangling the web of closure talk, I will define six types—or meanings—of closure. This will be our nomenclosure. Stay with me. It will be less painful than chemistry class.

When people use the word "closure," they generally do not stop and explain what they mean by it. Usually people assume that others know. Assuming everyone understands the word the same way is one reason why there is confusion and frustration with the concept.

Closure implies an end to something, but what is it that we are trying to end? Some people are trying to end a particular task associated with death. Others want to end a relationship because of a breakup or divorce. Still other uses of closure imply ending bad emotions. The breadth of what people are trying "to end" is far reaching. Furthermore, the different rituals proposed for *how* to end whatever it is people are trying to end are also unlimited.

Table 2.1 lists the six types of closure talk; identifies the types of endings within those categories; and gives examples pulled from businesses, politicians, and others who make the claims about how to find closure. I use the term "closure talk" to refer to how people use the concept of closure and to emphasize that closure is a part of storytelling. It shapes the story: here is what the problem is and here is how to solve it. However, I am not arguing that these suggestions will work for people. I only mean to demonstrate the various ways in which closure is used. Importantly, these categories are not mutually exclusive; multiple meanings of closure are frequently used for the same situation.

Closing a Chapter

Closing a chapter is the first type of closure talk. As with all types, there are "unfinished" or "unresolved" issues that someone is trying to end. Closing a chapter often refers to finishing the ritual regarding the burial of a loved one, ending a court case, concluding the grieving process, or formally closing a relationship. The idea behind this type of closure talk is that some aspect of a traumatic event is wrapped up. People often are advised to go through a ritual in order to mark the chapter's close. Then the person can start a new chapter in life.

In cases of death, suggested rituals for closing a chapter include funerals, viewings, and burials. Funeral directors rely on the concept of closure by closing a chapter as they sell their services. For instance, the question/answer section of a preplanning guide for Moles Funeral Home emphasizes that embalming and viewing the body can help give closure and allow people to express their grief.[17] Home funeral advocates, however, suggest that taking care of a loved one's body in the home is the proper ritual for helping to find closure.

When relationships fail, friends and experts often borrow death rituals when counseling divorced people or ex-partners—have a relationship funeral, write an obituary, or have a religious divorce ceremony. All these rituals strive

TABLE 2.1   NOMENCLOSURE

Types of Closure Talk	What Needs to End?	Examples of Specific Rituals
Closing a chapter	• Unfinished tasks • Unresolved court case • Painful relationship • A life • Grief	• Getting through a funeral • Burying a loved one • Viewing a body • Taking care of deceased loved one • Executing killer to end all trials • Ending a relationship with rituals • Throwing a divorce party • Having a relationship funeral • Accepting loss and moving on • Counseling
Remembering	• Fear of forgetting • Fear others will forget	• Getting a memorial tattoo • Planning memorial services • Starting scholarships, foundations • Participating in public memorial • Buying memorial ad in newspaper
Forgetting	• Painful reminders • A relationship • Other people's pain	• Burning love letters after breakup • Burying wedding rings after divorce • Razing a school after shooting • Telling people to "get over it" • Stopping public memorials
Getting even	• Sense of injustice • Anger, pain	• Convicting a killer • Executing a killer • Watching someone die • Humiliating someone • Acting out symbolic revenge

Knowing	• Haunting questions:
	  What happened? Why?
	  Who did it? Last words?
	• Worry
		• Ordering an autopsy
		• Talking to a killer
		• Reading a suicide note
		• Finding the body
		• Securing perpetual care
		• Having a private cremation
		• Using leakproof caskets
		• Knowing loved one is in heaven

Confessing or forgiving	• Guilt • Shame • Anger/bitterness	• Confessing to a crime • Acknowledging life of aborted baby • Apologizing • Receiving an apology • Forgiving someone

to close the chapter on a relationship so one can move on. Not all rituals are serious. Some like to close a chapter by throwing lighthearted divorce parties for their friends. Closure talk and the desire to close a chapter also show up in politics. On his last day in office, President Bill Clinton admitted that he gave false testimony under oath and agreed to pay a fine and accept a suspension of his law license. He told the nation: "I hope my actions today will help bring closure and finality to these matters."[18] Politicians have also used closing a chapter to advocate for the death penalty. They argue that the death of the offender is needed for the victim's family to close the chapter and move on.

Remembering

Remembering seems like a paradoxical type of closure talk. At face value, the word "closure" implies closing something. So you might ask, How does remembering help one to close anything? In this case, one is trying to end the fear of forgetting. People often fear forgetting a loved one after he or she has died, and they speak of closure when describing bringing an end to that fear of forgetting. Other things we are afraid of forgetting include love, relationships with our dead, memories of our dead, memories of ex-partners, lessons learned, peace, pain, and redefined meanings attached to a relationship. Closing the fear of forgetting means feeling assured that you have figured out how to remember. You can assure yourself that you have memories and rituals to show respect to your loved one. Those who grieve sometimes want others to remember, too. Some seek closure by participating in public rituals of remembrance.

Memorials ensure remembrance through such devices as roadside crosses and body tattoos. Public memorials help us remember wars, terrorist attacks, or school shootings. Individually, people rely on newspapers or, more recently, the Internet to create memorials remembering loved ones. Have you ever noticed the short poems or memorials in the newspaper recognizing someone's death—one year ago, five years, ten years? People do not want to forget their loved ones. They want others to remember, too.

Remembering as a type of closure talk is prevalent in the memory business. Those individuals selling products that help memorialize a loved one rely on people's fear of forgetting. You do not have to buy other people's products to memorialize a loved one. However, those in the business of selling memorial products work to create the impression that "proper" memorialization comes through their services. And so we come to believe in the ability to find closure through remembering.

Forgetting

Forgetting is the third type of closure. Finding closure through forgetting appears to contradict the strategy of closure through remembrance. Whether one wants to remember an event or person—or forget it—is subjective and contextual. Emotions, memories, and people you might want to end or leave behind include other people's pain, your pain, images of tragedy, anger, political scandals, guilt, abusive partners, ex-partners, testimonies, and other events during criminal trials.

Forgetting as a type of closure might mean getting rid of reminders of something that caused a lot of pain, such as razing schools or classrooms after school shootings, getting rid of personal belongings reminiscent of a past relationship, or burning wedding dresses and love letters. The theory of forgetting is that reminders get in the way of closure. Therefore, getting rid of those painful reminders helps us move on. Forgetting bad relationships also fits this category. Did you ever break up with someone only to find personal reminders all around? Did you burn the letters and gifts as a way to forget?

Forgetting also represents what people want to do about others' pain. Have you wished there would be closure to some discussion because you were tired of hearing about it? Wanting to move on from other people's grief is a type of closure that many seek. Brian Pilant, a twenty-eight-year-old bagpiper from Arizona, is tired of 9/11. "Shut up about it!" he grumbles in reference to talk about 9/11. "We need to drop it. Talking about things that we can do and take care of, OK. But stuff we can't do anything about—like the fact that it happened—we can't change that."[19] Brian and many others have expressed frustration with 9/11 public memorials. They want closure on it. For them, closure means forgetting that it happened, or at least not having the reminders. For others, closure to 9/11 may never happen. Or they might feel that they can only find closure through remembering, which includes public memorials and reminders.

Getting Even

A fourth type of closure talk is *getting even*. Some arguments for closure say people need to end the injustice, pain, and/or anger in their lives through revenge. Those who are hurting are told by others that they can find closure when the person who hurt them suffers punishment and/or physical pain and, in some cases, death. Getting even is also a common thread in closure talk regarding bad relationships.

Revenge or vengeance has long been a staple of politics and popular culture. The concept of "therapeutic vengeance" has offered new language and motivations to seek revenge in the name of closure and healing. Mock vengeance, a cousin of revenge, is also used to sell closure for bad relationships. I use the term "mock vengeance" to describe rituals and behavior that are targeted at someone's reputation or memory but do not physically or financially affect another individual (although learning of the events could emotionally affect that person).

Death penalty supporters tell others that an execution will provide closure. For example, a pro–death penalty website states: "The death penalty gives closure to the victim's families who have suffered so much."[20] In a letter to the editor in the *New York Times*, Stephen Sultan argues, "The victim's family is entitled to retribution and closure."[21] Other examples of "closure by getting even" include voodoo dolls, casting spells, humiliating someone on the web, virtual revenge, and spite-themed parties. The description of the book *The Revenge Seeker's Handbook* ties revenge and closure together: "Forget about turning the other cheek, revenge is good for you. It brings closure to traumatic events and stops you agonizing deep down that you should have done something, but never did."[22]

Knowing

The problem of unanswered questions frames the fifth type of closure talk—*knowing*. After a death or during a missing persons case, family members live with haunting questions. Some people argue that having answers to these questions will provide closure. "Knowing" is supposed to end the unresolved questions and worries. Most of these questions revolve around what happened during a death: what caused the death, why it happened, who is responsible, and what last words were spoken. Specific examples include the following: Where is my daughter's body? Is she dead or alive? Who killed him? Did she suffer? Why did he die? Did the doctor make a mistake?

Traumatic deaths or deaths that leave behind questions provide a group of potential customers for people selling investigative services such as autopsies, psychic readings, and private investigations. Many hope that finding answers to these questions will provide closure. In this quest, people order autopsies, talk to offenders, or search for missing bodies. They also hire wrongful death attorneys, psychics, or other investigative consultants.

Examples of this type of closure talk come from individuals who are grieving: Carmina sat in her Geology 104 class at Northern Illinois University the day Steven Kazmierczak walked in and shot twenty students and the teacher.

She just wants to know why he did it. Carmina says she needs an explanation for why he did it in order to have closure.[23] Other examples come from people selling services to those who grieve, such as those selling their autopsy services to lawyers and individuals to help uncover "the real cause of death." This information may lead to lawsuits and/or closure. A forensic pathologist in Bedford, Texas, advertises "second private autopsy" services. "The autopsy in fact will give the family closure about the actual cause of death of their loved one."[24]

Confessing or Forgiving

The final type of closure talk centers on *confessing or forgiving*. Advocates for this type of closure argue that confessing or offering an apology can provide closure by ending guilt or shame. Similarly, receiving an apology or forgiving someone helps one find closure by ending anger. Closure through confession, forgiveness, or apology is intended to affect one's emotions and state of mind and, in some cases, provide new insights into crimes.

Advocates of memorials to the unborn use closure in their abortion rhetoric: confessing to an abortion, acknowledging the life of that baby, and receiving forgiveness are the way to achieve closure. Religious discourse on closure frequently refers to confession and/or forgiveness. Some restorative justice advocates commonly refer to forgiveness as a way to find closure and healing. The New Mexico Coalition to Repeal the Death Penalty takes this perspective: "We know executions won't bring back our loved ones and they won't provide 'closure.' We have learned through very painful personal experience that closure only comes with healing and forgiveness."[25]

Closure has reached the isolation of death row, too, according to reports of last statements made by more than a few offenders in Texas. Some offenders hope that their apologies and pending execution will bring closure to the victims' families. Before his execution in 1997, David Herman said: "It was horrible and inexcusable for me to take the life of your loved one and to hurt so many mentally and physically. I am here because I took a life and killing is wrong by an individual and by the state, and I am sorry we are here but if my death gives you peace and closure then this is all worthwhile."[26]

Closure and Feeling Rules

Throughout this book, I will give examples of how these types of closure are used in narratives about how to respond to loss. Before going into more examples, I will discuss what they have in common and how they shape feeling rules.

In spite of the range of interpretations reflected in the six types of closure, all six types imply that closure exists and carry the assumptions that closure is (1) possible, (2) good, (3) desired, and (4) necessary. Closure encourages the idea that grief is bad and therefore something that needs to end. These assumptions, and the larger narratives that carry them, build feeling rules for how we are supposed to respond when bad things happen.

In the early 1980s, sociologist Arlie Hochschild challenged traditional theories of emotion by writing about emotions as social objects that are shaped by individuals and society. Instead of believing that emotions are instinctual, sociologists explain that emotions are shaped through our social interactions. Although there are emotional physiological responses that happen, the way we label these emotions and how we judge the appropriateness of them are shaped through social expectations.

We attempt to manage our emotions in different situations in an effort to look and feel the way we think we are supposed to feel in any given context. Hochschild uses the concept of feeling rules as a way to explain the consequences narratives have on people's emotions.[27] Feeling rules are informal guidelines we learn about how we are supposed to feel and how we should show that feeling in specific situations. We learn about feeling rules through previous experiences and cultural narratives. Cultural narratives are the stories and advice passed along through media, professionals, family, and friends. We use these narratives or stories to make sense of our own lives and our emotions.

An example of a feeling rule about grief is the common belief that one should be visibly grieving at a funeral. The truth is that sometimes people might go to a funeral and not feel an emotion they recognize as grief (or that others recognize). Or one might be grieving but not crying. Sometimes people will try to make themselves cry to match what they think others expect.

Feeling rules are informal expectations of how we think we should feel. When the feeling rules fail, or do not produce the emotions promised, individuals may experience emotive dissonance—a disconnect between what they feel and what they think they should feel. For example, in many cases, funeral directors tell family members that particular rituals for viewing a body and holding a funeral service will provide them closure. So if you are told that you will find closure after a funeral, you might expect peace and healing. However, it may be that the feeling that you associate with the concept of closure does not come after the funeral. You have a disconnect between what you expected to feel and what you actually feel. The degree of disconnect will vary among individuals depending on relationships to the deceased, prior experiences, and also the initial general expectations of what a funeral will provide. Even though we are exposed to similar narratives about grief, we do not embrace them in the same way.

In this book, we will explore the narratives about closure that tell us how we are supposed to respond when bad things happen and uncover what it implies about grief, pain, and healing. Closure is not the only narrative in our culture for understanding how to respond to trauma, but it has become a dominant one. Threaded throughout this book are examples of closure narratives that reflect the six types just discussed. There are times, for some people, when stories about closure may be helpful. I am not arguing that discussing closure is always bad. However, we will also learn how closure narratives shape feeling rules for grief and, at times, set up false hope, which leads to an emotional disconnect.

How we are supposed to feel—feeling rules—are frequently followed by suggestions for how we should accomplish those feelings. In discussions about closure, politicians, advocates, entrepreneurs, counselors, family, or friends are often quick to offer specific steps or rituals to follow in order to find closure.

The message frequently heard is that people should seek closure after bad things happen. What happens when that closure is not found? What if closure does not even exist? Or if closure is not what people really want?

Lessons about how we are supposed to react to bad things lead to confusion and, at times, anger. Not everyone agrees with the assumptions that closure is possible, good, desired, and necessary. Some even disagree with the simple premise that closure exists. Closure talk can elicit intense negative reactions from people because of the assumptions underlying the concept. When the feeling rules fail, or do not produce the emotions promised, individuals may experience a disconnect between what they feel and what they think they should feel.

To help understand feeling rules and the impact closure talk can have on emotions, grief, and relationships, we need to explore grief theories and popular ideas about "normal grieving." Chapter 3 explores research on grief and introduces examples of people who say they cannot find closure (the Walking Wounded) and those who say there is no closure (the Myth Slayers).

3. The Walking Wounded and Myth Slayers

Those Who Say There Is No Closure

The Internet brings a world of information to our fingertips. You can discover how to do just about everything. In fact, that is the slogan for eHow.com, a website devoted to easy steps for doing almost anything.[1] The day I browsed the site, the top "eHows" included how to get strawberry stains out of clothes, how to set up and monitor a child's e-mail, and how to check for termites. Skipping over those pages, I turned to "how to get closure." Here is the initial advice: "Losing a loved one or having a relationship end is a difficult thing to endure. Getting closure once you have suffered any tragedy or loss is key to getting your life back together and moving on to happiness and fulfillment."

There are more specific instructions on the pages for grieving over a child or sibling. Each topic is rated for difficulty level. Grieving a child is rated as "moderate" difficulty. From personal experience, I do not know of anything harder than grieving for a child, so it is hard to grasp why it is classified as just a moderate level of difficulty. The introduction does suggest a higher difficulty level: "The death of a child is one of the most difficult things a parent will ever have to deal with." The introductory remarks acknowledge that people are likely to think about their child every day of their lives. Then one is told that the first step is finding closure.

Prior to explaining the steps for grieving, eHow conveniently lists "things you will need." For grieving the loss of a child, you will need a grief counselor, a memorial fund, friends and family members, and a picture of your child or an item that belonged to him or her. There are eight steps to follow. The first one is find closure: "One of the easiest things to do to find closure is simply say goodbye to your child at a funeral. It's OK to talk to a tombstone or picture." The other steps are (2) cry, (3) speak at your child's funeral, (4) talk to a grief counselor, (5) talk to other family members about the death, (6) remember happy times, (7) keep an item that reminds you of your child, and (8) set up a memorial fund in honor of your child so his or her friends can make donations.

A separate eHow page describes how to grieve the loss of a sibling. The steps are similar to those for grieving the loss of a child, although it includes this addition to the "crying step": "It's fine to be sad when you think about your sibling, but don't let it disrupt your daily life too much." In step 8, a grieving sibling is advised to "talk to an accountant or financial professional if you've inherited anything from your sibling."

Let's look at why this type of script for finding closure may upset people. First, the eHow page may sound like a cruel joke to someone who has lost a child. How can anyone put ending the incredible pain into such simplistic steps? Language such as "one of the easiest things to do is to find closure" or "simply say good-bye to your child" grates on those who are grieving. How can grief be put into an easy-step formula in the same way that you would tell someone how to remove stains or find termites? It is confusing, if not infuriating, to hear people talk about closure when all you want to do is desperately hang on to your loved one. It angers many who are grieving to hear others mention closure as if there is an easy 1-2-3 formula.

Second, once particular "steps" or "procedures" are established for finding closure, some people will be left out, even if they believe in the closure promised. Usually, advice on finding closure suggests that you need to meet certain "criteria" in your circumstances to attain closure. You need a physical body to mourn and bury, or answers to relieve haunting questions, and so on.

Grief advice like that found on the eHow website offers support for the dominant assumptions about closure: that it is possible, good, desired, and necessary. Grief is often described as a particular task you need to complete in a specific way, and not following that path suggests something is wrong with you. Closure has become shorthand for the goal of grieving. In spite of not knowing what closure really means, it is routinely used to describe where we should end up, what we need, what we lack, or what we should help others find.

Despite these confident formulas for closure, many people who are grieving nevertheless experience a disconnect between what they are experiencing and what they read in advice columns such as eHow. Whether people do not believe in closure, do not want it, or do not fit the proposed criteria for finding it, they know that they do not feel what they are supposed to feel according to these constructed rules. This disconnect leads some people to say, "There is no closure" or "There is no closure for me."

Now you might be thinking, "How seriously should we take eHow anyway? It's not like it is a research-based narrative for grief." While it may not have the highest standards of research for each page, it is actually not a far stretch from the perspective of some grief theories. In this chapter, I show how bereavement research has helped shape popular notions that closure is needed for normal grieving. Then I introduce examples of individuals who argue that there is no closure: the Walking Wounded who cannot find closure even though they want it and the Myth Slayers who say closure does not exist. The Walking Wounded and the Myth Slayers are not actual organizations or groups, but rather terms I have created in order to explain two general perspectives that illustrate trouble with the concept of closure.

Is There a Road Map for Grief?

Bereavement research generally goes in one of two directions. There are those who say there is no universal road map for grief—we find our way through our own unique experience. Each person's grief is uncharted territory. People's experience with grief is affected, and thus made distinct, by many things, including the circumstances of death, relationship to the deceased, characteristics of the bereaved individual, quality of social support, and cultural differences in mourning rituals and expectations.[2]

Taking a different approach, there are those who present a universal road map for grieving, predicting the terrain, and identifying people who go "off-road." Popular translations of these theories often describe closure as the destination. And, as is typical in our fast-paced society, we are given an estimated time of arrival for reaching closure.

A road map for grief is often described as "grief work" and includes criteria for "normal grieving." The assumption is that grief work is the process by which an individual moves from grief to post-grief, which may be described as acceptance, recovery, readjustment, resolution, or closure, depending on whom you ask. From this perspective, we have those who define stages to go through or tasks to accomplish as people grieve.[3]

Perhaps the most famous of these theories is Elisabeth Kübler-Ross's five-stage model, which she developed in 1969 to explain what people experience when dying.[4] She later decided to apply those stages to grieving even though her original observations concerned the dying. Her final stage is "acceptance," which could be considered an earlier form of closure talk. Although Kübler-Ross never meant for the stages to imply that grief progresses in neat, orderly steps, many people who use her ideas interpret them that way.

People continue to develop new models of grief that suggest particular steps the bereaved need to go through before they supposedly will resolve their grief. For example, William Worden suggests four "tasks of mourning" that people need to accomplish after someone dies: (1) accept the reality of loss, (2) experience the pain of grief, (3) adjust to the new environment where the deceased person is missing, and (4) withdraw from the deceased and reinvest energy in life.[5] Thinking about grief as progressing through stages or accomplishing particular tasks is a dominant popular narrative for grieving. Failing to follow the "rules" or "stages" for grieving may lead experts (or friends and family) to say that a person is not grieving in a healthy way.

Psychology professor George Bonanno critiques the stages of grief perspectives and says there is no evidence to support them.[6] He says many people may not experience these stages, and that is not a problem. He argues that a majority of people have a "natural resilience" to guide them through grief. However, the more dominant perspective in psychiatric research would seem to place less trust in human resiliency or in a person's ability to find his or her own way through the pain—or along grief's road—without a road map provided by professionals.

Some scholars attempt to identify and label people who deviate from the established road map. When people travel a different route, park too long in one spot, or do not want to go in the direction others suggest, they are often labeled as abnormal. At times, the concern is that people are not getting to the "closure destination" fast enough. Other times, people are taking a different route, which might concern those around them. When we establish a particular road map for grieving, it is inevitable that there will be those who do not follow it.

Defining criteria that measure some distinction between normal and pathological grieving shapes expectations for what is the "right way" to grieve and what is "wrong." This move reflects the medicalization of grief, which refers to a perspective that views grief as a disease that needs to be cured.[7] With the medicalization of grief, terms and models emerge that explain normal grief versus problematic grief. We continue to see a growth in labels for grief that indicate something other than "normal": complicated grief, pathological grief, morbid grief, unanticipated grief, prolonged grief, neurotic grief, traumatic grief, unhealthy grief, abnormal grief, delayed grief, absent grief, inhibited grief, exaggerated grief, conflicted grief, unresolved grief, distorted grief, masked grief, sudden grief, and chronic grief.

A recent battle among psychiatrists involves the creation of "complicated grief." There are two groups of psychiatrists competing to establish the officially recognized criteria for diagnosing people as having the disorder of complicated grief, which they view as dysfunctional. In an earlier version of complicated grief, psychiatrist Mardi Horowitz and colleagues proposed measuring "complicated grief" by surveying people only fourteen months after the loss of a close loved one (e.g., spouse, parent, child). People are suspected of having complicated grief if, after fourteen months from the death, they still experience such symptoms as unbidden memories of the lost relationship, pangs of severe emotion, strong yearnings for the deceased, feeling alone or empty, or loss of interest in activities.[8]

In an effort to develop their own criteria and diagnosis, psychiatrist Holly Prigerson and her colleagues changed the term to "traumatic grief" and then to "prolonged grief." They also shortened the time limit for resolving grief. Whereas Horowitz's model waits until after the first year, Prigerson's model allows for a diagnosis of a disorder if certain symptoms are still present after six months. They originally had set it at two months after a death but decided to give those who are grieving a few more months to find a balance in life. You might be diagnosed as having "prolonged grief" if you experience some of these symptoms: "intrusive thoughts about the deceased, yearning for the deceased, searching for the deceased, loneliness as a result of the death, feelings of futility about the future, numbness, feeling life is empty, feeling that part of oneself has died, impaired functioning in social, occupational or other important areas."[9]

In another significant move, we are seeing the expansion of complicated/prolonged grief as a category that is being proposed for the next edition of the *Diagnostic and Statistical Manual of Mental Disorders* (*DSM*). The draft of *DSM-5*, scheduled for release in 2013, recommends a change that would significantly affect how psychiatrists treat grief. It would allow the diagnosis of depression even if the individual is grieving the recent loss of a loved one. What would currently be considered normal behavior following a death could become labeled as a mental disorder. This is a clear example of the social construction of problems. The behavior and experiences of people grieving do not change but the way we label them does. What is viewed as "normal" in 2010 may become a "disorder" in 2013.

The *DSM* is the psychiatric source that doctors, psychiatrists, legal experts, and insurance companies use to determine whether someone is normal or abnormal, well or sick, dangerous or safe, mentally ill or dealing with life's stress. Mental health professionals rely on the labels in the *DSM* in order to get their clients covered through insurance. If someone's condition falls under a mental disorder as described in the *DSM*, then it is more likely to be reimbursed.[10] The *DSM* is also important to drug companies as the expansion of previously unlabeled "disorders" opens new markets. With almost every new edition of the *DSM*, more and more behaviors are categorized as disorders.[11] The *DSM* also plays a role in shaping popular beliefs about what type of behavior is viewed as acceptable and what is considered wrong or dysfunctional.

Until the *DSM-5* proposal, bereavement had been seen as an exception to the criteria used to diagnose major depression. In other words, grief often shares many of the symptoms of major depression, but the circumstances following the loss of a loved one make those feelings and experiences "normal" or "expected" as opposed to a mental disorder. The proposed changes would eliminate the understanding of these grieving responses as normal. Advocates for the change argue that feeling depressed because of someone's death is no different from feeling depressed for any other reason.[12] They argue it would allow clinicians help in getting insurance companies to pay for them to treat clients. It also would open up the flood gates for pharmaceutical companies as a whole new wave of people, who used to be seen as "understandably upset" by a death, could then be diagnosed with a disorder and perhaps prescribed drugs.

Ridiculous, argues psychiatrist Allen Frances regarding the proposed changes. Frances, who chaired the *DSM-IV* Task Force and thus intimately understands the process, warns, "Medicalizing normal grief stigmatizes and reduces the normalcy and dignity of the pain, short circuits the expected existential processing of the loss, reduces reliance on the many well established cultural rituals for consoling grief, and would subject many people to unnecessary and potentially harmful medication treatment."[13]

Although his background is in psychiatry, Frances aptly represents a more sociological critique of the ever-increasing number of problems that are labeled as medical disorders. There are dangers for our society when we start medicalizing every issue people experience.[14] Scarce medical resources, including therapists, would be diverted from those who need them most. Diagnosing and medically treating every problem someone has decreases our tolerance for pain and the struggle of life. Frances poignantly states: "It seems patently absurd to create a diagnostic system which makes normality an endangered species."[15]

There are some people who suffer from grief in a way that would raise the need for medical help. I do not deny this—I would want these individuals to receive help. For people who suffer from severe mental health conditions at the point of grief, there are already "disorders" in the current *DSM* that would allow for this diagnosis. However, the concern about including all bereaved people under a label of mental disorder is that rather than respecting the pain of loss and difficulty of grief as a typical human response, we medicalize the pain of grief and deny the normality of it.

To be fair, grief scholars who are defining criteria for labels such as complicated grief try to set distinctly identifiable symptoms that need to be met at a severe enough level in order to prevent using too wide a net in labeling those who grieve. Most advocates of the complicated grief label argue that only 10 to 15 percent of those who grieve experience this type of grief. However, it is not just the psychiatrists' decisions that shape how we label others' behavior. Their "scientific criteria" get turned into simplified explanations for how to distinguish between normal and abnormal grief.

As psychiatrists battle on regarding specific criteria and labels for grief, their larger framework for the medicalization of grief trickles down into popular culture and training manuals for those working with grieving people. Because most people are not going to be reading the research articles that lay out the specific criteria for trying to measure grief, shorthand descriptions are used to explain what normal grief looks like. The broader research ideas translate into the universal road map we are expected to travel while grieving.

Psychiatry has dominated narratives about how to grieve, and our family, friends, and coworkers, who sometimes act as "grief police," further reinforce these narratives.[16] In many cases, "closure" has become the shorthand way to distinguish between normal and abnormal grief as we see reflected in eHow's pages for grieving. Can you find closure or not? Have you achieved closure or not? Even though closure (or lack of closure) is not yet part of the *DSM*, we see closure used in some grief research and certainly in many interpretations of the research.

Here are two examples of prolonged/complicated/chronic grief translated in reference to closure. First is an example from a 2008 textbook, which is used to explain "prolonged grief": "Sometimes the feelings of hurt, loneliness, and guilt are so overwhelming that they become the focus of the survivor's life to such an extent that there is never any closure and the grief continues to interfere indefinitely with one's ability to function."[17] Or take this perspective from an article that is meant to help funeral directors understand grief and know how to identify people who are experiencing complicated grief. The article describes complicated grief or chronic grief as "when a person's grief does not come to a finality or closure."[18] Here is an example given in the article for what is considered a "chronic grief reaction":

At age 29 Mary had her first child, Samantha, who lived six months and then died of sudden infant death syndrome (SIDS). After Samantha's death, Mary spent every morning with a cup of coffee, looking out the family window while holding Samantha's blanket to her cheek. This grief ritual continued day after day. With the blanket against her cheek, Mary would think about all the things she had wanted to do with Sam, the places they would go, Sam's first date, driving a car, college, first job, marriage—all those occasions typically shared by mother and daughter.

Mary is described as grieving abnormally and advised to seek assistance to provide closure to her grief.[19] Funeral directors are told in this article that Mary's behavior is not normal.

Achieving closure has been defined as a "normal grieving process" whereas abnormal grief is defined as an inability to find closure. The medicalization of grief has led to language and grief models—our road map—that imply proper ways to grieve within expected periods of time. "Normal" grieving is supposed to end after a relatively short period of time after which we have received closure on the experience.

People who do not find resolution to their grief within the expected time period can encounter resistance on a number of fronts: their grief may be labeled as pathological, abnormal, complicated, or chronic; intolerant employers may wonder why they are not "over it"; increasingly insensitive family and friends may not understand why they cannot just get closure and move on.

But what if their experience with grief is not pathological but just different from the feeling rules that have been constructed? What if people are not dysfunctional when they deviate from the standardized criteria but rather are just taking a different route through their grief? There are alternative ways of understanding grief.

The process of establishing a universal road map for grief is an example of social construction—a group of people, in this case predominantly psychiatrists and psychologists, are deciding what "normal grief" is supposed to be. When a particular set of ideas about grief becomes dominant, alternative perspectives get pushed aside. Because someone does not follow the universal road map, however, it does not necessarily mean he or she is dysfunctional.

What constitutes "normal grief" varies across cultures and changes over time. Feeling rules about grief often reflect larger cultural beliefs. Sociologist Tony Walter explains that there is a striking similarity between technical descriptions of complicated grief and popular beliefs about grief. Walter notes, "This reflects popular notions that grief is something one should get over quickly, and that it is embarrassing and/or inconvenient if colleagues' or family members' functioning is impaired by grief for extended periods. Indeed, it reflects a widespread duty in American culture for its members to be self-determining individuals and, moreover, happy."[20]

Is the universal road map really about what is best for those who are grieving? Or does it have to do with what is more convenient and comfortable for others?

There are scholars who criticize closure as a destination. They say it is the journey that is important, not the destination. Further, there is no schedule for how fast you need to travel. A road map that leads to a particular destination of closure implies that there is an end to grief. Kenneth Doka dismisses the goal of closure: "Distrust any counsel that suggests or promises that elusive 'closure.'"[21] Frank Ochberg, a psychiatrist specializing in traumatic stress, describes closure as a myth, a bad word that implies an ending to something that never ends: "You don't get closure on trauma, tragedy, the impact of human cruelty, but you do grow, you do get sadder and wiser and you do, more often than not, get the opportunity to help fellow travelers. Closure is a myth, but progress is not."[22]

Robert Neimeyer, professor of psychotherapy, believes that whereas traditionally we thought it was important to focus counseling on forgetting the loss and moving on, he now says it is clear that we try to continue bonds of love with our deceased loved ones. He adds, "We are less wedded to seeking closure, to the idea of saying goodbye to the one who died. We now recognize the importance of finding healthy ways to sustain a relationship with a deceased loved one, to maintain continuing healthy bonds, for example, by carrying forth their projects. Closure is for bank accounts, not for love accounts."[23]

Sometimes it might be social expectations that complicate one's grief, which is different from saying the grieving person is dysfunctional. It may be that the standardized criteria offered for how to grieve, or the closure destination sold to people, make the grief terrain rockier.

Whenever we define the "normal criteria" for grieving, people will inevitably be left out because of their circumstances. There are social expectations and, at times, regulations for how and when we grieve. There is a diverse range of experiences of loss and death that do not neatly fit social norms about grief. To better understand how someone can be grieving but not have that grief acknowledged, we go back to the concept of feeling rules. Through our experiences and social interactions, we learn what and whom we are allowed to grieve. We might think of this as social regulation of grief or the policing of grief.[24]

We will still feel loss and intense grief even if others do not acknowledge our loss. However, we will not have the same public outlets and rituals to process that grief. We have informal, unwritten rules about whom we grieve, how, and for what length of time. Again, these rules do not necessarily affect how we experience the hurt and pain but rather affect how we can share it with others—or not share it.

Some circumstances regarding a loss are more likely to fall outside of the standardized criteria for grieving that have been shaped by society. We turn to two areas of study that explore these concerns—ambiguous loss and disenfranchised grief. Pauline Boss defines ambiguous loss as loss that has no verification of death or no certainty that the person will come back. Although Boss says she is not a fan of the word "closure," she uses it to help distinguish types of loss. She defines ambiguous loss as the type of loss that has no closure and contrasts it with "normal loss" that does have closure.[25] She defines two types of ambiguous loss. First is the loss that has a physical absence but a psychological presence, such as missing persons, natural disasters, and separation from family due to divorce, adoption, or immigration. The second type of loss includes physical presence but psychological absence, including cases of Alzheimer's, brain injury, autism, mental illness, memory loss, and coma.[26]

Disenfranchised grief is defined as grief that is not publicly recognized or acknowledged by society. Kenneth Doka argues that disenfranchised grief generally involves relationships that are not recognized or socially approved (e.g., lovers, friends, coworkers, gay/lesbian); loss that is not recognized (e.g., miscarriage, abortion, adoption, pet loss, divorce); an individual who is not recognized as having the capacity to grieve (e.g., very old, very young, disabled); or death that is stigmatized (e.g., murder, suicide, AIDS).

Doka and Boss both caution against the concept of closure. However, those who discuss disenfranchised grief do not always pick up on these warnings. In the way people use the terms, they describe "having no closure" as the problem rather than having feeling rules and standard criteria for how we define normal loss and grief in our society that are too strict.

In spite of some scholarly and professional voices who actively criticize the notion of closure, people who are grieving are more likely to hear the popular ideas about "grief work," "stages of grief," and "finding closure." The universal road map for grief remains the dominant narrative for how people should grieve. And even though there are different routes in which people might travel, the ultimate destination, in most scripts, is closure. One of the most dominant themes of current feeling rules for grief is that people need to find closure.

How do people react to this universal road map and expectation that they need to find closure? Some people may not think much about it. They grieve a loss with sadness but not necessarily life-altering changes. Many people experience what would fit under the criteria established to describe "normal grief" or "uncomplicated grief." Many of them may also have no trouble with the term "closure."

Others might find their grief and loss alienating because they do not fit the standardized criteria. The universal road map does not work for them, so they feel abandoned on the side of the road. These are the Walking Wounded.

The Walking Wounded

The *Walking Wounded* are those who believe closure exists, and who want closure, but think they cannot obtain it. They believe closure exists in some form for some people, just not for them. The Walking Wounded long for closure; they feel less than whole because they lack closure. They accept three of the four assumptions constructed by others: closure is good, desired, and necessary. But they believe, for them, it is not possible. Their understanding of closure is shaped by the dominant narratives about grief and loss, which often get translated into the concept of closure. These narratives shape feeling rules and expectations for how they are supposed to grieve and what is needed in order to grieve properly.

Thus, the Walking Wounded see their grieving process as stalled or impossible because they cannot find closure, which they are convinced is necessary. The concepts of disenfranchised grief and ambiguous loss both refer to types of circumstances that affect the Walking Wounded. Significantly, not all people who experience ambiguous loss or disenfranchised grief believe that they need closure. The Walking Wounded represent those who believe they need closure and continue to search for ways to find it. Or they are stuck in a holding pattern internalizing the belief that without closure they cannot move on with life.

The Walking Wounded describe their losses as lacking closure. By assuming that closure is necessary but unattainable, they have difficulty finding language and rituals to help them express their grief. The Walking Wounded assume "normal" death is easier than other types of loss because closure is possible. The Walking Wounded may go down one of three general paths: (1) they may never find what they consider closure but continue to seek it; (2) they may go on to "find closure" through creative processes; or (3) they may decide they do not need what others have defined as closure, similar to the perspective of Myth Slayers whom we will discuss shortly.

Importantly, most individuals will neither fit neatly nor remain permanently in any of these categories. I use these labels and paths to help us understand how and why people argue they cannot find closure or they do not want closure. Grieving individuals will likely find themselves drifting from one perspective to another as they continue to find their way in their grief journey.

Using the examples of divorce, adoption, missing bodies, and wounded soldiers, I show how people talk about the lack of closure and, at times, the creative rituals used to try to find it. We also see further reinforcement of "normal loss" as that which has closure and "complicated loss" as that which does not. This not only legitimates the concept of closure but also ignores those who reject the need for closure (or struggle to find it) in circumstances of "normal loss."

Divorce: "The Corpse Is Still Walking Around"

The lack of closure is emphasized in many descriptions of why divorce is hard. Some argue that divorce or separation is worse than death because there is no closure. Here people assume that closure is found after death, which contradicts the claims of many who grieve. Nonetheless, there is a common comparison between divorce and death.

One website, which encourages both parents to be involved with children after a separation, implies that divorce is worse than death: "Children are distressed and damaged more by the loss of a parent through separation than through death. With death there is a closure and it is accompanied by good memories. With separation there is no closure and often on-going bad feelings."[27] Barb Hepperle, a divorce coach, said, "I was told from someone who lost a beloved child that her divorce pain was worse because the 'corpse' from her dead marriage still had the audacity to keep walking around! A common problem in the ending of a relationship is often there is no closure. This only adds more agony to the already broken heart."[28]

In a comment on a divorce support discussion, John compares divorce to death: "When your wife dies, hopefully you have happy memories and still feel loved by her, a funeral quickly brings closure." (You can imagine the frustration widows and widowers have with John's assumption of quick closure.) John goes on: "In a divorce, many people feel just as bereaved, and in addition to feeling the loss, they also suffer feelings of betrayal, hurt etc. and there is no swift closure, there are endless expensive visits to solicitors, court hearings etc."[29] On another blog about divorces, a similar comparison is made: "Here is the deal, with divorce there is no closure, they're still out there doing what they do. You never know when they are going to just pop up in your life. Now if they died well that's over it's done. You never have to be concerned about what they are going to do next. You can have closure it's just very sad for a while."[30]

Adoption: "No Acknowledged Grief and No Closure"

Parents who grieve the loss of their children to adoption are among the Walking Wounded. On a website about women who grieve over adoption, they argue that losing a child to adoption is far worse than losing a child to death, including miscarriage, because "there is no closure."[31] Other grieving mothers describe the pain of adoption this way: "When a mother loses her child to closed adoption, it feels as if her child has died, yet there is no wake, no funeral, no sympathy cards, no public acknowledgment. There are no friends or relatives to offer comfort and support. There is no obituary, no grave to visit, no flowers to bring, no grieving permitted and no closure."[32]

Adopted children may also experience unacknowledged loss. David Kirschner, an advocate for children who are placed for adoption, describes the pain for adoptees: "Consequently in adoption, there is too often *no* acknowledged grief, *no* meaningful mourning, and *no* closure. Just a festering wound that cries out to be healed, so that the adoptee can truly bond, give and receive love, have a solid sense of self and identity, and not get stuck in pathological grief and unrealistic fantasies (of birth parents) that may last a lifetime."[33] Author Sherrie Eldridge describes adoption this way: "It can be likened to a toddler losing both parents in an automobile accident, only there is no acknowledged grief, no funeral, no closure. Just a deep wound that needs to be healed." Family therapist Jeffrey LaCure says, "The difficult part for adoptees is that they never got the chance to say goodbye, to put closure on the relationship with their birth parent. It is like having a relationship with a stranger for years that is never completed. And that has a lifelong impact."[34]

At times, closure becomes a political battlefield. In the case of adoption, various groups fight over which adoption process will provide more closure for those involved. Advocates of closed adoption argue that keeping files closed will allow all involved to move on with their lives, which is an example of closure as "forgetting." Those who want open adoptions claim that having access to knowledge about the child, birth parents, and adoptive parents helps everyone maintain closure and peace of mind, which reflects closure as "knowing." Of course, those who are against any adoption claim that closure can never be found and argue that it is best to never separate a child from his or her biological parents.

Missing People: "Still Waiting for Closure"

Those waiting for confirmation of death are examples of the Walking Wounded. These individuals include those who are looking for missing persons or who presume a loved one died but have no physical proof. Media reports on missing persons often comment on families waiting for closure. In an article titled "No Closure for Family of Missing 11-Year-Old," the reporter writes: "More than three years after 11-year-old Nordex Wilkinson went missing family members are still waiting for closure, since even though they are almost sure she is dead they want confirmation of this so they can move on with their lives."[35] In another case, the report features the family's wait for closure: "It was two years ago today that Allison Jackson Foy of Wilmington went missing. At this point her family has assumed the worst, but is still waiting for closure."[36]

The attacks on September 11, 2001, led to a type of ambiguous loss for many families. During this time, family members continued to wait for identification of bodies or body parts in order to confirm the death of their loved ones. At the site of 9/11, forensic scientists worked hard to identify body parts to allow families to have some physical remains to bury. When this failed, other routes were explored. As an attempt to help the Walking Wounded, some churches and officials tried to help families find creative ways to have funeral rituals in an effort to find closure. Even the Catholic Church overlooked its usual rules and allowed people to display a photo instead of a coffin or to bury objects instead of bodies.[37] Pauline Boss counseled grieving families in New York following the attacks of September 11, 2001. She shares this story about a wife who was still looking for her husband six months after the attacks. At the time, the wife said, "I would be happy just to have a part of him to bury—even if it's just a finger nail." Boss says that when she met this woman, she reported that she had received his heart and buried it in a full-sized coffin in order to have the ritual of a funeral.[38]

While writing this chapter, I have been following the sad case of a missing college student in my community. Jon Lacina was last seen January 22, 2010. Finally, on April 14, his body was found. Closure was central in reporting his found body. The president of Jon's university said: "We all held out hope that Jonathan would be found alive and well, but while that hope no longer exists, Jonathan's family and friends can now begin to bring closure to this terrible ordeal." Jon's family graciously replied: "All we as Jon's family can do in return for all this is to express our gratitude, but please know it is heartfelt. We believe the care shown and the effort to bring closure for us is the touch of God through all of you to provide comfort in the face of the chaos of life."[39] It is too early to know whether Jon's family feels like they have found closure or even whether they want it.

Wounded Soldiers: "Do They Want to Go Back to Get Closure?"

Some of the Walking Wounded claim to find closure through alternative rituals. Creative closure describes a process of creating new rituals to try to achieve this emotional state of closure, however it may be defined. Sometimes people will create new rituals in an attempt to help people find closure when standardized rituals are not available. People's motives for selling closure rituals vary, as we will explore throughout this book.

An example of creative closure is Operation Proper Exit, which aims to help wounded soldiers find closure. Founded by the USO and the Troops First Foundation in June 2009, it is a program designed "to return the injured to the scene of their battlefield injuries to help them find psychological closure."[40] The program is supposed to "give wounded heroes a chance at closure by taking them back to the war zones that have left physical and emotional scars."[41]

Sometimes creativity can be risky. Operation Proper Exit was kept quiet when it was first started because no one was sure what might happen when returning wounded soldiers to the place where they were injured during an ongoing war. It was at best a tenuous experiment. After seeing what were considered positive responses, the program went public. Colonel David Sutherland said, "The amount of developmental growth and closure was phenomenal." Dr. John Olsen, an Army surgeon, said that the Army surgeon general referred to the program as an important psychological step. However, he acknowledged that there is no medical research that supports "the therapeutic value of sending wounded veterans back to a conflict zone."[42] Despite the perceived positive outcomes of the program, there is currently no research on the long-term effects of returning wounded soldiers to an active war zone to see the place where they were injured.

Richard Kell, executive director of the not-for-profit Troops First Foundation, developed the idea while talking to injured troops at Walter Reed Army Medical Center. As Kell states, "The first thing you hear from some of the wounded warriors is that they want to go back because they want to be with their buddies. Then later, as they heal physically . . . they say they want to go back to get closure." He says that some wounded soldiers move on without a need to return but that others never got to say good-bye properly.[43] Sloan Gibson, president of the USO, says that after participating in Operation Proper Exit, soldiers "return home knowing that their sacrifice is meaningful and that the men and women they've helped to protect and serve are truly grateful."[44]

Sergeant Rob Brown, who lost part of his leg and almost his life while serving in Iraq, now trains for the 2012 Olympics in kayaking, which he describes as a peaceful way to let go of past memories. "I had pretty much the entire chaplain corps standing over my head giving me my last rites. It was kind of disheartening." Rob explains part of the difficulty in recovery: "When you are ripped from a place that is part of your daily life, you tend to have a lot of regret. It is like that open chapter in your book of life that never gets finished and yet you've started another one." In reflecting on his return visit with Operation Proper Exit, he says, "The big portion of closure for me was the fact I could walk on my own two feet out of there as opposed to leaving on a stretcher. I didn't want the bad guys basically saying when I could leave. I wanted to be the one that did that on my own terms."[45]

Closure has also become a reason for awarding veterans a Purple Heart, which is a medal given to those who are wounded or killed in the line of duty. Wilbert "Shorty" Estabrook, a former prisoner of war during the Korean War, led a campaign to get a bill passed that would present a Purple Heart to all soldiers who died in captivity. He used closure as a reason why families need the Purple Heart awarded posthumously: "When someone died while a Prisoner of War that is as final as you can get and the Purple Heart offers at least some closure for the families!"[46] In a letter supporting the bill to change who gets a Purple Heart, Harold Fencl said, "The next of kin of these people recognize the Purple Heart Medal as final closure. No other medal says it like a Purple Heart. Most of the next of kin of those who died as prisoners of war have been told very little about their loved ones. They are searching for closure now."[47] Congress passed the Honor Our Fallen Prisoners of War Act in 2006, which changes who is eligible for the Purple Heart to include those who died while a prisoner of war.

Sixty years ago John Erickson was wounded in the Korean War and spent thirty-three months as a prisoner of war. But it was not until August 2010 that John received a Purple Heart. A friend and chaplain said, "For him, [the Purple Heart] is closure. He thought it would be awarded posthumously. This now makes him feel complete."[48] National Public Radio (NPR) hosted a discussion about the need for soldiers with traumatic brain injuries to receive a Purple Heart because it is the most powerful symbol to show that one has been wounded in action. However, the army has not given soldiers with traumatic brain injuries a Purple Heart, allegedly because it would cheapen the award. NPR reporter Daniel Zwerdling says that the soldiers and families he has talked to report that "they'd feel some sense of relief and closure" to receive a Purple Heart.[49] The debates about who should receive a Purple Heart and who needs closure continue.

These previous examples of the Walking Wounded involved circumstances of divorce, adoption, missing persons, and war wounds. But there are many other individuals who might be categorized as part of the Walking Wounded because they do not think they can grieve "normally" or find closure. A mother who experiences a miscarriage. A child whose parent was deported because he is an illegal immigrant. A young man who lost his home and all his possessions in a tornado but people ignore his loss when they keep saying how lucky he is to be alive. A young woman whose fiancé died but does not feel acknowledged as a grieving widow, even though she feels that way. A man who grieves for his dog but is afraid to share his pain. All these individuals will be searching for ways through their grief. Some may decide they can find closure through particular rituals. Others may never find what they think of as closure. Still others will decide that closure is a myth and not needed. We meet some of those people next.

Myth Slayers

Myth Slayers are people who claim, "There is no closure." Some of them may have a history of expecting closure, but at some point discovered that closure did not exist. Myth Slayers counter each of the assumptions that underlie dominant claims about closure. They argue that closure is not possible, not good, not desired, and not necessary. Closure is not possible because the pain never completely goes away. Closure is not good because it provides a false hope. Even if it does exist, they argue it is not desirable because people do not want to forget the good things about their loved ones. Closure is not necessary because there are other ways to find hope and healing without subscribing to the myth of closure.

Myth Slayers may feel compelled to warn others that closure does not exist and that it is a problematic concept. Importantly, these same people do not reject hope or healing. They report a lessening of pain over time and hope for healing. However, they use different concepts and language, besides closure, to talk about it.

Closure Is Not Possible Because the Pain Never Goes Away Completely

The most dominant point in the Myth Slayers' argument is that pain does not end and therefore closure is not possible. Gordon Livingston knows something about grieving loss. In 1991, his oldest son committed suicide after struggling with bipolar disorder. Six months later, Gordon's six-year-old son, Lucas, died from complications of leukemia. A psychiatrist and a grieving father, Gordon writes, "Like all who mourn I learned an abiding hatred for the word 'closure,' with its comforting implications that grief is a time-limited process from which we will all recover. The idea that I could reach a point when I would no longer miss my children was obscene to me and I dismissed it. I had to accept the reality that I would never be the same person, that some part of my heart, perhaps the best part, had been cut out and buried with my sons."[50] From both a professional and a personal point of view, Gordon rejects the idea that somehow you achieve closure: "The process of mourning requires that we keep fresh the memories of our child." He refers to visits to a grave over the years to illustrate one pattern of continual mourning: "Commonly this effort is played out in graveyards where birthday flowers are renewed and our footprints in the snow mirror the footprints in our hearts."[51]

Myth Slayers are angered by the notion that one can simply stop grieving. To them, closure implies an ending point in their grief, a place at which they can leave the pain and move on. As Amy Florian writes, "For many in our society, closure means leaving grief behind, a milestone usually expected within a matter of weeks or months. Closure means being 'normal,' getting back to your old self, no longer crying or being affected by the death. It means 'moving on with life' and leaving the past behind, even to the extent of forgetting it or ignoring it. For we who have experienced death, this kind of closure is not only impossible but indeed undesirable."[52]

The pain does not go away, Myth Slayers argue, because the love remains. Myth Slayers do not want to close the love, which is what they think others imply when pushing closure. Author Kevin Caruso explains this argument: "The love that you have for your angel will never 'close.' And thus the pain will never 'close.' No, there is no 'closure.' There is just love."[53]

In grieving for his brother, Joseph Dougherty argues against closure: "Closure implies that some day, all the sorrow and pain will be forgotten, and along with it, the feeling of emptiness created by the loss of one who we love so much. And also the memories of the good and the bad, the triumphs and the failures, the joys and the redemptions." He clarifies that closing memories includes not only the painful ones but also the good times. By suggesting closure, some assume that all memories are closed. Joseph explains that this is impossible and undesirable: "Closure implies finality, something ending or in completion. I challenge those of you who have lost a loved one to tell me if a single day passes when that person hasn't been in your thoughts, even if only for the briefest moment. Closure never occurs, because as long as all of us here today live, we will carry a part of this man in our hearts and our souls."[54]

From grief counselors to grieving parents, we see people working to end the myths about closure. Grief counselor Sherry Russell dismisses it: "Closure is supposed to be a finalization. It is supposed to tie up all the loose ends neatly and orderly, making some kind of sense out of what has happened. Where did it ever become acceptable to say grief had a 'closure'?"[55]

A support group for suicide rejects closure: "Suicide is extremely painful. And it is very difficult to move on after a suicide. And looking for 'closure' after a suicide is a natural thing to do. But I would suggest that you not focus on closure, because it will never happen."

Many bereaved parents hate the word "closure." Darcie Sims's son Austin died from a brain tumor at age one. Darcie argues that there is no such thing as closure and would like to banish the word closure from grief language. She says that the only thing that closes in death is the casket.[56] There is hope, peace, and healing, but not closure. A father of a murder victim tries to educate a journalist who asked him about closure: "'Don't use that word with me,' he said. 'I hate that word. I don't know who made that word up. There is no closure. So many people don't seem to understand that. There is no closure.'"[57]

Closure Is Not Good Because It Promises False Hope

The term "Myth Slayers" also captures people who are frustrated not only because they view closure as impossible but also because it provides false hope for people who are grieving. They fight against the concept of closure because when other people tell those who grieve to find closure, it can lead to more stress.

Jonathan Wallace writes about 9/11 on his web page and zeros in on the problem with our culture's conception of closure: "Despite the candy-sweet operations of hope, I do not believe that there has been any 'closure' or can ever be. Closure is a psychological fraud, a phony and poisonous by-product of hope, an artifact of a culture in which the most dangerous crisis must be resolved by the end of the television hour (or no later than the end of the television season). It is the concept, which has little to do with human reality, that stories have an ending."[58]

Myth Slayers reflect on the additional stress and, at times, the insults that come when people encourage closure. As Diane Leonard, whose husband, a Secret Service agent, died in the Oklahoma City bombing, said, "The word 'closure' is offensive to those involved personally in the bombing. There is no such thing as closure. It just doesn't happen. I'm finding the more people expect us to have it, and the more we expect ourselves to have it, the more frustrating it is that we can't reach it. It creates additional issues for us."[59]

Some websites warn people not to expect others to find closure. One website that offers advice on how to help parents who lose a baby lists prominently under the heading "What NOT to Say."

> "You need closure." . . . Think of closure as an ending point, and then remember that grief after losing a baby doesn't really ever end. Sometimes people will think that the purpose of mourning is to find closure, however, in the case of perinatal loss, there is no real end. You can have closure after completing a task such as making funeral arrangements or obtaining information about what may have caused the loss, but you don't really get closure of the love you have or the hopes and dreams for this baby. . . . "Closure" implies that there is an ending point. Grief softens and eases but doesn't really end. It evolves as life changes and moves forward. Parents mourn the loss of their baby, then they continue to revisit this loss as their lives unfold and they think about what would have been and what should have been.[60]

Friends and family are encouraged not to build up false hopes or unreal expectations by telling grieving parents to find closure: "Often when parents are seeking 'closure,' they are disappointed, frustrated, or confused when they find that this type of grief doesn't end. We all wish the pain could end, but it is usually more helpful to allow parents to talk about how they feel, to talk about their baby, and to grieve freely and without judgment rather than to impose time limits or a plan to seek closure."[61]

Some of the most passionate and intense claims against closure come from families of homicide victims who oppose the death penalty. One of their main concerns is that the argument for closure in the case of execution promises families false hope. We will learn more about family members of homicide victims in chapter 7.

Closure Is Not Desired Because We Do Not Want to Forget

Some Myth Slayers argue that even if closure did exist, it would be undesirable because they do not want to forget their loved ones. To them, closure implies not only an end to grief and pain but also an end to remembering their loved ones. They tend to be those who are grieving the death of a loved one, and they assume closure means forgetting. When people who are grieving think closure refers to ending memories or a relationship, they often reject it. Because closure is a socially constructed concept, we need to know how individuals interpret the meaning of closure in order to understand their responses.

Mazie Lawson went to the Pentagon on September 11, 2007, to participate in the sixth anniversary memorial service of the 9/11 attacks. She said that she grieves for her daughter, Cecelia, who died in the attack on the Pentagon. Speaking through her tears, Mazie told reporters, "Some people will say they want closure. I never want closure, because to me the word closure means to forget, and I don't want to forget my baby girl."[62] Nina Bennett shares Mazie's feelings as she expresses her love for a granddaughter: "If closure means moving on and leaving the memory of [my granddaughter] behind, then I will never have closure. Maddy is a very significant part of me, and I will carry her along for the rest of my life journey."[63]

Reverend Al Miles has counseled many people in their darkest hours of grief. When people ask him when grieving parents reach closure, his answer is "never." One of the people Miles has counseled is Larry, whose twenty-two-year-old son died from cancer. After awhile, people started pressuring Larry to find closure to his grief. He wondered, "What do these people mean by 'closure' anyway? Do they really think there'll come a time when I'll forget my son's life or death? Do they actually believe one day I'll no longer feel the pain of my loss?" Larry questioned why he would stop loving, missing, or thinking about his son. "If closure means forgetting my son, then I want nothing to do with this concept."[64]

Among those who think about closure as forgetting, grief counselor Sherry Russell argues that to accept closure is to end all memories and feelings. Who would want that when grieving a loved one? "If closure were possible, we wouldn't learn the lessons grief teaches."[65] Similarly, author Robert Shimabukuro criticizes the closure rhetoric that politicians used to describe the financial redress to Japanese Americans who were incarcerated during World War II, arguing that remembering this incarceration is an important political lesson that should not be forgotten. Supporting this view, an anonymous Seattle Nisei said: "I was against redress then, and I'm against redress now. There's no sum high enough that could compensate. And I don't want closure. I want people to remember the horror of what was done, every minute of every day. There should never be closure."[66]

Closure Is Not Necessary in Order to Find Hope and Healing

One of the problems with the closure narrative, as some Myth Slayers point out, is that it prevents people from thinking of other paths to healing after a loss. Myth Slayers offer hope and encouragement through a different path by explaining that the pain of grief eases over time. This, however, is different from closure. In fact, they argue that staying open to grief, as opposed to seeking closure, brings important experiences with it.

In her article for Atlanta's Compassionate Friends, Amy shares how grief eventually lessens its grip but still remains and eludes closure.

> Eventually we realize we are taking the past, with all its pain and pleasure, into a new tomorrow. We never forget, and in fact we carry our beloved with us; he or she is forever a cherished part of who we are. We are changed by the experience of having loved this person, by the knowledge of life's transience, and by grief itself. We become different and hopefully better, more compassionate, more appreciative, more tolerant people. We fully embrace life again, connecting, laughing and loving with a full heart. Still, there is no point of "final closure," no point at which we can say, "Ah, now I have finally completed my grief." Or, "Yes, now I have healed." There is no point at which we will never cry again, although as time goes on the tears are bittersweet and less common.[67]

We return to Jonathan Wallace's comments about closure in his reflections on 9/11. He dismisses closure and explains that though the bereaved will move on and grief will ease, there will still be no closure.

> Closure is in particular a fraud on the bereaved, as it preaches that there will—there *should*—come a moment when grief is over. In reality, though we may go on with our lives, remarry, bear new children, and laugh at silly jokes again, there is no reason ever to stop mourning or to forget what we have lost. Grief may recede; instead of being the ocean we swim in, it may be a vial of ocean water in the cabinet of wonder, but it is always there. Balance, yes; closure, never.[68]

Myth Slayers suggest that those who push for closure have never experienced intense grief themselves but rather want others to get over the pain and move on. It is the "other people" around those who grieve that want the closure to happen. They argue that the larger cultural phenomenon does not translate well to individual grieving.

In an article for the *New York Times*, Anna Quindlen poignantly captures frustration with closure: "The world loves closure, loves a thing that can, as they say, be gotten through. This is why it comes as a great surprise to find that loss is forever, that two decades after the event there are those occasions when something in you cries out at the continuous presence of an absence."[69]

As a self-described life coach, Quinn McDonald tells clients that there is no closure to grief. She says, "As a culture, Americans are big on closure. Something awful happens to us, and we look for a ritual that allows us to tie it up neatly, claim we are 'just fine,' and go back to work." But she tells her clients that there are no instructions for grief: "We have to write our own. And there is no closure, no sign that we get that mourning is over and we can go back to our regular lives. When we lose someone we love, when a medical problem blows up our routine, lives do not get glued back together." [70]

Myth Slayers often point to people who have not experienced grief as the ones who push for closure. Joseph Dougherty talked about this point at his brother's funeral: "When we see or read news stories about families suffering tragedy and loss, a modern term for dealing with those losses is often used: 'closure.' Closure. A nice, convenient word to describe what some believe other people achieve after a devastating loss. What's apparent to me is that those people never knew what it means personally to suffer a loss such as the one we all experienced this past Sunday morning. There is no closure."[71]

Myth Slayers are charting their own journey through grief. They reject the road map that points to closure as a destination. Myth Slayers find healing and peace during their journey, but do not use closure to describe this experience.

Grief Is Complicated and Normal

For sure, there are complicated circumstances and how we grieve the loss of our relationships differ. There is a difference in grieving for a child who was murdered and grieving for a ninety-six-year-old mother who died in her sleep. There is a difference in grieving for a loved one who is presumed dead but whose body has not been found and grieving for a loved one who died after living with cancer for five years. My point is *not* that some deaths are easier to grieve than others but rather that there are many differences in how people die and how we grieve. Too often, though, these different experiences receive similar responses from friends, family, and counselors in terms of how people are expected to grieve. It is true that grief is often complicated. It is also the case that complicated grief is most often normal.

Medicalizing grief and labeling people as having a disorder further privatizes the grieving process. Rather than encouraging cultural rituals that increase social support from friends, family, and cultural groups, we further individualize the experience of grief by labeling people as pathological in need of psychiatric care and/or drugs.

Myth Slayers face an uphill battle in light of the *DSM* and its official label of "prolonged grief" as a mental disorder. The Walking Wounded will increasingly feel detached from the "normal standards" for grieving. And so they will look for new ways to heal. Philosopher Thomas Attig says, "With each detail we identify that troubles us, we can use our imaginations to think of ways to relieve our hurt or find some resolution or closure."[72]

Creating new rituals for grieving is not necessarily a bad thing. We should be open to people creating their own road map. As a society, however, we tend to favor the universal road map that says, "Destination: closure." If the Walking Wounded focus too intently on closure as described by standardized feeling rules, they may get stuck on the side of the road because they cannot follow the map. With this dominant narrative about grief, we see a market for those selling closure.

Even those whose grief others acknowledge and who face a loss that is clear and typical are surrounded with advice and marketing campaigns for how they can best grieve and find closure. Those who do want to use a universal road map for grief are not sheltered from the contradicting messages about closure.

In contemporary U.S. society, we increasingly see people and institutions develop and sell policies, products, and services in the name of closure. It is not just therapists and psychiatrists who get involved in "treating grief," but, as we will see in later chapters, a whole range of individuals and businesses claim to be "grief experts" and sell products and services promising closure. All along grief's road are people selling closure. Some are selling products and services as we will see in chapters 4, 5, and 6. Others are politicians and advocates using closure in political rhetoric, which is explored in chapters 7 and 8.

No guidelines or licenses are needed to sell closure. We ought to examine what these narratives say to people who are traveling along grief's road. In the next chapter, we see how those who are in the business of death care—such as funerals, cremation, memorialization, and pet grief—are guiding people in their grief journey. A challenge for people is that the signs along the road that read "this way to closure" often have arrows pointing in opposite directions.

4. From Embalming to Teddy Bear Urns

Selling Closure in the Twenty-First-Century Death Care Industry

When I was a teenage exchange student in Japan, my host family's grandfather died. I was struck by the differences between his three-day Buddhist funeral and funerals I had witnessed back home. The Japanese ceremony occurred at home: The family placed the body in a wooden box, arranged flowers around it, and then took turns nailing the box shut. The next day they took the body to a crematory and ate lunch during the cremation. Afterwards, family members took turns removing pieces of bone from the ashes with chopsticks; the bones were placed in a ceramic urn to be buried. The entire family took part in the ceremony, and they seemed at peace when it ended. Today, some might say they had found closure.

My experience in Japan reflects cultural differences in caring for our dead. Even in the United States, there are many ways to care for our loved ones when they die. People make choices about death care as they navigate the sales talks of those who are in the business of death. Often as part of their sales pitch, they sell themselves as experts in helping people grieve. Contemporary marketing of these services relies heavily on selling closure. This chapter discusses how funeral home directors, home funeral advocates, ash-handling businesses, and the pet grief industry use the concept of closure and, in the process, help shape feeling rules for grieving. In particular, we will see how the businesses use competing—and contradicting—arguments for what brings closure.

Professional Funeral Homes

In the twentieth century, professional funeral homes became the dominant way of caring for our dead—moving our society away from families taking care of deceased loved ones in the private home. The funeral industry emerged during the Civil War with embalming as its cornerstone. Prior to the war, embalming was used in medical schools to preserve bodies for instruction. Other than that, embalming, or the preservation of a dead body, was not acceptable. Value was placed on the integrity of the dead body; no interference with the body was wanted.

Two things happened during and after the Civil War that changed the way many Americans viewed embalming. During the war, families who could afford it found specialists who helped preserve the bodies of dead soldiers, offering families the chance to see their loved ones again before burial even though they may have died far away from home.[1] This opportunity gave emerging undertakers practice and public acceptance for their craft. A second critical event was the death of President Abraham Lincoln and the cross-country journey of his preserved body. Well-known death scholar Gary Laderman describes this event: "Hundreds of thousands of people filed past the viewable body on display in cities from Washington, D.C., to Springfield, Illinois, and newspaper reports provided the public with graphic details about embalmers, whose methods were central to preserving a sacred relic that ritualistically united Americans after the divisive and bloody war."[2]

In time, embalming became the linchpin of the funeral industry. Once people became convinced that embalming was a necessary part of caring for the dead, it was no longer feasible for ordinary citizens to take care of their own dead. Today, however, some people are questioning the necessity of embalming and traditional funerals.

In the twenty-first century, new trends in death care increasingly challenge funeral directors' ownership of the death care industry. As (often less expensive) cremations have become more popular, funeral homes have had to step up their marketing to keep their profits from going up in ashes. Funeral directors and related businesses are creative in using the concept of closure to sell their services.

According to the National Funeral Directors Association, in 2009, 37 percent of deaths resulted in cremation as the choice for final disposition in the United States. It predicts that, by 2025, cremation will account for 59 percent of dispositions. There are several possible explanations for the increase. First, cremation generally requires fewer services, products, and materials and therefore costs less than a traditional funeral service. A typical cremation package costs between $1,000 and $2,000 compared to a traditional funeral that can easily cost on average $6,500 and may run well over $10,000. Second, some religions have become more accepting of cremation. For example, in 1997, the Roman Catholic Church agreed that cremation ashes could be present at a Catholic funeral mass. Third, environmental concerns, including land use and avoidance of chemicals released in the ground from embalming, have also raised interest in cremation. (There are also competing concerns about the environmental damage from cremation, so the debate continues.) Finally, our society's increasing mobility could lead to higher rates of cremation as people feel less of a need or ability to have a family plot. Cremation ashes can be moved easier than bodies if families want to keep loved ones near them.

Some countries have a higher rate of cremation; in Japan, the rate is almost 100 percent. Major religions, such as Buddhism, Sikhism, and Hinduism, encourage cremation as a final disposition, whereas other faiths like Christianity, Judaism, and Islam may discourage it in favor of burial. In some Christian denominations, however, there is an increasing openness to cremation as an acceptable final disposition. Religion is a crucial, though not exclusive, factor in shaping how people choose death care rituals. If following a culture or religious community that shapes the rituals for death, one has to make fewer decisions about what to do when a loved one dies. The cultural rituals, whether religious or other, may provide guidance. In Japan, people do not have to rely on death care businesses to guide their grieving. When a culture does not provide such dominant guidelines, death care businesses have more influence in shaping choices following a death.

In the United States, there are many religious and nonreligious views about death. Cremation and alternative memorial services are competing with the traditional funeral and burial. The trend toward more cremations is a concern for funeral homes because they lose money if families choose "direct cremation," which means no public viewing or additional services. The profits are in high-end caskets, embalming, and other cosmetic and viewing services. The traditional funeral service usually includes extra services and products that add to their profit. For example, a list of products and services for the "traditional full-service funeral" from Bryant Mortuary in San Francisco reads:

> Casket; local transfer of the deceased to the funeral home; embalming; dressing, cosmetology and other care of the deceased; professional support and administrative staff assistance; preparation of the necessary permits and death certificate; receiving and arranging

floral arrangements; use of the visitation rooms; general use of the facilities for the service and arrangements; funeral service; use of the funeral coach; limousine; utility/flower cart; register book; acknowledgment cards; and memorial folders/programs or prayer cards.[3]

As this list makes clear, the cremation option circumvents many of these costs and is therefore less lucrative to a funeral home.

In an effort to combat this trend of direct cremations, funeral directors increasingly describe having a funeral as essential for gaining closure. DeVoe Funeral Service Inc., located in New Jersey, highlights closure in its description of a funeral: "A funeral is an opportunity for relatives, friends and neighbors to reflect upon and celebrate the life of the deceased and gain personal closure."[4] The Minnesota Funeral Directors Association describes a funeral as a step toward a separation from the deceased: "The funeral is oftentimes a good means of closure for the living, a time to say goodbye, and a time to begin living again without the loved one." Ross, Burke, and Knobel Mortuary, located in Nevada, states: "A 'closure' of sorts must occur to help survivors adjust to their loss and recognize that a death has occurred."

Funeral homes cannot just rely on traditional funerals for their profits, so they are working to stay involved with cremation and provide other services to go with it. With the increase in cremations, funeral home directors need to convince people that at least some of the traditional funeral services are still needed.

Embalming and viewing has been marketed as necessary for closure, even if family members choose cremation as the final disposition. Such efforts from the funeral industry help shape one of the most dominant feeling rules about grieving—you need a formal viewing complete with embalming in order to gain closure. Embalming continues to be an important part of a funeral home's business and needs to be preserved through careful marketing. Current marketing for embalming stresses two themes: (1) embalming is an art that provides peace of mind and closure for the family, and (2) viewing is necessary for people to reach closure, and thus embalming is needed for viewing.

Although embalmers literally perform physical closure on their dead clients, they also sell emotional closure to their living ones. Some embalmers describe their work as an art. Deborah Bluck, a funeral director and embalmer, says that her work is a positive thing that helps people through difficult times: "Viewing a loved one helps with the healing process. The family has an easier time with closure and it sinks in that they are really gone. It eases their mind."[5]

Those who sell embalming as an art and a means to closure rely on the belief that seeing the loved one looking "natural," "pleasing," and "peaceful" will hasten the grieving process. According to the International Cemetery, Cremation and Funeral Association (ICCFA), "embalming is a temporary preservation of a dead human person." It describes the process as "a surgical-like technique of injecting chemical solutions into the deceased's vascular system, thus producing a natural life-like appearance."[6] The chemicals in the body from embalming give a deceased person the fullness and color that reflect the living more than the dead.

Sometimes embalming includes efforts to reconstruct a badly damaged body. Vernie Fountain has been an embalmer specializing in postmortem reconstructive surgery for over thirty years. According to the website of the Fountain National Academy of Professional Embalming Skills, in 1990, Fountain started his mission to turn the previous "closed casket situation" into an "open casket situation." Faye Bonini, the professional development coordinator of the National Funeral Directors Association, argues, "Family members don't want their loved ones buried appearing the way they died. They want to remember them how they appeared when they were living."[7] Fountain agrees and says that he hopes his seminars designed to teach mortuary students about postmortem reconstructive surgery do more than just teach the practical skills.

Fountain wants to educate the public on how embalmers give closure to families of the deceased. "I've had instances where family members came up to hug me and cry on my shoulder because of the joy that their lasting image of their loved one was not a gunshot wound," Fountain says.[8] He passionately argues that an embalmer's ability to offer an open casket "makes a huge difference in the happiness of the family."

One family who is grateful to Fountain lives in Iowa. Their twenty-two-year-old son committed suicide by placing a rifle in his mouth and pulling the trigger. The damage was severe. There was no note. The family wanted to see their son once again to say good-bye. The family's local funeral director called Fountain and asked him to come restore the young man's image. The funeral home director said that the family and community needed to see the young man for a final moment. In a testimonial letter to the funeral home, the family thanked Fountain for helping them find closure.[9] They appreciated that Fountain could repair their son's face and said that the open-casket funeral provided "a great deal of closure" for their family and others.

Of course, most people do not incur such disfiguring wounds. And not all families have the need to see their loved one embalmed. Nonetheless, they will also likely be encouraged to have a viewing.

In the case of professional funeral homes, the "viewing" typically refers to those that funeral directors arrange for the public, which include embalming and other services. It is possible for family members to "view a body" without having all services added such as embalming. However, when funeral homes discuss the "viewing," they usually encourage a family to have a public time of viewing with the formally presented and embalmed body complete with cosmetics.

Although the law does not require embalming in the majority of situations, most funeral homes will not allow a public visitation unless the body is embalmed. It is not usually explained, but families can have a private viewing of the body even if there is no embalming. Refrigerating a body to delay decomposition instead of embalming could be an option in most cases if funeral homes would offer it.[10] The public viewing of the body is touted as necessary for closure to help maintain a need for embalming.

Occasionally, a funeral home will acknowledge in person or in its marketing literature that embalming is not legally required but will argue that it is still important. As explained on the website of the Springfield Funeral Home in British Columbia,

> While embalming is not mandatory except in some specific instances, it is our sincere belief that healing is best promoted by adequate closure of a relationship. The grief journey includes spending time with the loved one's body, that part of them that gave us access to their soul. As the body is viewed and we bid our farewell, the reality of death is impressed upon us visually, and so we are able to begin our sad journey through grief to a new kind of wholeness.[11]

Funeral home and crematory directors tend to sell "viewing the body" (which implies, but need not describe, embalming) as the way to find closure. The graphic language and difficult images surrounding embalming make it a tricky bit of marketing. Therefore, convincing mourners of the importance of "viewing a body" is critical to selling embalming services.

Kohut Funeral Home, located in Pennsylvania, states on its website that "viewing is part of tradition for many people who consider it part of closure." It also cites unnamed sources in declaring that "most grief specialists felt that it helps the grieving process by making the bereaved recognize the reality of death." After acknowledging that there are other forms of final disposition, it then claims that "the traditional viewing and funeral service associated with burial help to bring closure to friends and family."[12] Other funeral homes suggest that friends and family "may be in shock or denial" and that a viewing of the body "can bring a sense of closure to the bereaved."[13] Bliley's Funeral Homes in Virginia calls viewing "a very literal way for the living to find closure and say their good-byes."[14]

With so much at stake, many funeral home directors do not rely solely on encouraging people to have a viewing. They go further in warning potential clients that "direct cremation" may not provide closure. Iowa's Hugeback Funeral Home characterizes direct cremations this way: "The best known option is 'direct' cremation. However, 'direct' emphasizes no viewing or visitation, no service, no casket or burial, and sometimes . . . no closure."[15] Other funeral homes repeat the line that direct cremation offers no closure. In fact, the same paragraph is repeated word for word on many websites because huge corporations now own so many smaller funeral homes and use the same marketing information. Funeral homes often also cite unnamed research studies to make their argument, as in this example: "Researchers have found that people who did not go through a funeral or memorial service or did not have a physical place to place flowers or other memorabilia found it harder to bring closure to the loved one's death."[16]

Other crematories explain that direct cremation alone may not provide the closure you need. Benedict-Rettey Mortuary & Crematory in California encourages clients to do more than cremation: "You may select cremation only. This entails simply meeting with us to arrange the details. However, we hope you consider the benefit of some type of formal or informal service, for the support it can bring to family and friends, as well as the closure it helps to provide."[17]

Some funeral homes offer cautionary tales of regret when discussing their warning about direct cremation. Iles Funeral Home in Des Moines, Iowa, shares its concern with potential clients: "Although direct cremation without any type of gathering or service is an option, many people later regret this decision because it ignores the need for closure."[18]

"There is still hope for closure" is the message that typically follows the warning. Tennessee's Atchley Funeral Home assures clients that "families who choose cremation instead of burial can still fulfill the need for closure by having a funeral ceremony and/or visitation."[19] Hugeback Funeral Home tells clients: "Viewing the body brings closure to friends and family, allowing them to accept the death."[20] And, if clients decide on the viewing, it means they are buying additional services, including caskets, embalming, facility use, and other handling charges.

Funeral industry professionals have been claiming for decades that the traditional funeral, including viewing and embalming, are important for the grief process. Funeral homes continue to make this claim but now connect it to the popular concept of closure. Interestingly, some of their competitors also use closure to sell alternative forms of funerals. One response to the dissatisfaction with the funeral industry is a movement toward home funerals. Once again, we find lots of talk about the need for closure and claims that only home services can offer true closure.

Home Funerals

Home funerals reflect an earlier era of death care, a time before professionals were called to take care of our deceased loved ones. Modern advocates of home funerals are selling a philosophy about death care: the family should take care of their loved ones after death. There are a growing number of these advocates, or as some call themselves, death midwives, around the country willing to shepherd families through a home funeral. One of them is Jerrigrace Lyons.

Lyons is an ordained minister who operates Final Passages, a home funeral advocacy business. She also gives workshops to teach others how to be home funeral advocates. When Howard Kopecky was diagnosed with terminal cancer, he knew that he did not want his family to spend a lot of money on his funeral. He saw an ad in the paper for midwife Lucy Basler—who had been trained by Lyons. When he died, Howard's wife and his family were able to give him a meaningful service for under $1,000.[21]

On her website, Lyons explains that home funerals promote healing and closure for several reasons. For example, she says that the process of family and friends constructing or decorating a wooden or cardboard casket or urn is a "healing act of closure." She also claims that community participation and a home ceremony allow more time for closure.[22]

Katherine Foster, a doctor on the Kaiser Bioethics Committee, testifies that Final Passages offers a "valuable step in a cultural shift toward allowing families to reclaim the process of closure on the life of their loved one." It is significant that she argues that it is the process of closure that needs to be reclaimed and not merely the rituals of caring for our dead. Once again, we see the importance of closure elevated in grief narratives.

On homefuneral.com, advocates claim that "being physically involved in the process helps in grieving. It gives more closure to the loss of a loved one. And it's a relief to many people because they can 'do something' rather than sitting idly by waiting for a funeral home to take care of arrangements." Lyons explains the process that brings closure:

Fear of having the body nearby is the hard issue. They're concerned about odor and seeing the body deteriorate. They're afraid it will melt right in front of their eyes. Over a couple of days the body does change, usually in subtle ways. It starts to look more like a shell. But having a wake and caring for the body in the home is the way we used to do it. Another fear is looking at our own mortality. People don't want to do that. But bathing the body of a family member or friend following death, sitting beside their body, talking to them, maybe crying beside them, all helps us come to terms with their passage. We begin to receive the information with many of our senses, helping to bring some closure to the initial shock that death can bring.[23]

Elizabeth Knox tragically stumbled into the business of home funerals. In 1995, her seven-year-old daughter Alison died in a car accident. Refusing to turn over her body to strangers, Elizabeth found a way to take care of her daughter with the help of a funeral director who showed her how. She describes the process: "I cared for her at home for three days, bathing her, watching her, taking in slowly the painful reality that she has passed from this life, and sharing my grief with her classmates and brothers and grandparents and our wonderful community of friends, before finally letting go of her body."[24]

That experience, simultaneously tragic and beautiful, led her to create Crossings, a home funeral and green burial resource center. Ken Picard interviewed Elizabeth and shared these insights about home funerals:

The sense of closure that comes from doing a home funeral should make sense to anyone who has lost a close friend or family member. During a time of mourning, especially after a sudden, unexpected death, people want to feel useful. But all too often, the expression of condolence—"Is there anything I can do?"—has no response. In this country, where 99 percent of all deaths are handled by funeral directors, there's rarely anything of substance for friends and family to do. But, as Knox explains, giving people a task—picking up the death certificate, buying more dry ice, building the coffin or digging the grave—provides a physical way to work through grief.[25]

Tim Matson, author of *Round-Trip to Deadsville*, shares a cautionary tale with others: "Whether you build a coffin, bury a body or help plan a service, it's essential to play a part in funeral preparation to achieve a sense of closure." The caution comes when he recalls a friend who still regrets being rushed through all the funeral preparations for her father. His friend lamented, "He [the undertaker] handled everything. I don't feel like I was really involved, it happened so fast."[26]

Tracy French is a former board member of the Funeral Consumers Alliance of Humboldt in California. She explicitly tells people that embalming is not needed. In fact, she pushes the perspective that spending time with a loved one's body is what allows closure.

> There's no good reason for embalming. One of the things we learned about was keeping a body cool on dry ice, wrapping it in towels and laying a blanket or something over it. They say you can keep a body for several days, but it depends on the climate. Up here three or four days should be no problem. It can be very healing for the family to sit with the body rather than having it whisked away. You can let it sink in, find closure.[27]

In the case of home funerals, advocates also emphasize the need for viewing the body, but not in the way funeral homes talk about it. Home funeral advocates argue that embalming is not necessary and that the actual work of taking care of a loved one's body is what brings closure for family members. Furthermore, some advocates would say that viewing the natural process of death—that is not temporarily halted by embalming—is an important part of people's grief process.

Rhetoric in the professional funeral homes and the home funeral movement describes closure as an emotion that can only be achieved through the proper rituals. The confusing and contradictory advice offered to those grieving a loved one may not end with choosing between professional or home funerals. If you decide to cremate a loved one, you will have to decide what to do with the ashes. There are plenty of businesses willing to help you make those decisions. Again, you will notice that the arguments for what provides the best closure point in different directions.

Ashes to Ashes: Caring for Remains

The increase in cremations means more families have to decide what to do with the ashes. Should you scatter ashes over a favorite place? Bury them in a secure location that allows generations to visit? Keep them in an urn on your mantel? Or turn your loved one into jewelry or other keepsakes? If someone follows religious customs, family traditions, or other cultural rituals concerning death care, then the decision for handling ashes may not be as complicated. My host family in Japan knew exactly what to do with the cremation remains and was not left wondering which option to choose.

In the United States, however, many people remain open to exploring alternative options regarding cremation remains. A growing number of businesses have seized the opportunity to tell people how to properly care for loved ones' ashes in a way that provides closure. The stiff competition over ash handling has also complicated grief narratives as businesses fight over the proper way to reach closure in the process of caring for loved ones' remains.

Aerial Burial

Aerial burial is a popular way to scatter ashes. There are airborne scattering businesses across the country providing options for grieving families. Several common arguments are made in the sales rhetoric of these businesses: aerial scatterings provide closure, maintain a dignified process, offer a superior memorialization than other methods, limit family members' mistakes, and set the loved one's spirit free.

Kelly Murtaugh, president of the International Scattering Society, says that the best part of scattering ashes is providing people with peace of mind and closure.[28] Air Legacy, a scattering business located in Colorado, claims, "Aerial Ash Scattering is perfect closure."[29] Everlife Memorials in Texas advertises the scattering of ashes on its website: "Aerial scattering offers a means of closure to families who are ready to take the final step in the grieving process."[30]

Scatterings, a California business that scatters cremated remains, claims, "Airborne scattering above a memorable setting gives closure while providing peace and comfort to those left behind."[31] An "unattended scattering of ashes" ranges from approximately $195 to $325, depending on the desired site of the scattering. If you want to go along when the ashes are scattered, it will cost more. Scatterings encourages clients to ride along in the airplane in order to find closure. The following quote is the company's description of participating in the release:

> You will be able to pour the ashes from their urn, however you will typically not see the ashes as they are released beneath the aircraft. It can be emotional to take part in the actual scattering of the ashes, and the small space, noise and bumpy ride in a small aircraft can heighten those emotions. However the views from the aircraft and participating in the release can provide for powerful closure.[32]

A flight that families attend is $725 or higher depending on the number of people and other services chosen.

Homeward Bound Aerial Services in Colorado describes its purpose as helping "in the bereavement process, creating a lasting memorial to loved ones by professionally scattering ashes from an airplane. This helps to bring closure and peace of mind to family and friends."[33] Final Flights, a scattering business in California, promotes its business as "a dignified scattering of your loved one's ashes from the air, returning them to the earth or sea." Then in boldface letters is the following promise of closure: "Bring peace and closure with a moment of dignity and beauty."[34]

In addition to closure, scattering businesses argue that airborne memorials are better than other memorials. Scatterings promotes aerial scattering of ashes as a superior memorial to a loved one compared to more traditional choices: "For those left behind, the focal point of the memorial becomes not a marker in a cemetery, but the memories of the person, and the place of scattering, as they are encountered during the patterns of daily life." It describes an airborne scattering as offering a wide-reaching memorial: "When the remains of your loved one are scattered by air, each sunset becomes an ongoing memorial, no matter where you are when that sunset is observed."[35]

Another argument airborne scattering businesses make for their services is that they help loved ones release the deceased's spirit. Final Flights says that while some people choose to keep loved ones at home or in a mausoleum, others want the scattering of ashes, which releases the spirit. "While scattering from a boat in the ocean has become quite commonplace, scattering from an aircraft is rather unique. Ashes dispersed from an airplane cover a much larger area, enhancing the feeling that a loved one's spirit is being set free in Nature."[36] The claim that scattering sets a spirit free implies that closure comes from knowing a loved one is now free.

There is clearly an entrepreneurial motivation in many of these businesses. While some specialize in the scattering of ashes, others use it as a way to broaden their services. Clearwater Flight Services in Florida sells a range of distinct services, including a Mile High Club (which allows a couple to engage in sex in flight), as well as Ashes over the Sea, which it says is performed with "dignity and sensitivity." Clearwater Flight Services claims, "A memorable setting gives closure to the cremation process while providing peace and comfort to those left behind."[37] The Mile High Club costs $275 per hour. Ashes over the Sea costs $300 for an unattended scattering. An attended scattering costs an additional $100 per person. It appears that sex is cheaper than death. Or perhaps it is the closure that costs more.

Eternal Ascent in Florida offers the airborne release of ashes by balloon. Its sales pitch leans heavily on the battle over which service provides the best closure for the most people. For example, it claims that scattering ashes from a single-engine plane provides no closure. Likewise, reef balls (which will be discussed shortly) are very expensive and do not provide much closure. Fireworks, or rather shooting ashes up with fireworks, are described as "Very expensive. Not very peaceful. Not a lot of closure." And, interestingly, keeping an urn at home is described as "Not inclusive, limited closure for others. Only for one or two people and usually not passed down to anyone." As for how its services do in providing closure, Eternal Ascent has this to say:

> Closure: While we can't guarantee closure, we can provide a visual that will be sure to help you with the grieving process. When you see your loved one's ashes ascending up to the heavens, you get a sense of closure, peace, and pride along with satisfaction that you've done the very best for your loved one. Our method is a celebration of life which will surely bring to you "Peace of Mind" and a deep sense of closure. Everyone who has attended what we call a "Release," has commented that they think it is so beautiful and fills them with memories of their loved one whenever they see a sunset, rainbow, or lone cloud.[38]

Although the first sentence of this passage says that Eternal Ascent cannot guarantee closure, other parts of the same passage promise it. As with other businesses, Eternal Ascent combines the assurance of dignity with the promise of closure. In its description of a memorial of a lifetime, it states: "We celebrate a life by providing you with the most fitting and unique farewell. Our method is both dignified and affordable. A truly joyful tribute which brings a deep sense of closure when you thought you never could."[39]

A business in England offers the scattering of ashes in a fireworks display. Heavens Above Fireworks customizes fireworks to include human or pet remains, allowing for what it calls "a spectacular memorial event and happier farewell." Displays range from the "Grand Finale" to "A Simple Farewell." It also provides memorial spaceflights in which people can send ashes into space.[40]

Memorial Spaceflights in the United States also provides services to send ashes into space. In the first memorial flight in 1997, a symbolic sample of ashes from twenty-four people, including Timothy Leary and *Star Trek* creator Gene Roddenberry, were sent into space. For some of the later flights, a link was added to the Memorial Spaceflights website to show where the flight was orbiting. On its website, the creators posted this note from one of their clients: "I wanted to thank all of you and the whole organization for all you have done for my family and the other families involved in the launch. It was truly a moment of closure for all. God bless!"[41]

Burial at Sea

Aerial burial businesses face competition from those offering burial at sea. Nature's Passage emphasizes that its sea burials offer closure in a way that other services cannot provide: "Your sea burial ceremony will be held in a de-institutionalized setting—at sea . . . a dramatic, serene and intimate setting while family and friends participate in the ceremony that facilitates grieving and encourages healing and closure an experience that you wouldn't see in a funeral home or cemetery."[42] Serenity at Sea in California is another example of a business specializing in ash scattering. According to Serenity at Sea, it is "the organic nature of the ocean" that brings people closure.[43]

Some businesses expand their other aquatic services by offering ash scattering. In addition to weddings, dinner cruises, and sailing, California Cruisin' offers closure through ash scattering: "The scattering of their ashes at sea provides a meaningful and memorable closure in which we feel connected to nature and the cycle of life."[44] For $750, Island Bound Cruises in New Hampshire offers closure for those who are grieving: "A Burial at Sea helps bring closure to the loss of a loved one by celebrating the spirit of their life with the ever-present spirit of the ocean, the water that connects us all. The scattering of ashes at sea combines a sense of finality and a new beginning."[45]

Eternal reefs, or reef balls, are another way to bury loved ones at sea. For eternal reefs, human remains are mixed with concrete to make a casting that is later lowered into the ocean to attract ocean life. Family members can help make the cast and even leave handprints or written messages in the concrete.

The reefs are held up as a means for closure. As Don Brawley, owner of Eternal Reefs in Georgia, says, "We are in the closure business, we get people back in touch with the process."[46] Don describes the option: "For families and individuals that choose cremation, Eternal Reefs offers a new memorial choice that replaces cremation urns and ash scattering with a permanent environmental living legacy."[47] The "permanent" concept is combined with environmental friendliness and a new beginning. Larger reefs cost over $6,000 but can accommodate several sets of remains, making them available for spouses to share. Smaller reefs are available for around $2,000. Journalist Sylvia Cochran describes the eco-friendly burial of eternal reefs as a "wonderful means of offering closure to a family ready to celebrate a life well lived, rather than merely mourn the loss of a loved one." The language she uses challenges people to not "merely mourn" but "celebrate a life."[48]

Do-It-Yourself Scatterings

The question may be raised: Why do you have to pay other people to scatter ashes in order to seek closure? There may be something to the expertise in scattering ashes. It is not always so easy to dump a bag or urn of ashes in the air and not have them fly back into your face. In a memorable scene in *The Big Lebowski*, the Coen brothers illustrate this problem when The Dude and Walter are trying to scatter Donny's ashes only to have them blow back all over them.

However, air scattering businesses go beyond the potential messiness of scattering ashes and work on shaping people's emotional expectations. They warn that some methods of keeping ashes are not dignified, including having family members handle the ashes. One ash-scattering business explains why you should hire professionals to scatter ashes rather than just leave it to family members.

> Unless you have been specific with regard to your wishes, the finality of scattering can paralyze, and often the result is that nothing is done. The ashes are taken by surviving family members and kept on a shelf in a closet. The closure that is so necessary in the grieving process is never achieved. The ashes may not comfort, and can become a silent burden. The airborne release of cremated remains offers closure in a legal, dignified manner, over a location that is scenic or holds special significance, and does so in a manner that is in keeping with the philosophy of cremation.[49]

Air Legacy cautions people about the "generational concern" of leaving ashes in the hands of family members. A loved one may keep your remains on a mantel or in storage. The next generation might do something even "less dignified." It also describes air scattering as more dignified than "simply just spreading the ashes on the ground." In sum, it claims, "Ash Scattering is perfect closure."[50]

These warnings do not keep everyone from do-it-yourself scatterings. Some people choose even more unusual, and often illegal, places to scatter ashes of loved ones. In November 2007, Disneyland employees noticed on camera a woman scattering powder while riding the Pirates of the Caribbean.[51] Officials quickly shut down the ride and cleaned up the ashes with a vacuum purchased for that job. The vacuums have special high-efficiency particulate air (HEPA) filters that pick up the ash as well as any bone fragments left. Disneyland officials use the code "HEPA cleanup" to let others know that they need to clean up cremation ashes.[52] Avoiding "HEPA cleanup" would be a good argument for professional ash handlers to use in convincing people that true closure comes only through proper scatterings.

Other people ask loved ones to scatter their ashes over favorite sites such as golf courses, parks, ball fields, backyards (even if they no longer live there), oceans, and so on. Olympic gold medalist Misty May-Treanor scattered some of her mother's ashes on the sand volleyball court after winning gold in Athens in 2004 and Beijing in 2008.

President Barack Obama knows about scattering ashes. Barack's grandmother, Toot, died two days before he was elected president. A few weeks later, Barack and his half-sister Maya returned to the spot where he had scattered his mother's ashes a decade earlier. They climbed over a wall and went down a rocky shore to a spot called Lanai Lookout to scatter his grandmother's ashes.

In an anonymous online comment to the *Los Angeles Times*, David describes how he scattered his mother's remains. Because not all her remains fit in the urn, he made a list of a dozen places, private and public, that were special to her. He then went to those areas and left a little of her behind. He says, "As I got near these places in normal travels, I'd visit, put my hand in a coat pocket and remove a handful or two of ashes from a plastic bag and surreptitiously scatter them in a lawn or garden area and say a prayer. It helped give me some closure."[53]

More Warnings from Funeral Directors and Other Entrepreneurs

With the rise of ash-scattering businesses, more traditional funeral home directors have started to warn clients about the dangers of scattering ashes. Funeral homes do not make the same profits when people cremate and scatter ashes, so they caution clients that the scattering of ashes will not provide closure. Bud Coglianese, director of the Coglianese Funeral Home in Illinois, says, "With a funeral, families are often provided with a sense of closure but with spreading of ashes that may not be as easy to obtain. If you scatter ashes, there's no place to go if you ever want to return to that place."[54]

Herman Meyer, a funeral director in Kentucky, warns clients against scattering ashes. He argues that it is a basic human need to be remembered and to have a focal point for that memory. Meyer, along with many other funeral home directors, uses rhetoric from the ICCFA regarding questions about cremation.

For example, one question from the ICCFA discussion guide asks: "Why is having a place to visit so important?" The answer lends itself to the argument that families should not scatter ashes but rather bury them.

> Because it provides a focal point for memorializing the deceased. To remember, and be remembered, are natural human needs. Throughout human history, memorialization of the dead has been a key component of almost every culture. The Washington Monument, Tomb of the Unknowns and Vietnam "Wall" in Washington, D.C., are examples of memorialization which demonstrate that, throughout our history, we have always honored our dead. Psychologists say that remembrance practices, from the funeral or memorial service to permanent memorialization, serve an important emotional function for survivors by helping to bring closure and allowing the healing process to begin.[55]

Also in the ICCFA discussion of ashes are cautionary tales about what might happen to areas where remains are scattered.

> If, for instance, you scatter the cremated remains in your back yard and then decide to relocate to another home or even another city, it is nearly impossible to gather up the cremated remains once they are scattered. If you were to scatter the cremated remains in a park or just an empty section of land, what would happen if the area was later developed into a shopping mall or housing development? Any of these situations could make it extremely difficult if not totally impossible for loved ones to visit the site in the future. It is vital when you discuss the scattering of cremated remains, you consider all possible difficulties that may potentially arise for your loved ones in the future.[56]

Wait! Don't scatter the ashes. Keep them with you. This is the type of warning you might hear from the founders of Phoenix Diamonds as they advise us that "scattering ashes may be TOO much of a final closure."[57] Phoenix Diamonds argues that after spending many years with loved ones on earth, you may not want to ever forget them. The solution is to make diamonds out of your loved one's ashes: "What better more fitting way could you remember them forever than with a real memorial diamond made from the last remnants of their existence—diamonds are forever they say."[58]

If you prefer gardening, you can have loved one's cremains turned into planting soil. Businesses selling memorial soil stress that turning cremains into soil brings a whole new meaning to death—the promise of new life.

Other options for keeping ashes with you include teddy bear urns—specially made stuffed teddy bears with a pouch inside to hold cremains. One version is the Brown Huggable Heart Teddy Bear Cremation Urn. The owner of Huggable Urns started her company after her father died. She said her dad inspired her to create something soft and cuddly to hold his remains: "It gives me such comfort to be able to pick up my Teddy Bear and give my Dad a hug anytime I want to especially during my personal hard times. By having my Dad in my Huggable Teddy Bear I can bring him with me to all of our family gatherings."[59]

Teddy bear urns are marketed to all—including pet owners—but perhaps especially to parents who have lost children. Huggable Urns includes several testimonials of parents who share how much they appreciate being able to hold their child's remains in a soft bear.[60]

One mom wrote on her blog that after her miscarriage, finding a teddy bear to hold her baby's ashes helped with closure: "The teddy bear can be held and snuggled. I can't see that being an option with a pewter or marble urn. I ordered the bear with two day shipping. I need this to be over as soon as possible. I need our family to have closure."[61]

We have seen the death care industry expand in services for funerals, cremation, and ash-handling businesses. Pet grief is another area that has seen tremendous growth in business opportunities regarding death. Once again, closure is an important argument for hiring professionals. Pet grief is quickly escalating from a type of disenfranchised grief to one that is aggressively targeted for a variety of products and services.

Pet Grief

Growing up on a farm, I experienced the death of many pets. As a child, I built my own pet cemetery and painted cement blocks to mark the shallow graves. The animals were not even placed in a box let alone a beautiful casket that protected against the elements. I dug a hole and placed them in it. According to professionals in the pet funeral business, my actions were undignified and incomplete. I did not properly memorialize my cherished friends and their remains would not be protected forever. If you are to believe the pet grief industry, I am still lacking closure.

Although there were a couple of pet cemeteries in the early 1970s, most pet grief businesses selling cremation or burial services and memorial products started after 1998. Some funeral homes expanded their services to include handling dead animals and serving the bereaved pet owners. Other pet grief businesses started independently of traditional human funeral homes.

One overarching theme in the pet grief industry is "pets are people, too." This argument asserts that our bonds to pets are like our bonds to people. The logical sequence goes like this: Pet grief is normal, natural, and devastating. Because pets are like family, losing them is similar to losing a human loved one. Pets need dignified endings, and pet owners need proper services and support to help with grief and to find closure and peace of mind.

Some pet grief businesses advertise closure as their primary mission. Whispering Pines Pet Cemetery in Nebraska intertwines the need for closure with its service: "It's just a dignified goodbye. People need closure. That's why pet cemeteries have been in existence for over 2,000 years." Fairwinds, which offers pet cremation and other services in Arizona, uses closure as one of the main topics on its website: "Closure, hand in hand, finding peace." Similarly, All Pets Crematory and Remembrances in Connecticut states that it is "offering the access to gain closure in an understanding and professional atmosphere." Heaven's Pets in Louisiana combines its personal attention to pets with its service of offering closure: "We treat every pet and situation as our own, and it's such a privilege to help families reach closure when they lose their loved ones."

In pet grief rhetoric, owners are responsible for giving their pets "proper endings" and for taking care of their own emotional health. Closure emerges as a primary way of describing this emotional health. Memorials.com makes an explicit connection to the pressure to spend money and your family's emotional health: "So today's experts—and just those who speak from experience of having a lost a pet—highly recommend that, when you have lost a pet, the best thing to do for your families [*sic*] emotional health is to invest a few dollars in some sort of memorial and give your cherished friend a memorial befitting the treasured memories."[62]

Sometimes closure is promised through a specific service or product. Angel Ashes in California tells pet owners: "A memorial pet urn can help you achieve closure and give back a little of what your companion gave to you." Pet Urns Unlimited in Michigan claims that a beautiful urn will not only be a wonderful memory but will also help you achieve closure. More lighthearted urns in the shape of a fire hydrant are also available. Dignified Pet Services in Oregon recommends: "A funeral, memorial service, burial, or placement of the ashes encourages healthy closure to the loss process." In Ohio, Pet Dignity Pet Funeral Services tells people that although pet visitation does not have to be formal, it may help bring closure. A pet cremation business in Nevada informs people that cremation grants a pet owner closure.

Gently informing pet owners that they need closure is not always enough for some businesses. At times, horror stories and cautionary tales are used to get the point across. The most common horror stories involve landfills, garbage bags, dumpsters, and rendering plants.

Memorials.com warns pet owners that others have been careless in how they treated their dead pets and have come to regret their actions later. Its website cautions, "As many a commentator on the Internet has noted (often with disappointment), it is common today for families who have lost a pet to simply pay a 'disposal fee' to a municipality or veterinarian office and, well, be done with it." The marketing rhetoric continues to shape feeling rules for pet grief by defining proper grieving rituals, which depend on buying its products: "Many pet owners have stumbled upon pet cremation jewelry, pet grave markers and other such products many years after the death of a pet and bemoaned the fact that they did not adequately memorialize their cherished pet."[63]

If those mild cautions are not enough to get people to buy its services, Memorials.com turns up the pressure in telling people how to find closure and prevent horror stories. The following quote from its website graphically defines what it considers improper dispositions for pets:

> Investigative reporters across North America have made a number of attempts to find out just exactly how dead pets are disposed of, and some of their results are startling: some reports say that many bodies of pets end up in rendering plants where they are mechanically stripped of their fur and flesh (sometimes while still wearing their collars and other such items), and each part ground up and churned into a variety of other products, ranging from fertilizer to, yes, pet food. While these reports are usually denied by leaders of the rendering industry (which does recycle farm animals), they are so numerous that they seem plausible at least in some cases. Even if the bodies are not sent to a rendering plant, however, they are typically unceremoniously cremated—often in ovens with many animals at once—and the ashes are informally disposed of in a simple dumpster or even open air outside the crematory.[64]

Marketing in the pet grief industry tells pet owners that they need to find closure in order to grieve properly. Of course, the way to find closure includes buying services and products. Other ways of burying and remembering pets fall under such descriptions as undignified, improper, and uncaring. Traditional, and less expensive, ways of caring for pets when they die—such as burying them in your backyard—are framed as lacking dignity and failing to provide closure.

Read the Fine Print: Selling and Buying Closure

When considering any sale or contract, one is advised to read the fine print. The same is true for closure sales in the grief and death care industries. What are they really saying when promising closure? What is already an emotionally difficult time may be further strained in a tug-of-war contest about closure in the death care industry. Marketing rhetoric in this industry tells people that closure exists and can be found. It is not just a question of whether or not people need closure after a death but rather how people are supposed to handle their loved one's remains in order to find closure. The various death care perspectives spar over whose method offers the best closure. Furthermore, many of the marketing narratives argue that choosing other dispositions will deny one closure. If we look at the six types of closure talk identified in chapter 2, three of them show up prominently in the death care businesses: remembering, closing a chapter, and knowing. Each type is used to sell products, services, and feeling rules.

Entrepreneurs rely on the need for *remembering* in order to sell death services. The debate about what to do with a loved one's physical remains shapes feeling rules about remembering. Aerial burial businesses tell people that closure comes through "letting go" of their loved ones in a way that allows them to remember their loved ones in every sunrise and sunset or anytime they look up at the sky. Other death care "experts" tell people that the proper way to remember their loved ones is through burial so that there is a place to visit. And still others suggest using human remains to make jewelry so people can literally hang on to their loved ones.

In cases of keeping loved one's ashes with you through jewelry, gardens, or teddy bears, it would seem this choice is the opposite of closure. Yet many people use the word "closure" to describe their experience. This is "closure as remembrance" by ending the fear of forgetting. If you have ashes with you, or products that were made out of ashes, then theoretically you never have to let go. However, maintaining ashes or objects made out of ashes can also raise the risk of losing those things. What happens to one's grief process if the life gem jewelry gets lost or stolen? How does one feel when the tree that is planted with the memorial soil dies? How does it feel to have an urn break?

Or accidentally spill? It is possible that these unfortunate situations lead to a renewed loss.

The importance of remembering is also used to sell memorial products. Using the rhetoric of closure, memorialization is becoming increasingly professionalized as people are told how to "properly" remember their loved ones in "dignified ways" worthy of their love. Of course, people do not need to buy any specific products to create memorials and keepsake items to remember their loved ones. However, the death care industry markets the professionalization of memory as necessary in order to expand its services and products.

Another interpretation of closure is *closing a chapter*. Death care workers encourage families to choose the "right" rituals for the last chapter of someone's life in order to provide closure. For example, this strategy is seen in debates about why you should not choose direct cremation without a viewing as this is not a proper way to say good-bye. Or why you should not keep a loved one's remains in an urn on your mantel because it denies other people from experiencing the release of the loved one's spirit. And the same goes for pets. People are told to follow specific ways of saying good-bye to their pets in order to find closure.

Funeral directors rely on the idea that traditional funerals are a proper way to close a chapter and find closure. The "art of embalming" perspective argues that closure comes from seeing a dead body as if it were alive, but sleeping. Peaceful. Natural. At times, mourners have been known to comment on how a person looks better in the casket than he or she did before dying. One might ask if creating the picture of a lifelike dead loved one might make it harder to let go. Does embalming help us deny the natural process of death? And, if so, how does that affect our grieving process? Home funeral advocates argue that we should experience the natural process of death. They agree that "viewing the body" helps the living. In fact, they recommend helping to take care of the body. But how will people feel about themselves if they cannot manage that type of care? Are we setting up false expectations about closure and death care?

Death care businesses also rely on *knowing* as a type of closure, which refers to having the answers you need to gain peace. They claim you can find closure by having peace of mind in knowing you did the right thing. Death care professionals encourage you to buy the expensive casket that is leakproof so you do not have to worry about nature's elements (even though no casket can prevent decomposition or water leakage). Pet owners are encouraged to find peace of mind through knowing they did everything they could to show how much they loved a pet.

Death care workers also talk about people needing certain rituals in order to *know* that their loved one is actually dead. Funeral directors imply that without viewing a body, loved ones will have a harder time knowing and accepting that someone has died. They shape the expectation that viewing a body, and thus *knowing* someone has died, will bring closure. Home funeral advocates also talk about knowing as closure but through different rituals. From their perspective, helping to take care of a loved one's body gives a person time and action to *know* that the person they loved has departed the shell of the body. This, they argue, is closure.

Finding ways to keep someone's life meaningful after he or she is dead leads people to create a diversity of memorials and perform a variety of rituals. This is not a new phenomenon. People who grieve are often interested in rituals that help uphold their loved one's memory. What is more recent is the professionalization of these activities and the link to closure talk as a way to market this need. You do not have to buy other people's products to memorialize a loved one. However, if you are in the business of selling memorial products, it is important to create the impression that "proper" memorialization comes through these services. Linked to the rhetoric of what is proper is the promise of closure.

There is no one final disposition that fits every person and every family. Some people love the idea of an eternal reef while others want a traditional funeral. Some parents want to take care of their child as part of a home funeral while others want a professional embalmer to reconstruct their son's face so they can see him one last time. It is important to hear people's stories about burying a loved one or scattering the ashes so that we understand that people's situations are different and their needs following a loss cannot be summed up in a marketing strategy.

What is not clear is whether or not people can find this "closure" by following the professional advice. It is more likely that those around them assume the proper rituals did lead to closure; therefore, they mistakenly believe that the hardest part of grief is getting through the funeral and final disposition of the body. This is typically not the case for those close to the deceased. Grief continues long after a funeral, which is often not understood when funeral rituals promise closure. Using closure to sell death care services fails to capture most people's responses to loss.

People in the death care industry are not the only ones talking about peace of mind and closure as a way to market services. In the next chapter, we turn to those who are not only explicitly selling "assurance" in the form of knowledge but also creating worry as a way to generate more business in the name of closure.

5. The Assurance Business

Creating Worry and Selling Closure

When loved ones die or go missing, we are often left with haunting questions. Why? How? What were his last words? Did she suffer? Did the doctor make a mistake? Where is she? Is he dead or alive? We search for answers. At times, we become desperate to know what happened and are willing to pay almost anyone if there is hope that we will learn something.

Lingering questions about death and loss are nothing new. Generations of families have wondered why and how people die. What has changed is our ability to pursue those questions and the pressure to do so.

Three major changes in the last generation have shaped our ability to find answers to these "How?" and "Why?" questions. First, scientific and technological advances such as medical tests, DNA profiles, computers, and the Internet offer new opportunities for knowledge. This does not necessarily guarantee more satisfying answers, but it does provide access to more information. Whereas our grandparents may have had to say, "We'll just never know the reason," today, the sheer amount of possible information might tempt us to search continually for those answers.

Second, we are more likely now, compared to a generation ago, to be told we can find closure by gaining knowledge to these haunting questions. Journalists declare that a family will reach closure when a suspect is captured, a body is found, or new evidence comes to light. When that information is not available, people might feel like the Walking Wounded because they are told you need answers to find closure. What is not often discussed in these stories is the lack of closure some feel when the answers do come.

Third, the quest for closure has sparked a new way to sell knowledge. I refer to individuals and businesses that are in the market of selling peace of mind and answers as the *assurance business*. People in the assurance business claim that they help others find closure. Lawyers, psychics, medical consultants, forensic pathologists, and private investigators all use closure as part of their sales talks. Politicians, officials, and journalists also use closure as an argument for policies needed to gain more information.

We do not need to buy professional services to look for answers. Most of us participate in an everyday version of the assurance business. As a mother, I am often trying to assure my children. Friends, family, pastors, doctors, teachers, and others work at assuring us in times of worry or need. Furthermore, there are professionals whose job it is to find answers whether or not private citizens hire them to do so. Police investigate murder cases. Doctors perform autopsies. Officials help search for a missing child.

In this chapter, I focus specifically on people who are in the business of selling answers and peace of mind as an enterprise and who use closure as a marketing strategy. Securing knowledge that ends worries is the type of closure advertised. There are concerns about this marketing strategy and how it shapes feeling rules for grief. Let's look at a specific example of who might be targeted.

On April 2, 2008, as she returned home from her classes at the University of Wisconsin at Madison, twenty-one-year-old Brittany Zimmermann was killed in her apartment. Six months later, Brittany's mother, Jean, told reporters that she was still waiting for information. Who killed Brittany? How did she die? Why? "Until we have justice for Brittany, there is absolutely no healing that can start," said Jean. "We have no answers. I don't even know what happened to her." Jean and her family say they will do whatever it takes to find answers. "If it takes money, we're going to try to raise the money."[1]

People like Jean and her family are potential customers for those selling answers. Many look to technology, science, and other expertise to get the answers desperately sought for closure and peace of mind. Unwilling to settle for ambiguous circumstances or to entertain the possibility that we will never know why something happened, we search for answers in the hope of finding knowledge that might allow us to hurt less.

How do we balance what is helpful in pursuing these answers and what is causing more harm than good? People like Jean, and countless other family members who are searching for answers, are the target audience for those in the assurance business. People selling services ranging from psychic readings to autopsy reports are tapping into our fear and hope and promising closure along the way.

I am not opposed to people having services available to them to help find answers. I would never tell a mother who does not know where her daughter is or how she died to try to stop worrying about those questions. People's desperate need for those answers is understandable. Nor am I proposing that we limit the services, experts, and technology that might be able to help us find answers to these difficult questions.

However, it is because the need for answers is so great and makes people so vulnerable that I raise these concerns. We need to at least pause and think about how it affects our grieving and healing process when so many people are selling answers even when it is not clear that they can provide the answers—let alone closure.

Selling Closure in the Assurance Business

Closure is sold in a variety of packages within the assurance business. Entrepreneurs use closure to sell services and products. Politicians use the closure argument to lobby for expanding state authority in gathering knowledge. These marketing strategies use the promise of closure to sell "answers" by exploiting the fear, pain, and hope of those who have the questions. Even worse, we have people creating doubt and questions in order to sell the answers. If there is no doubt or lingering questions that raise a person's need for answers, then businesses may propose questions and create worry. Some go further by using horror stories, anticipatory regret, and dire warnings to get people to hire them.

If someone wants to sell services such as autopsies, private investigations, psychic readings, or wrongful death lawsuits, what does that person need to say? Developing a sales talk requires establishing a need and targeting a potential client's emotions. Once someone has his or her heart set on getting something, it is hard to talk that person out of it. People do not want to be sold things; they want to buy them. An old sales saying is "Sell the sizzle, not the steak." Closure is the sizzle.

Selling Autopsies

There are several reasons why closure is useful in the marketing world. First, selling closure is a nicer, more comfortable idea than selling other services or products such as autopsies, expensive caskets, private investigations, and DNA profile kits. An autopsy is a perfect example of this strategy.

Think about it. How do you sell an autopsy? It is not likely that you will see a commercial for an autopsy during your favorite television show although the role of autopsies in many hospital and crime shows may implicitly sell the idea. But how do you delicately sell the decidedly indelicate process of cutting up your loved one's body for hundreds if not thousands of dollars, especially when the process is not covered by insurance? One answer is closure.

Journalists have helped set the stage for this idea. Heath Ledger, a popular young actor, was found dead in his apartment on January 22, 2008. It seemed that the world waited for the autopsy report as people speculated on how he died. About two weeks later, on February 6, the Office of Chief Medical Examiner of the City of New York announced the cause of death as an accidental overdose. Monica Gaza, an entertainment news editor, described the news as closure, saying the autopsy report "will allow all those who love Heath and are devastated by his death some much-needed closure and maybe help with the grieving and the healing process."[2] We see the same formula in other celebrity deaths. Someone dies and we wait for the autopsy report. When it comes, media stories announce that we can now have closure.

Journalists are not the only ones to describe an autopsy as a path to closure. Those who are selling autopsy services use closure talk. You might be wondering, "Who *buys* an autopsy anyway?" Legally, there are times when an autopsy is ordered by the state, particularly in cases of sudden, violent, ambiguous, or suspicious deaths. And hospitals, particularly those connected to medical schools, may request consent from a family to perform an autopsy in order to learn more about a death. However, the rate of autopsies performed has dramatically declined in the past few decades. It is estimated that before 1970, autopsies were done in about 50 percent of all hospital deaths compared to only 5 percent today.[3] For overall deaths (not just those in the hospital), autopsy rates went from about 19 percent in 1970 to 8 percent in 2003.[4]

Many reasons are given for the decline. Significantly, starting in 1971, the Joint Commission for Accreditation of Hospitals no longer required a 20 percent autopsy rate for a hospital to be accredited. Other factors include hospitals' reduction of costs (they did not want to pay for as many autopsies), doctors' concerns about medical malpractice lawsuits (families get angry over information gained from an autopsy about incorrect treatment), and the availability of new technology that provides information about death (rather than just depending on an autopsy report).

The decrease in autopsies performed in hospitals has opened up a market for private autopsy providers who sell their services to family members, lawyers, funeral home directors, and insurance companies. Immediate family members can request an autopsy so providers may market directly to them.

They also may go through wrongful death attorneys and funeral home directors to indirectly reach family members. For example, the owners of Pathology Support Services tell funeral directors that in order to help a family they should recommend an independent autopsy be performed to help family members understand what happened: "Our goal is the same as yours, help the family through the grieving process and bring closure."[5]

Forensic pathologists may also market their services to wrongful death attorneys who, in turn, encourage clients to request an autopsy in order to find information for lawsuits. Furthermore, autopsy providers market to insurance companies in order to help them gather information, which could help them avoid payouts. Sometimes life insurance policies vary depending on the cause of death. Of course, the same providers may market their services to family members arguing that they might find information to help them receive higher insurance benefits.

The services are not free. Toxicology reports (blood and urine tests for drugs) start at approximately $400. Partial and complete autopsies range from $1,500 to $6,000. In many cases, insurance will not cover an autopsy that is performed by a private provider. The bill can be high—so the need for closure needs to be higher.

Closure and peace of mind (often packaged together) are the main focus in describing why someone would want an autopsy performed on a loved one. In an article on MedicineNet.com, a WebMD site for people searching for medical information, autopsies are credited with providing tangible and psychological benefits: "Psychologically, the autopsy provides closure by identifying or confirming the cause of death. The autopsy can demonstrate to the family that the care provided was appropriate, thereby alleviating guilt among family members and offering reassurance regarding the quality of medical care."[6]

Three different autopsy providers all frame their services through closure. The Memory and Aging Center at the University of California at San Francisco claims "an autopsy may provide closure for family members since the final and most accurate diagnosis may otherwise be left unknown."[7] American Autopsy Services sells its services to families, funeral directors, and attorneys. It states multiple times, in each section on its website, that autopsies can help the family find answers for closure: "All existing technologies and procedures are available to shed light on remaining questions and end uncertainties to help bring about final closure."[8] Autopsy Pathology Services claims there are many reasons to perform an autopsy: "To determine the extent of disease. To determine the cause of death. To diagnose the specific type of dementia. Peace of mind. Closure."[9]

For family members who do not have much doubt or many questions about why someone died, some autopsy providers try to create concern. One strategy is to raise doubts about the quality of medical care received by the deceased. Pathology Support Services fosters the need for more information and the distrust of hospitals or care centers. Its website states, "There are approximately 40 percent serious errors in the diagnosis of hospitalized patients who die and are autopsied and two thirds of the undiagnosed conditions were considered treatable."[10]

Another strategy to raise the need for closure is to suggest that survivors might experience guilt about whether they provided adequate care or harbor lingering questions about why the person died. Some autopsy providers suggest that enhancing a family medical history through knowledge generated by an autopsy can provide answers for other family members. For example, American Autopsy Services claims: "An autopsy also forestalls questions that may arise after burial or cremation, and the autopsy often discloses vital information, such as the status of inheritable diseases that will assist surviving family members with their health care."[11]

If you live in the right area, you might have the option of calling 1-800-Autopsy, a mobile autopsy service. Vidal Herrera started the private autopsy firm in 1988. Herrera says that an autopsy can give a family a sense of closure because it tells them the truth. His motto: "The deceased must be protected and given a voice." Herrera says the autopsy business is growing and recession-proof. He operates three franchises in Florida, California, and Nevada. Herrera claims, "People that are hurting need to find closure, pursue litigation or even get a second opinion."[12]

Herrera travels around in a white minivan with 1-800-Autopsy painted on the side. Inside the van is everything needed to perform an autopsy. A former investigator for the Los Angeles County Coroner's Office, Herrera lost his job because of a back injury. Only qualified to assist in an autopsy, he employs freelance pathologists to perform them. He reports that his business completes over 700 autopsies a year. Herrera sells other services such as toxicology tests and paternity testing. As another service, for about $900, plus any costs for exhuming and transporting a body, he recovers DNA from bodies to complete paternity tests.

The autopsy services are part of a larger business for Herrera. He runs Morgue Prop Rentals, which rents out autopsy/morgue equipment to film producers. Herrera also started the business Coffin Couches, which, as the name suggests, recycles coffins into couches and sells them for around $4,000. And, on his 1-800-Autopsy website, there is a gift catalog that includes clothing, shirts, hats, thongs, and other gift items with the company logo as well as plastic body part–shaped key rings, brain and hand gelatin molds, and other odd offerings.

Pet owners may also be in the market for buying autopsy services. An animal autopsy is called a necropsy. The costs for these services range from $500 to $1,500. In the past decade, closure has increasingly been used to market necropsy services to pet owners.

In 1998, Marcia King argued that a necropsy, or animal autopsy, is recommended "to help give the owner closure by determining the definitive cause of death."[13] Writing for a 1999 pet column for the College of Veterinary Medicine, University of Illinois at Urbana-Champaign, Sarah Probst claims that "finding out the cause of death of a horse will bring closure to many horse owners who might be grieving the loss of their beloved horse."[14] Necropsy is for the birds, too. In their article for *Winged Wisdom*, Sandy and Bill Harrison say the most important reason to get a necropsy is for peace of mind and closure.[15] The same is true for bunnies. Nancy LaRoche, writing for the Colorado House Rabbit Society, says that one of the three things a necropsy does is "bring closure to those who are grieving."[16]

In 2008, Dr. Bill Spangler founded Necropsy Services Group (NSG) "to fill a previously unmet need in veterinary medicine and to provide a complete necropsy service to veterinarians, pet owners and the legal services."[17] This "need" that the website argues has not been met before is in part constructed by closure talk. In the following description of its services, closure is one of the important reasons for a necropsy: "Knowledge of the underlying pathology associated with the death of a veterinary patient often provides emotional closure for the pet's owner as well as offering valuable retrospective information to the veterinarian who managed the case."

Autopsy and necropsy providers are not the only ones who use closure to sell their services. We also see closure marketed by wrongful death attorneys, private investigators, and psychics.

Wrongful Death Attorneys

Many wrongful death attorneys are selling themselves as grief counselors when they promise closure. Take the introduction on a website advertising legal services for a firm in Florida: "It is the phone call that no one wants to get, bearing news that no one wants to hear. However you received the news, it changed your life forever. Now, you and your family are left to deal with the consequences. At Larmoyeux & Bone, we help you recover from your loss. Although we cannot bring your loved one back to life, we can help you get the closure that you deserve."[18]

A Texas wrongful death attorney uses this tagline: "We help you get the closure that you need."[19] An attorney in Illinois encourages potential clients to "get the closure you deserve after the loss of a loved one." He goes on to say you need that closure to move forward after a tragedy.[20] Wrongful death attorneys in Minnesota offer help during a time of grief: "Obtain closure in the midst of a difficult time. Rely on the support of the wrongful death attorneys at Johnston and Martineau."[21]

Closure is described in part as understanding what happened to cause a death. Wrongful death attorneys claim that they can help find the answers and therefore give families closure. A law firm in Colorado argues, "Many grieving families want to know exactly what happened. A wrongful death lawsuit can help bring out the details that led up to the accident. Understanding the circumstances can help bring closure."[22] Again, before their contact information, the lawyers offer closure: "Do you need a lawyer? In a wrongful death case, an attorney can help you find closure after a traumatic loss and help your family secure financial relief."[23]

Many wrongful death attorneys use a combination of "closure through knowledge" and "closure through payback" in their marketing. Closure through payback can mean either financial compensation or punishment of another person.

Associating justice with closure is a familiar strategy. We see the link between justice and closure in criminal legal rhetoric. Wrongful death lawsuits also add the lure of financial compensation, which is linked to closure. Attorneys at Reardon & Reardon in Massachusetts claim that they "work diligently on your behalf when you are in the middle of emotionally trying times. By tenaciously working to secure compensation for financial loss and conscious pain and suffering, our lawyers can help you find some closure in the midst of loss."[24]

Wrongful death lawyers at Drivon, Turner & Waters in California connect closure with punitive damages: "In addition to providing the victim's family a sense of closure after the immeasurable pain they have suffered, punitive damages discourage the negligent party from acting irresponsibly again."[25]

Other law firms describe closure more generally but clearly as something that you need and deserve. Wrongful death attorneys in a Florida firm have a boldface heading on their website that reads: "Helping you achieve the closure that you need."[26] A law firm in Virginia emphasizes closure as the most important benefit of its services: "More than anything else, pursuing a wrongful death lawsuit often provides families with the peace of mind that they need for closure."[27]

Wrongful death attorneys in a Houston law firm recognize the difficulty of forgiving a drunk driver. In contrast to those advocates who may say forgiveness brings closure, this law firm argues that you may never forgive but you can find closure through a wrongful death lawsuit: "Whether you suffered a catastrophic injury or are grieving the sudden death of a loved one, you may never be able to forgive the drunk driver and move on entirely. However, by pursuing a personal injury or wrongful death claim, you may feel there is some closure that enables you to move forward."[28] Not only do these Houston attorneys use closure to sell their services, they also sow doubt in the minds of people wondering if it is possible to forgive those who hurt them.

Other "specialty lawyers" use closure to market their services. For example, a lawyer who works specifically on riding lawn mower deaths wants to help families find closure. John Gehlhausen states that he "is committed to helping surviving family members find closure and obtain justice and compensation in the wake of tragedy."[29]

Urgency is another strategy for creating a need to hire a wrongful death attorney. Warning: Even if you do not have the questions or need now to investigate a death, you might later. And then it will be too late.

The following cautionary tale on a wrongful death attorney's website warns people that they may regret not taking legal action.

> While understandable, the decision to forego legal action means that the family and survivors are deprived of the income lost and a sense of what many victims call closure, or justice. Often a family member will seek out a lawyer many months or years after the loss, only to find out that evidence has been lost, insurance adjusters are reluctant to open old claims, legal deadlines have elapsed etc. Indeed, one of the most common causes of our lawyers rejecting a claim is that it is too old. Thus, it is advisable to contact counsel as soon as possible after a fatal accident.[30]

In an already emotionally difficult time, people facing trauma may be scared by the notion that they have little time to find closure.

Private Investigators

What *really* happened? A private investigator will find the answers that will give you closure. Or that is what many private investigators would have us believe.

"Your Key to Closure" is the motto for a private investigator business in Columbus, Ohio, which claims "Through our polygraph examinations we provide closure to unpleasant or questionable circumstances."[31] In Boston, private investigators say, "the truth will be captured" allowing clients to have closure.[32]

Matt Tyson, a private investigator in California, says that people come to him with questions and he finds the answers. As a tagline on his website, he sells the idea of closure: "We can fully investigate for you and get to the truth. Find closure, satisfaction and an end to your hassle."[33] In an article about accident reconstruction investigators, readers are told bluntly that closure will only come through information. "The truth is: you will never get the closure you need unless you find out what really happened in an accident."[34]

Private investigators may also market themselves as "infidelity experts" who provide closure through information. Nationally known speaker, author, and "infidelity expert," Bill Mitchell tells people that his book can teach them "how to spot a cheater, how to garner proof, create favorable demands and leverage, win negotiations and get immediate closure—all in as little as one week."[35] In other media reports, Mitchell says he understands how to investigate marital cases and bring closure swiftly and to your advantage.[36]

Private investigators also raise questions and attempt to create fear in order to sell their services. TM Morgan Investigations alerts potential clients to their risks and explains how it can help: "Discovering an affair in your relationship is hard enough, but that's just the beginning of what you will face. A family court ruling will be rendered either for or against you and your children. A judge will decide for you based on the evidence, who is the best custodial parent. If you suspect your spouse is cheating, you need professional investigative help!" TM Morgan follows up on this concern with its promise that investigators work closely with clients to ensure closure.[37]

A private investigation firm in New Jersey also raises questions to create interest in its services:

> Are you sick and tired of the lies? Are you tired of your spouse trying to convince you that you are crazy? Are you tired of the stress? Is it consuming your every thought and having difficulty concentrating on work? Are you tired of your spouse playing you for a fool? Are you ready to learn the truth? You deserve to know the truth! Eventually you will get to the point where you decide to take action in an effort to obtain the proof that will provide you with closure. If you are reading this then that means that your spouse is already underestimating you. You are close to learning the truth![38]

Some businesses specialize in catching cheaters. Affair Investigations welcomes readers to its website with the headline "We Catch Cheaters!" and "Me and Mrs. Jones" as background music. It also tries to raise concerns through these claims: "Infidelity is higher today among happily married couples as couples with marital problems." And "Almost as many women have affairs on men as men have affairs on women." Then we are assured that Affair Investigations can conduct "a covert, cost effective infidelity investigation that offers closure and answers your suspicions."[39]

Another infidelity specialty business starts its marketing with some statistics: "According to the *Journal of Couple and Relationship Therapy*, approximately 60 percent of men and 50 percent of women will have an extramarital affair at some point in their marriage." It also mentions that most people are not aware of their partner's cheating. Hiring a private investigator, it says, will provide closure to your suspicions or fears.[40]

As with other sales talks, those marketing private investigations contain a price buildup. Author of the article "Hiring a Private Investigator to Catch a Cheating Husband," Dean Cortez explains that catching a cheater will not be cheap, quickly adding: "But this can also be the best investment you will ever make. If you've been tortured by the thought of your husband cheating, then you truly can't put a price tag on getting closure and being able to move ahead with your life."[41]

There are other products related to investigating infidelity. Chase Investigations, Inc. gives you the power to be your own private detective. For $50 you can buy a CheckMate Infidelity Test, which detects semen. Its website tries to raise your need for answers by including this question: "Do you suffer from the nightmare of suspicion and doubt caused by the infidelity of a cheating spouse? Find out what's really going on the quick and easy way with the CheckMate semen detection test kit. He or she brings the evidence home to you without even knowing it." In boldface letters, it encourages you to "place an order now to find closure."[42]

AccuTrace also sells a semen detection test and an infidelity test. It encourages you to think about doubts people have in their relationships: "They suspect infidelity; however, they do not have any proof. AccuTrace offers an answer to this question so that closure can be obtained, and the relationship can move forward based on solid facts."[43]

Psychics and Out-of-This-World Closure

Lawyers and private investigators are not the only ones selling answers and promising closure. Psychics also use closure talk. Did someone die before answering your questions, therefore preventing closure for you? According to many psychics, you can still find that closure by "communicating with angels" or speaking to people "from the other side." Or perhaps you just need psychic help in finding the hidden messages of your life to bring that elusive closure.

Annette Martin describes herself as a "psychic detective." Closure is not just her motto but also her business name: Closure 4U Investigations.[44] Other psychics describe closure as their service. Traci, a spiritual advisor, says she delivers closure to her clients. She believes that bringing inspirational messages from the other side for those seeking closure is her responsibility. Testimonials on her website refer to the closure they received after finding answers to their questions. Bev from Sacramento says, "You have no idea how much closure you gave me." Lisa from New Mexico says the reading "gave me closure on the situation with my niece and made me feel so good to know that she is okay and that she sends her love."[45]

Psychic services range in price depending on what you are seeking. For $50, you can join Carole Obley for her psychic seminar on understanding death. She promises "a powerful experiential exercise using a photograph to help you heal and embrace emotional closure with those in spirit."[46] For $80 per thirty minutes or $130 for an hour, you can hire an "earthbound conduit." Psychic medium Nadine says, "I consider myself an earthbound conduit/telephone line linking people to Angels, their deceased loved ones or the Universal source of wisdom to receive closure to unfinished business, healing from the past and guidance for the future."[47] Skype readings are coming soon according to her website. (I assume she is advertising future Skype readings with her, the psychic, and not with loved ones who have died.)

Psychic Debra of northern Kentucky offers her services to help others find closure and insight in their lives. A two-question e-mail costs $20. Online readings cost between $20 and $75, depending on how long they take. An in-person reading costs $75 per hour. She accepts payment by credit card, Paypal, check, or money order.[48] Lady Magdalena of Heavenly Visions also sells closure. For $25, you can receive a ten-minute reading or increase your time all the way up to sixty minutes for $150. She says, "If you need help or advice and have been unable to receive the information that you need; if you need to bring closure to a situation with a past loved one, then I invite you to contact me for an accurate, unbiased reading on what matters to you most."[49]

Whether psychics or autopsy providers, so far I have discussed individuals and businesses that use closure to sell services and products. Closure talk is also used politically to gain knowledge and expand legal rights and state power. We turn to these examples next.

Closure and Knowledge as a Political Argument

When I was growing up, I remember going into our small-town post office and reading the FBI "Most Wanted" posters. It was a thrill to read about these criminals, but now the method of gathering information through posters appears not just nostalgic but amazingly low-tech. As a child, I never would have imagined how advances in technology would change the methods used for tracking people.

Low-Tech Knowledge

About sixty years ago, on March 14, 1950, the FBI started its list of the "Ten Most Wanted Fugitives" that relied on public cooperation to help capture "the worst of the worst." According to the FBI, 494 fugitives, or "Top Tenners," have been on the top ten list and 463 (94 percent) have been captured or located. The FBI claims that about one-third of those captures are a direct result of public information that resulted from people responding to the list.[50]

Today, the top ten list still exists, but it is not limited to the post office. The FBI uses Facebook, Twitter, digital billboards, widgets, and other social networking tools to spread the "Most Wanted" list. You can even sign up for e-mail updates regarding new fugitive information.

Printing pictures of missing children on milk cartons is another low-tech method for gathering information that I remember from my childhood. The milk carton campaign was started by a dairy farmer in Des Moines, Iowa, in the mid-1980s and joined by other dairy farmers around the country. It was short-lived—about two years—and then dairy farmers wanted to promote different issues. Other initiatives are now used to search for missing children. The AMBER (America's Missing: Broadcasting Emergency Response) Alert System is one example. However, parents can still create their own "virtual milk carton" online to raise awareness for a missing child.

At the time of the milk carton campaign, closure was not used as a reason for gathering information. Only more recently do we see closure connected to this campaign. Etan Patz was the first missing child to appear on the milk cartons. In 1999, stories about Etan included the following: "Twenty years after little Etan Patz vanished, there remains no closure at all."[51] Although the concept of closure was retroactively applied to the solving of Etan's disappearance, the term was absent from the original public awareness campaign.

Similarly, in 1950, closure was never part of the FBI's rationale for soliciting information about fugitives. Today, however, we not only see a change in methods for gathering knowledge, but we see closure as a prominent reason for expanding legal rights or state power as part of the process. Closure is now used to justify using both low-tech and high-tech methods for gathering knowledge on crimes.

Homicide is no game, but officials hope that playing cards might help bring justice. Several states have developed "cold case playing cards" that feature pictures and information about unsolved cases. They give the cards to inmates in prisons and jails hoping someone will pass along information about the cases. Cold case playing cards are an example of a low-tech method of gathering information. State governments rely on people who are using the cards to share information about the unsolved cases.

The main market for the cards is jails and prisons, but anyone can buy a deck. Closure is used as an argument for developing these cards, giving them to inmates, and selling them online to others. The company that produces them, Effective Playing Cards and Publications, hopes that the cards will solve some murders and offer families closure. On the website it says that purchasing cards can help "Bring a Murderer to Justice. Bring Closure to a Grieving Family."[52]

One Florida deck features Bobbi Jean Tew on the four of diamonds. Her body was found two years after her disappearance, but her killer is still unknown. A local reporter says that her in-laws hope the cards will bring closure to the families. "The waiting, the not knowing is just pure hell. You just have so many different emotions and so many questions," said Bobbi Jean's former mother-in-law, Phyllis Jackson.[53] Florida's attorney general Bill McCollum offers hope: "These cards have been immensely successful in generating tips and two cases have been solved, bringing closure to the victims' families and friends."[54]

Family members of homicide victims hope the cards can help them find closure. At age thirty-eight, Sandra was seven months pregnant the last time she was seen at a shopping mall in 1994. Sandra's sister, Donna, has been looking for her since then. Donna's son, who is incarcerated in a county jail, called his mom one day to tell her that he saw his Aunt Sandy's picture on one of the jail's cold case playing cards. Donna had not heard of those cards before. She said, "I'm glad that they are doing this. When you're missing someone, there's no closure at all. You don't want to give up hope."[55]

Low-tech methods like post office posters, milk cartons, and playing cards have generated some knowledge for helping solve crimes. However, officials have also been busy developing high-tech methods for generating new knowledge. Along with the increased technology are ethical concerns. Closure plays a role in these debates, too.

High-Tech Knowledge: DNA

Recent technological advances offer new, cutting-edge methods for gathering information about people and crimes. DNA is a prime example of this type of knowledge. DNA stands for deoxyribonucleic acid. (Now you see why we just say DNA.) The information in DNA, which is located in the cell nucleus, provides hereditary material mapping out biological instructions for each individual. DNA sequencing converts DNA into messages similarly to how letters in the alphabet allow us to build words and sentences. Forensic scientists may try to use DNA from hair, skin, blood, semen, or saliva to identify victims and perpetrators. Sometimes people refer to this process as genetic fingerprinting or DNA profiling.

In order to match DNA from a crime scene to people, you need to have previously collected DNA from individuals stored somewhere. How do you do this? There are significant privacy concerns involved with collecting and storing citizens' DNA because most of those people are not volunteering it. There has to be a need for collecting DNA that rises above constitutional rights to privacy and other ethical concerns about DNA collection. This is where closure enters.

Winding its way through the crime victims' rights movement, death penalty rhetoric, and other court cases, the concept of closure has worked its way into legal decisions as a fundamental goal of law enforcement. The case for widening the net of those who have to give DNA samples rests in part on the perceived need for victims' families to find closure. Recent court decisions have claimed that compulsory collection of DNA from certain offenders is necessary to ensure three goals: rehabilitation, deterrence of crime, and closure for victims.[56] Politicians and advocates like the closure argument because it disarms critics when you can argue for healing and closure. Closure is used as an emotion claim in order to expand state authority.

For several years, most states have been collecting DNA samples from anyone convicted of a felony. Those profiles are then uploaded to a national DNA database. However, in a rapidly increasing trend, states have also passed or introduced legislation that will allow them to collect DNA samples from people arrested for a variety of crimes even if not convicted. This raises concerns about violations of constitutional privacy rights. How much privacy do people have when arrested for petty offenses or when presumed innocent because they have not been convicted? The government is also collecting DNA from detained immigrants. The FBI predicts it will accelerate its collection of DNA samples to about 1.2 million new entries a year by 2012.

In the late 1990s, Attorney General Janet Reno requested that the National Institute of Justice examine the future of DNA evidence and how it can best be used. In 1998, the FBI started a DNA database that stored DNA profiles with the goal of matching evidence from one case to evidence from other unsolved cases. Since then, legislation continues to be introduced that expands who is required to give DNA for this collection. Closure for victims' families became a prominent argument in the push to expand the national DNA database.[57] In 2001, a report on the Combined DNA Index System (CODIS) reaffirmed the power of closure with this statement: "When DNA evidence is used to solve very old crimes, the closure provided to victims and their families is impossible to measure, although it can have a profound effect on those involved."[58] In a 2003 hearing before the Subcommittee on Crime, Terrorism, and Homeland Security, Representative Howard Coble, chair of the subcommittee, introduced DNA as the tool that can benefit everyone and provide closure to families who have lost loved ones.[59]

In 2004, in *United States v. Kincade*, the U.S. Court of Appeals for the Ninth Circuit determined in a 6–5 ruling that it is constitutional to force a parolee to provide a DNA sample for the FBI's DNA database. Judge Diarmuid O'Scannlain wrote, "DNA profiling of qualified federal offenders helps bring closure to countless victims of crime who have languished in the knowledge that perpetrators remain at large."[60] Disagreeing with the decision, Judge Stephen Reinhardt warned, "It is always tempting to grant the government more authority to fight crime. We all desire more effective law enforcement, less recidivism, and 'closure' for victims of heinous crimes. But that desire does not justify eviscerating the structural edifices of the Fourth Amendment—those barriers often constitute the only protections against governmental intrusions in the most intimate details of our lives. DNA contains such details." His warning, however, has so far not been taken too seriously.

A few days before Christmas in 2004, a robber killed Johnia Berry, a graduate student at the University of Tennessee, in her apartment. Johnia's parents write, "The anguish we went through is beyond words. We grieved while the sheriff's department interviewed more than 1,000 people and submitted more than 400 DNA samples from suspects. Time continued to pass—and we received no closure."[61] Three years later, the murderer was finally caught when he committed another crime and his DNA matched the DNA from Johnia's case.

Johnia's parents advocated for an expanded DNA collection to help other families avoid the traumatic wait they had to endure. In 2007, their advocacy paid off as the Tennessee Legislature passed the Johnia Berry Act, which allows the collection of DNA from those arrested for a felony (instead of waiting for a conviction). Johnia's parents call the legislation "life-saving" and say, "Any family who loses a loved one will be able to rely on this legislation to assist with closure and bring the correct perpetrator to justice."[62] Tennessee state representative Jason Mumpower agrees, "While the rights of the accused should and will be protected, the victims of heinous crimes and their families deserve the closure that comes with seeing a murderer brought to justice." Mumpower raises the level of expectation by implying that closure is possible and that families deserve it as a right.[63]

More court cases continue to uphold closure as a reason for expanding the DNA collection process. In 2008, a Minnesota court concluded, "The state has substantial interests in DNA collection, specifically identifying these interests as 'exonerating the innocent, deterring recidivism, identifying offenders of past and future crimes, and bringing closure for victims of unsolved crimes.'"[64] Also in 2008, a juvenile appealed a ruling that forced her to submit a saliva sample for DNA analysis. The Supreme Court of Illinois upheld the decision to force the DNA collection and cited the need to bring closure to victims as one of the primary reasons.[65]

On March 4, 2010, Ed Smart lobbied Congress to give states money so that police can collect DNA samples from all those arrested for violent crimes. People are more likely to know Ed as Elizabeth Smart's father. Brian Mitchell kidnapped fourteen-year-old Elizabeth Smart from her bedroom in Utah and sexually abused her for nine months before she was rescued. Now her father is advocating for greater legal capacity to collect DNA samples in hopes that other families can be spared the pain his family endured. He called the DNA legislation a tool that "will bring closure to some families, exonerate other families and most importantly, it will prevent this nightmare from happening to so many families."[66]

On May 18, 2010, the U.S. House of Representatives voted overwhelmingly to pass Katie's Law, also known as the Katie Sepich Enhanced DNA Collection Act. The bill would give money to states that expanded the collection of DNA from people who are arrested prior to any charges or conviction. The bill's sponsor, Congressman Harry Teague, says expanding DNA collection will bring closure to victims.[67]

A small Facebook group advocates making DNA profiling compulsory: "Every day women and children are raped and murdered and only a few find justice. Families don't rest because they get no closure. There are always traces of DNA found on helpless victims, but not everyone is listed. If every single person were profiled, criminals [*sic*] hiding places would get smaller and smaller! Help the innocent."[68]

The claim that we should collect more and more people's DNA, even from those not convicted of any crime, raises considerable ethical concerns. First, collected samples are stored indefinitely, and most states have no policy for destroying a sample even if the person is never convicted. Furthermore, the practice raises significant privacy issues. Many worry that the insights that DNA provides into diseases and other genetic markers are outweighed by the possibility of future genetic discrimination.

People often view DNA evidence as irrefutable, but there is more to solving a crime than matching DNA. Individuals could plant DNA evidence at a crime scene by leaving another person's DNA there. One possibility is to leave someone's cigarette butt or some hair at the crime scene. Either of these is easy enough to find. And, at many crime scenes, or even on a person's body, people unrelated to the crime leave traces of DNA. Furthermore, Israeli scientists are building evidence that DNA can be manufactured. Currently, forensic labs do not have the tests to determine if DNA samples are from humans or labs.[69]

The actual success rate of DNA profiling is much higher on television shows than in real life. First aired in 2000, *CSI: Crime Scene Investigation* has become one of the most popular television shows in America and inspired two spin-offs: *CSI: Miami* and *CSI: NY*. Other shows about forensic science include *Crossing Jordan, Forensic Files, Extreme Forensics, Without a Trace*, and *Cold Case*. How might shows like *CSI* influence the public's understanding of DNA and other forensic evidence?

Criminal justice professionals and scholars debate the "CSI effect," which has multiple meanings. Some prosecutors complain that jurors who watch shows like *CSI* expect a higher standard of proof in the form of DNA evidence before they will convict. On the other hand, defense attorneys have referred to a CSI effect described as jurors convicting on forensic evidence alone. Others describe a CSI effect of an increased number of students who want to enter the field of forensic science.

Of course, *CSI* is not the first television show to generate concerns about effects on jurors. Starting in the late 1950s, *Perry Mason* became a popular television series (also a popular character in novels and movies). Perry Mason was a defense attorney who typically defended someone accused of murder and won the case by demonstrating who the actual killer was. Defense attorneys expressed concern that Perry Mason raised expectations that the defense attorney need not just prove reasonable doubt but also identify the real guilty person.[70]

Although prosecutors and media reports caution about a CSI effect, defined as raising standards for a conviction, Tom Tyler is skeptical. Tyler, who is a professor of law and psychology, explains that the actual CSI effect might be an increased desire for closure. He argues that *CSI* promotes the need for closure, which he describes—in the context of a criminal case—as convicting someone. A conviction provides the most "psychologically satisfying resolution because an acquittal leaves the crime unsolved." Tyler argues that the popularity of *CSI* "lies in its ability to simplify the messy uncertainties of real-world crime. *CSI*'s plots are consistent with the strong psychological need to achieve closure following the commission of a crime."[71]

Crime shows often dramatize real-life stories, or cases "ripped from the headlines." Tyler gives the example of *CSI*'s dramatization of the Natalee Holloway case. Natalee was an American teenager who disappeared during a trip to Aruba in 2005. Six years later, her body has not been found and no clear answers have been given for what happened. On an episode of *CSI: Miami* titled "Prey," a fictionalized version of that case, the victim's body was found and DNA profiling from a sperm sample led investigators to the offender. Closure—found in just an hour.

Television shows like *CSI* and *Law & Order* affect people. Research consistently demonstrates that television plays a role in educating the public about the legal system although the specific effect varies. Some claim that shows like *CSI* give scientific evidence more validity than it should have. Professor Michael Mann argues that by holding up DNA and other forensic evidence as infallible, *CSI* convinces viewers that people may lie, but evidence cannot. The expectation, then, is that answers from high-tech knowledge will provide closure.[72]

Television producers are not the only ones to capitalize on forensic science and the push for closure. Next, we look at businesses using the promise of closure to sell services involving high-tech knowledge, such as DNA profiles, to the general public.

Selling Closure and Private DNA Testing

The talk show *Maury* has for many years relied heavily on "Who's your daddy?" themed episodes. A producer claims that the show—which uses paternity tests to reveal the biological father—has provided many people with closure.[73] But now, you do not have to appear on *Maury* to get a paternity test. Businesses are selling private DNA tests and, they claim, closure.

In 1993, Identigene first started unveiling DNA paternity testing for consumers, and by the early 2000s, several other businesses had followed suit.

For $150, Identigene guarantees professional results in three to five days, which might provide you with closure. Paternity Express promises results in two to three days, also for $150. In response to the question, "Who may use DNA testing?" its website states: "Someone wanting closure or peace of mind regarding his/her paternity."[74]

Advanced Paternity goes beyond paternity tests by attempting to create a need for tests to determine grandparentage for $500 (are you the grandparent?), avuncular for $400 (aunt or uncle?), siblingship for $600 (brother or sister?), or twin zygosity for $400 (are your twins fraternal or identical?).[75] In 2008, Rite Aid introduced a less expensive home paternity test ($20 test, $120 lab fee), but it is not legally admissible.

DNA technology has spurred new business opportunities besides paternity testing. Whereas paternity testing targets a present need for information, other businesses are selling future needs. Genetics Info describes the DNA profile services of Fairfax Identity Laboratories as "Closure in a DNA Profile."[76] In a blunt exploitation of fear, Fairfax Identity Laboratories sells personal DNA profiles: "Although we don't like to think about it, disaster can strike anyone at any time. During those times of personal insecurity, it makes sense to ensure in advance that there can be closure should the unthinkable happen."[77] The personal DNA profile is referred to as CID, or Confidential Identity.[78] Tapping into our fears of death and reminding us of past tragedies that others have experienced appears to be the strategy for constructing our need for these products. We are given an assurance that we may be able to prevent some of that horror by purchasing particular services. The staff at Fairfax reasons that the profile will serve as a basis of identification in case of a tragedy, which will give loved ones closure.

In an article designed to market home DNA tests, the headline reads: "Home DNA profiling test kits are an important tool in giving your family closure and guarding your estate and are easy to purchase and use." The article then claims that people need to prepare for tragedy by storing DNA information so that loved ones can identify them for closure.

> Tragedy isn't something most people want to contemplate—especially when it concerns the loss of their own life and how it could affect the loved ones they leave behind. Ever since the super tragedies of September 11, 2001 and the Southeast Asian tsunami, more and more people have asked themselves: "What would happen to my family if my remains were unidentifiable? What would they bury? How would they find a sense of closure?" Today, thanks to our society's

advanced technology, you don't have to worry any longer. Personal DNA profiling, accomplished through an easy and pain-free process, is the answer and ease to your insecurities.[79]

The business DNA Analysis also uses September 11, 2001, as a cautionary tale. Labeled under "fact" is this claim: "From 9/11 only half of the victims were identified. Had their DNA been stored, more families would find closure." DNA profiling and storage cost $350.

ID-Secure, another DNA profiling service, claims to establish identity and "in unfortunate circumstances" provide closure for relatives.[80] ID-Secure markets its services to organizations that have employees in high-risk situations. The owners of ID-Secure argue that their service "delivers that extra degree of assurance for each and every one of your employees" and provides "answers and closure for families if the worst should happen." Using a similar strategy, Rich Ulmer, president of InVitro International, describes the company's Guardian DNA testing system for children, "We hope parents never have to identify their child, but if they do, DNA can make emotional closure possible."[81]

Answers Are Important but Not Necessarily Closure

There are times when people benefit from services and products that provide knowledge. For example, I do not disagree that there are cases when an autopsy is important. When our son was stillborn, my husband and I decided to have an autopsy so that we could find out what happened. After the autopsy, we still did not know what happened. But there could have been information that might have helped us with future pregnancies. We were thankful to at least have that option. So we were among those who wanted an autopsy for more information. Then, again, we were never promised closure when making that decision. In fact, we were told that there was a 50 percent chance the autopsy would not provide any explanation.

Countless families have received critical information from an autopsy or private investigation. They may or may not describe it as closure, but in any case, many report being helped by these services. It is important that we have private autopsy providers who are professionally trained and properly regulated in order to give us more information about death when we need it. But this can be offered without promising closure. My concern is the potential for emotional exploitation of grieving family members.

Through the assurance business, marketing and political rhetoric continue to frame closure as something that is possible, good, desired, and necessary. Here are some examples of feeling rules that are shaped by the assurance business marketing: The more you know about life and death, the more peace you will have. Gaining answers to questions about a crime or death will provide closure. If there are questions, you should do whatever it takes to find the answers before it is too late.

It may be that answers can provide relief, peace of mind, and—depending on how you define it—closure. However, it is just as likely that people will receive answers that do not bring any closure. An end to the haunting questions is helpful and perhaps a huge step in the healing process, but it is often not "closure." For some, the "answers" may just be the beginning of grief. Let's look at why this might be the case.

First, as discussed in chapter 2, the word "closure" has different meanings. Forensic pathologists, wrongful death attorneys, and private investigators may be offering closure defined as answers to specific questions (knowledge). For families, answers to their questions might indeed provide some relief and badly needed information, but this is not necessarily closure for them as they might imagine it. Furthermore, answers to the initial inquiries may just raise more questions. If an autopsy report shows a completely different cause of death than expected, family members might go through another round of questions. This does not mean the autopsy was not worth it. The knowledge received may be very useful, but it does not necessarily mean closure.

Second, "official answers" about a death or a crime may not be the "right answers." If people disagree with an official report, then that knowledge is not going to provide closure. How someone died is sometimes a matter of opinion. We may have the information in front of us, but it does not always clarify motive or context. Was it a suicide, natural causes, accident, or homicide?[82] For example, officials declare a death a suicide, but family members insist that it was a homicide or an accident. In these cases, the official answers may cause more grief because an answer that says suicide carries stigma and emotions that the family must navigate.

Third, sometimes the "official answer" changes. Around the world, people mourned when Princess Diana died during an auto accident in 1997. People debated whether it was an accident. Nine years later, in 2006, an official UK police report found no evidence that Diana was murdered. Lord Stevens hoped that "the publication of this report will help to bring some closure to all who continue to mourn."[83] However, there was no closure to the public debate about how Diana died. Two years later, in 2008, an inquest jury returned a different verdict of "unlawful killing through gross negligence" blaming both the chauffeur and the paparazzi. Once again, Lord Stevens hoped this new report would bring closure to the case. Even though it reversed the previous report, he encouraged people to accept the latest report: "I do hope everybody will take this verdict as being closure to this particular tragic incident and the people who have died will be allowed to rest in peace."[84]

Finally, answers may only begin the grief process, not end it as closure often implies. Finding evidence that a missing person is dead is an important part of allowing a loved one to grieve. However, this is different from a neatly packaged view of closure. Not knowing who killed a loved one results in continued suffering for those who wait for answers. But even the arrest and conviction of offenders—though obviously crucial in the justice process—cannot guarantee that the victims' families will have closure to the pain and grief. Promising closure through specific information or particular law enforcement tools, such as a large DNA database, represents an incomplete picture of what it usually takes for people to heal.

Some Questions Will Remain, and We Can Survive Them

Is it possible that we can create more harm than good when insisting that there are answers for questions? Creating questions that might not otherwise be there should at the very least be suspect. Capitalizing on people's fear of the worst-case scenario in order to sell DNA profiles may not be the most useful way to think about the potential of high-tech knowledge.

I understand the desire to have questions answered. But there are always going to be some questions that have no answers. Or the answers we have are not the ones we want. If we do not like the answer we have, we may be more willing to believe (and pay money to) those who say they can find the answers to any of our questions. Certainly, there are questions that we should continue to answer when possible. Which questions we should answer and which ones we should not pursue is not a simple formula.

I do not want to minimize the tortured experience that families go through when they do not know where a loved one is, how he or she died, and so on. Clearly, there are questions that haunt us. Doing what we can to answer many of those questions is important. But it is also important to monitor those who are claiming to sell answers and to guard the grief narratives that accompany the promise of "closure through knowledge."

Even with advanced technology that gives us knowledge about why someone died or helps us identify who committed a crime, we cannot be guaranteed closure. This does not mean that we have to give up the technology that allows us to get more knowledge. But we need to be more intentional about how we connect knowledge and technology with grief narratives.

We can survive a loss even when there are some questions that remain. We can find some peace (even if not complete) and healing (even if pain lingers, which it does), without having all the answers. We will not always have answers. And even the answers we receive may carry lingering doubt. The trick may not be finding all the answers, but learning to live with some questions.

Whereas this chapter has focused on those who are selling assurance and answers as a way to find closure, we turn next to those who are selling the idea of revenge and symbolic death as a path to closure.

6. Bury the Jerk

Symbolic Death and Mock Vengeance as Relationship Advice

Traditional marriage ceremonies include the phrase "until death do us part." I am not going out on a limb to suggest that this phrase was intended to mean the physical death of one of the spouses. However, as divorce has become more common, people are linking death and marriage in new ways. Today, people may think of the marriage as dead, or the ex-partner as "dead to me." Now you can buy products to help "bury the jerk" through symbolic burials. You can have a divorce cake topped with a murdered groom being pushed off the cake by the bride. Or you can buy a wedding coffin to give those rings a final resting place. Are people seeking closure through the symbolic death of an ex or a relationship? Not everyone is buying it, but many are trying to sell it.

Bad relationships have emerged as a social problem in need of closure. Often, we think of loss and grief primarily in terms of the death of a loved one. But we grieve other types of losses, too, such as the ending of a marriage or other intimate relationships. What do we do with the pain, anger, humiliation, abandonment, or grief that might come with the end of a relationship?

There are a variety of perspectives on how to heal after a painful breakup. In this chapter, we explore specifically those who are selling symbolic death and mock vengeance as a way to find closure after a bad breakup. I define mock vengeance as rituals and behavior that target someone indirectly but do not physically or financially affect that person, although learning of the events could cause emotional harm. In chapter 2, I identified "getting even" as a type of closure talk. Some people believe that you can only find closure when you successfully get revenge. The idea is to balance out the injustice, pain, and anger you have experienced by causing someone else as much or more pain.

Many examples in popular culture and the media would have us believe that revenge or aggression is good for the soul. For instance, an emerging "divorce industry" caters to people seeking celebration and/or revenge after breakups. Part of the divorce industry rhetoric encourages people to believe mock vengeance directed toward an ex will bring closure. In addition to tapping into the belief that acting out aggression brings a sense of justice and healing, we see the adaptation of death rituals that will allegedly bring closure after a bad relationship. A particular appeal of these rituals of symbolic death and mock vengeance is that they are often couched in terms of a party or celebration; consequently, people may be more willing to engage in them.

Many businesses have borrowed from death imagery and rituals to sell the idea of closure for bad relationships. Options for grieving a relationship and finding closure include writing relationship obituaries, buying Wedding Ring Coffins, symbolically burying your ex, and planning end-of-a-relationship services and divorce ceremonies complete with divorce announcements and party gifts. Let's take a look at the variety of advice that promises closure through parties, especially those relying on mock vengeance and symbolic death.

Have a Party, Plan a Mock Death, and Get Closure

Historically, the word "party" in the context of divorce referred exclusively to a legal party. When divorce carried greater stigma, the newly divorced were not as public, let alone celebratory, about their divorces. Even though not everyone takes this approach, there is now a cultural option of celebrating a divorce, and a divorce party might refer to a celebration. Similar in purpose to a funeral or memorial service, a divorce or breakup party marks a death. However, unlike a funeral, divorce parties are typically advertised as upbeat, celebratory affairs.

Although divorce is nothing new, celebrating divorce is a more recent phenomenon, driven largely by businesses that exploit the pain and anger that often accompany a divorce or a bad breakup. In some circles, the shame of a divorce has turned into an opportunity to celebrate freedom and perhaps humiliate the ex-spouse.

By this point, it will come as no surprise that closure is an oft-used marketing tool for selling the products and services related to divorce parties, with one magazine even going so far as to call a divorce party "The coolest concept in closure."[1] A website devoted to divorce advice tells people, "You need closure. We mark important occasions with ceremonies, like weddings, christenings and funerals. Why not have a divorce party to officially end your marriage in a therapeutic way?"[2] People selling these products cite so-called experts who encourage the parties. An online article about divorce quotes clinical psychologist David Berndt: "Closure is one of the therapeutic benefits a divorce party can bestow. A divorce party can give a sense of finality."[3]

Frequently, suggestions for finding closure through divorce parties include mock vengeance. Not all of the advice for throwing a divorce party encourages mock vengeance. However, several businesses now include divorce party items, the majority of which employ revenge and/or humiliation as a theme. The advice often follows themes that reflect death—not usually grieving the loss—but a celebration of the death. First, you must announce the end of a relationship. Two popular options are a relationship obituary and a party invitation.

Relationship Obituaries and Party Invitations

Need to find a way to mark the end of a relationship? Write an obituary. Kathleen Horan started the website Relationship Obituaries after she broke up with her boyfriend. Two weeks after breaking up, Kathleen's dad died. She explains that writing the obituary for her dad brought comfort, so she decided to write one for the relationship, too. Other media reports connect this ritual to closure: "Looking for closure after a break up? Write an obituary."[4] Or "If you need closure on a dead love affair, a Web site allowing you to write a 'relationship obituary' might help in burying the whole thing for good."[5] Or "Searching for closure? How about writing the ultimate send-off; a relationship obituary!"[6]

Entries on the Relationship Obituaries website can be sad, funny, smart, and mean-spirited. The people and relationships described in the obits range widely. For example, one of the obituaries begins: "Heart Attack—T was a cardiologist. It took A, a photographer, 5+ years to diagnose that he had no heart himself." Another entry states the need for closure in the first sentence. "The Energizer Bunny Ran Out—I am here for much needed closure on a long term relationship that started with a match on E-Harmony over four years ago and never grew up." Other entries directly refer to the death of the relationship. "After almost two decades, Nicole Z. and Peter B. finally laid their love to rest. It was a long, drawn-out death, both suffering from fitful delusions. Acknowledging the truth brought them to a timely end, allowing them to pass on in peace. They met during their first year of college when he gave her the book, *School Is Hell*, featuring a single-eared insecure rabbit he would soon come to resemble."[7]

Party invitations can also announce the end of a relationship. For example, one card features two wedding rings chained together on the front. The inside of the card reads: "You're invited to a breaking free party. Help me celebrate my divorce." Another has a picture of beer bottles in ice with the description "The divorce is final . . . so let's celebrate." A more subtle choice is the card depicting cracked wedding bells on the front.

Cruder cards are also available for divorce parties. The web-based business Just Say It with Cards offers several breakup celebration cards. One of the cruder and more violent cards includes "The 'dickhead is gone' party! Come Celebrate with me," with a cartoon picture of a literal "dickhead" in a guillotine (*after* the execution). Another card with mock violence has four cartoon men pictured on the front with the saying "so many men . . ." and the inside says "so few bullets!" with one bullet going through all four heads. Another card says "It's an 'EX' burning party! Help me burn moments from my past as I look forward to my future."

There are also cards that allow one partner to tell the other he or she wants a divorce. One shows a picture of a smiling couple cutting a wedding cake on the front with the words "Remember when we were happy and in love?" The inside simply says, "I don't." Another card states, "I've taken a long look at our marriage. The Pro's, the Con's. And guess which list is longer? It only makes sense . . . Let's get a divorce."

Not sure how to select divorce party invitations? eHow.com has a page on that. Its description implies a celebration: "When you select your divorce party invitations, make sure they convey an upbeat feeling so that guests know it's a celebration. Invitations are your way of telling friends and family you're ready to make a clean break with the past and you want them to be there when you do."[8]

A divorce support website posted an article for readers called "Getting Closure: Throw Yourself a Divorce Theme Party." The directions encourage celebration: nothing sad or somber. The article says that one problem with divorce is that there is no ceremonial closure. A "divorce celebration" is a way to mark the closure. Music suggestions include Diana Ross's "I'm Coming Out," Elton John's "I'm Still Standing," and Ray Charles's "Hit the Road Jack."[9]

Let Them Eat Cake

No party would be complete without a cake. Here, too, we see themes of violence. Shanna Moakler, who told reporters that she held a divorce party to get closure,[10] served her guests a three-layer cake featuring a knife-wielding bride on the top layer and a bloodied groom on the bottom layer. "Blood" flowed down the cake layers and surrounded the groom. Because Moakler is a celebrity, several entertainment magazines reported on her party. A photograph that appears in multiple articles shows the happy divorcée laughing heartily as she gazes at the cake. Moakler's divorce party inspired increased public interest in celebrating the end of relationships.

Her famous cake sparked the interest of other cake decorators. On coolest-birthday-cakes.com, you can find divorce cakes. Using Moakler's murdered-groom cake as inspiration, the cake designer created a similar one but customized it for her friend whose husband was a musician. She describes the cake: "The blood is red icing with some corn syrup to make it more liquidy to pour on cake. The cake topper is actually a store-sold bride dragging the groom but when separated it looked like she pushed him off the cake. I smeared the icing to look like he fell off the cake and the bride smashed his guitars. This table centerpiece was a big hit!"[11]

A picture of the murdered-groom cake drew mixed comments on the website. Some people expressed outrage, which led the decorator to blur the image of the cake and direct people to another link if they really wanted to see it. But the majority of people posting comments loved the cake, although some thought the blood went too far. The idea of closure is intertwined with people's enthusiasm for the cake.

I love this cake! Even though a divorce is a very sad occasion, I honestly believe that one needs closure. This will make the perfect picture to put at the end of the wedding album of the divorced couple. Natalie

I am married, for 9 years now, and I love the idea! I am from a divorced family, and I have many divorced friends. It is a chance to celebrate the life you had with the "now ex" and put closure on it and move on! They wouldn't be getting a divorce if wasn't time to move on! Kellie

I never married but have been to many a divorce party and all of them were very upbeat, women who had been through the mill for way too long celebrating closure. Nuala

This cake is awesome! Humor has to be involved in every part of our lives so why not divorce! Keep the cake on your website :o) I would have loved to have a cake when my first marriage fell a part [sic] . . . closure! and maybe smashing the cake on my x would have been fun too. Anonymous[12]

While not all divorce cakes rely on a violent theme, many do. Slashfood. com shows several pictures of divorce cakes, including both cakes where the bride pushes the bloody groom off the top of the cake as well as the reverse, where the groom pushes a bloody bride. There is also a multitiered cake with the top having two separate small cake circles. The bride and groom are each on a circle pointing guns at each other.[13] Another divorce cake features a decapitated groom standing next to a bride who is holding the groom's bloody head.

Divorce Gifts and Party Games

If you are attending a party, you might want to bring a gift. Some stores have started divorce registries to help you figure out what to buy. Not all people who use a divorce gift registry are searching for mean-spirited items. But the practice of giving gifts to people who are divorcing has helped spawn a new market. Businesses cater specifically to those who are celebrating the end of a relationship by offering products such as ex-spouse toilet paper, voodoo dolls, and other revenge-themed breakup gifts.

Smashing Katie offers a range of breakup gifts. Its founder, Angie Schmidt, found out that her husband was having an affair with her neighbor. Five days after her divorce, Angie made a T-shirt that said "Ask Katie Where My Husband Is." Katie was the other woman. Angie said she wore the shirt around the neighborhood for revenge while she was walking her dog. Her experience inspired Smashing Katie, which she funded from money she received from the divorce.[14] One of the more explicitly violence-themed gifts is the "ex knife block set" priced at $99.95. Here is the product description: "Turn your kitchen into a crime scene without doing the time. This clever and artistic kitchen accessory holds 5 high quality stainless steel kitchen knives in a rather unorthodox fashion—stuck straight into the body of this wee little man. With every use, dedicate your knife block to your former wee little man and get the silent revenge you deserve." For $21.95, you can also buy the Exorcist Gift Collection, which promises to "breathe life into a dead relationship." The description: "Voodoo Doll Included: Need a prick me up? Yes, you can give your ex a migraine with the simple stab of a pin with this fun 9" voodoo doll."

Divorce Party Supply is an online gift store for those who want to indulge in mock vengeance. For only $17.95, you can buy the Ex-Wife Voodoo Doll. The description reads: "Whenever you feel your ex-wife needs to be punished, use one of the pins to put her back in line. Stick the pin into the activity that you want your ex-wife to stop doing and instantly she will stop acting like a bitch."[15] The Ex-Husband Voodoo Doll is also available.

Divorce-themed party games are another element of the divorce party culture. In an article on divorce parities, Jennifer DeMeritt describes these types of games: "If you crave more serious ex bashing, party suppliers have penis piñatas, pin-the-tail-on-the-ex games, voodoo dolls, and other devices to help you purge."[16]

Divorce party businesses appear to cater more to women than to men, although most products are available for either gender. Marketed for bachelorette and divorce parties, penis piñatas are evidently a popular item at women's parties—often marked as "best seller" or "sold out." Bachelorette Parties.com advertises the product as "The Penis Piñata—Whack It." There are typically two sizes available: small and large. Commentary on this party game frequently implies taking out your frustration or aggression. The Bach elorette.com website has this description: "Any woman knows there is a time to love a man. Men can be kind, strong, caring, and warm. We also know that there is a time to create a[n] effigy to men in the form of a piñata and to beat that piñata to a bloody pulp. Pick up a broom handle, sisters, and let this son of a bitch have it."

Several businesses offer the Pin the Tail on the Ex game. PartyCheap.com describes the game: "We've found the perfect way to let out your frustrations over a breakup. Play an outrageously fun round of the Pin the Tail on the Ex Game! A great activity for a divorce party and so easy to play." The playing board has a space to personalize it with a large photo of the "ex." In the book *Exorcising Your Ex*, an example of one woman finding closure involves this game. After playing Pin the Tail on the Ex, the picture of the ex used in the game was torn up and ceremoniously burned in the backyard.

Wedding Ring Coffins, Ex Plots, and Bury the Jerk Kits

Either as part of a party or as a separate ritual, several businesses sell ways to symbolically bury a relationship to help you find closure.

Has your marriage ended, but the pain remains? According to the founders of the Wedding Ring Coffin, you need to give your marriage a proper burial in order to find closure. After twenty years of marriage, Jill Testa was getting a divorce. She packed away her wedding pictures and other personal items from her marriage. She stopped wearing her wedding ring. Jill said she initially stuck the ring in a drawer, but it kept haunting her.

> I wore that ring every single day for over 20 years. That ring symbolized a marriage which was supposed to last until death do us part. That ring deserved more. I had a few ideas as to what to do with

it but it was after attending a funeral that THE idea came to me. My marriage had died and the ring that symbolized that marriage deserved a proper final resting place. And so, the Wedding Ring Coffin was born![17]

In April 2007, Jill and her brother Steve began selling Wedding Ring Coffins.

On the home page of the Wedding Ring Coffin website, browsers are encouraged to "give a dead marriage its proper, final resting place. The Wedding Ring Coffin is the perfect gift for yourself or a loved one for bringing closure after a divorce. It's time to bury the past and move on to a new tomorrow."[18] Jill describes the Wedding Ring Coffin as an "innovative divorce product that helps bring closure to people going through the pain of divorce." She says, "Most people just get it. If they're feeling sad, bitter, angry, it can provide closure."[19]

There are two styles of Wedding Ring Coffins. The original is a mahogany-colored coffin with a black velvet ring insert. The coffin has a lid that opens partially or fully. You can choose from stock messages for the attached plaque or customize a message. The stock messages include "Bury the past and move on to a new tomorrow," "Rest in Peace," "Gone and Forgotten," "I do . . . NOT!!" and "Six feet isn't deep enough!" Custom-ordered messages have included "I lost 140 pounds in three days. I divorced my wife" and "She should have learned to play golf."[20]

The second version is ivory colored with a burgundy interior. "The burgundy interior is a dramatic contrast to the pearl white finish. Like our mahogany coffin, it is ideal for burying the past and putting a marriage and divorce behind you. It can also be used as a unique way to propose marriage." The two stock proposals on the company website are "'Til Death Do Us Part" and "I Can't Live without You." Logic would suggest that you could buy the ivory coffin for a proposal and have it ready for burial in case of divorce.

The website offers a step-by-step guide for celebrating your divorce. After a celebration, the Wedding Ring Coffin owners promise that "you'll feel a real sense of closure and it will help you to 'bury the past and move on to a new tomorrow.'"[21] The business also sells divorce party invitations—ten for $13.95. The front features a picture of the mahogany Wedding Ring Coffin with the words "You're invited to my divorce party! Join me as I close the lid on my marriage."

You can also "bury" your ex online. Ex Marks the Plot is the first cyber cemetery available for burying exes. Abby Waters, one of the creators of the

site, explains, "Whether it's a bad breakup or a bad boss, people can experience healthy grieving by putting closure to the past with the ones who don't
last."[22] Waters claims, "Ex Marks the Plot accelerates the grieving process and
provides the much needed closure and freedom from guilt to help people
move on from the grief and loss in their past."[23] In order to "lay your past
to rest," you can buy a $14.95 package that includes a tombstone with an
epitaph and name, a burial certificate, a eulogy scroll, and an option to send
links to friends or the deceased. For an extra $1.99, you can order an autopsy
report. Waters assures people that the closure can be undone. If you get back
together with your ex, she will take down your tombstone and undo the
death. Eventually, she hopes to add a resurrection section for those who want
to raise their ex from the dead.

Similar in format to Ex Marks the Plot is AshHoles.com, which encourages you to use its service for closure: "You can bury your anger here, at Ash
Holes.com. It is therapeutic and it provides closure. It helps break the energy
so you can go on with your life."[24]

Bury the Jerk describes itself as a business for "Relationship Closure and
Recovery." Its mission is "to help individuals find closure after the loss of a
relationship by providing quality services and products which promote comfort and healing through a ceremony attended by those who offer support
during this time of loss."[25] For $24.97, you can get the Traditional Relation-
ship Funeral package, which includes a basic jerk doll, a coffin that the doll
rests in, a tombstone, personalized eulogy, certificate of closure, eight custom
programs, and eight notes for the newly single. If you want the deluxe package, for $64.97, you can receive the formally dressed jerk (as opposed to the
basic jerk), all the other items in the basic package, plus the power princess kit
and the complete party kit. On the tombstone, you can choose the following
epitaphs: "Gone and Forgotten," "Loser," "He Never Did Last Long," "Stu-
pid," or "Waste of Time." The company allows a limited range of diversity
for your jerk. Options for the "basic jerk" package include Caucasian blond,
African American, or Caucasian brunette. The business also offers a Bury the
Bimbo kit for men.

The story behind Bury the Jerk includes a personal testimony about finding closure. One of the founders shares her story:

> Bury the Jerk LLC had it's [sic] christening event at the fall of a long
> "on again off again" relationship. Closure for this relationship was
> overdue and would never be obtained with my ex; I would have to
> find it on my own. Words spoken by a friend after my first husband's
> death came back to me "at least you're not going through a divorce."

I thought the statement crass at the time, but when I experienced divorce, I understood completely. When someone dies it's final, there's no negotiating anymore . . . you participate in long standing traditions that encourage you to grieve and find closure. With this in mind, I knew what had to happen. We were going to have a "relationship funeral."[26]

It is striking that the author's first husband died, yet she describes divorce or a bad relationship as more difficult because it lacks the traditional closure rituals that come with death.

With your jerk kits, you will receive a certificate of closure suitable for framing. The bottom of this certificate reads, "You are being awarded the right to start over!"

Other Options for Revenge

Strategies for seeking closure through revenge run along a continuum. Some of the suggested activities for seeking closure through "getting even" are best described as mock vengeance. They are meant to humiliate someone but not cause serious injury or consequences. Other advice for revenge is more severe in terms of the results the actions might have on another person.

One form of revenge targets a person's reputation, which can result in mild to more serious problems for that person. Some websites allow you to post stories about a breakup. Charles and Dwayne, who call themselves "e-closure professionals," run a website called e-closure.com. They solicit breakup letters to post on their pages. They say you will receive closure after posting your pain. They give a definition of e-closure as "the act of gaining emotional finality by sharing a story of a breakup with the world, via the Internet (specifically through e-closure.com)." The following is their example of someone reaching e-closure: "Johnny was tired of pining over his ex-girlfriend from 8 years ago, so instead of hanging himself in the barn or torching his old love letters, he sent them to a website, and got some e-closure."[27]

The website ReportYourEx.com offers the opportunity to tell the world what a bad person your ex is. The site claims that reporting your ex "will give you all the closure that you need to get revenge on your ex. Tell everyone what a bad person they are."[28] There are similar sites available to report on employers.

On the website HowToDoThings.com, there is a section called "How to Make Your Ex Mad." The creators of this site claim that feeling anger or hate is normal: "One of the worst feelings in the world is when your loved one breaks up with or dumps you. This can really create feelings of depression, bitterness, and hate. In other cases, it becomes a powerful motivation to enact revenge." Then they get to their advice on finding closure: "Sometimes, the road to total closure with an ex can be through revenge and making him mad. This will lift up your spirits knowing that you can, at a certain level, make your ex feel miserable and even the same way you do."[29] Following this narrative are specific strategies for making your ex mad.

Revenge is not just for ex-boyfriends according to *The Revenge Seeker's Handbook: Everything You Need to Know about Getting Even.* Adam Russ says that his book offers "inspirational examples of real-life revenge" for everyone ranging from "sacked employees and cheated house owners, to golf widows frustrated at being left at home with the kids yet again."[30] The description of this book ties revenge and closure together: "Forget about turning the other cheek, revenge is good for you. It brings closure to traumatic events and stops you agonizing deep down that you should have done something, but never did."[31] Russ says he packed the book with "tips, advice and strategies about getting your own back in a number of different situations when you've been wronged. Most importantly, it shows you how to take your revenge and get away with it. Whether it's a college roommate that needs to be gotten rid of, a local company that needs bringing into line, or the person you love/loved, this book gives a suitable remedy, striving at all times to stay within the law."[32]

A variety of other websites sell products and services designed to get revenge on someone. You can pay someone to send dead flowers or dead fish to anyone you want to upset. ThePayback.com advertises such services: "There's nothing that gets your message across better than a smelly, nasty dead fish! These packages are very popular and are most often sent to ex-boyfriends/girlfriends, backstabbing friends, or anyone who has pissed you off."[33] A dozen dead roses cost $24.99 plus shipping. One dead smelly fish costs $19.99 plus shipping.

RevengeLady.com offers stories, advice, and products to help gain revenge. Revenge Lady says, "Get mad . . . then get even. It's justice, plain and simple. Revenge is healthy. Don't listen to those mealymouths who tell you otherwise." The website promotes *The Woman's Book of Divorce,* saying, "There's only one way to get over the pain of divorce . . . and that is to make your ex suffer instead." Here is a description of what is called the perfect gift: "Give your unfavorite person 'The Finger.' Or let us mail it for you. The recipient will receive an elegant gift box. Nestled inside is a realistic-looking severed human finger with a nifty little gift card. He or she will get your message loud and clear! Great for ex's, bosses, landlords . . . anyone who's done you wrong!" Giving someone the finger costs $11.99 plus shipping.

Seeking Vengeance

Not all advice for grieving a bad relationship recommends vengeance. You can find articles that offer ideas for gaining closure after a divorce that do not promote humiliation or revenge. Alternative narratives to finding closure after a bad relationship generally focus on redefining the relationship and/ or making peace with the ending. Some advice focuses on private "closure rituals" that allow you to make peace with the end of a relationship. Other nonvengeful rituals include religious services or mediation that help a couple to separate amicably. Some advice on throwing divorce parties discourages the mean-spirited activities and themes directed at the ex.

It is hard to estimate how many people are holding divorce parties and what percentage of those who have a party focus on the vengeance/humiliation angle. Given the recent growth in the divorce party industry, however, it would appear that plenty of people are out there buying the various products geared at mock vengeance.

How did we get to the point where people are celebrating the "death of a relationship" and encouraging mock vengeance (and sometimes more serious revenge) as a way to find closure? Although the use of the term "closure" may be more recent, vengeance has a rich history. Seeking closure through vengeance after bad relationships is rooted in other beliefs about aggression and anger. A cultural belief often referred to as the catharsis theory claims that anger, pain, and frustration can be relieved through acting aggressively. The word "catharsis" comes from the Greek word *katharsis*, which means a cleansing or purging. The belief is that viewing aggression or acting out aggressively will purge you of negative feelings.

Aristotle taught that viewing tragic plays could give people emotional release. Contemporary media advocates borrow the same argument. Some defenders of violence and aggression on television and in the movies use the cathartic theory. Alfred Hitchcock wrote, "One of television's great contributions is that it brought murder back in the home, where it belongs. Seeing a murder on television can be good therapy. It can help work off one's antagonism."[34] In the 1990s, Paul Verhoeven, director of *Total Recall*, said, "I think it's a kind of purifying experience to see violence."

Video game producers have also jumped on board, saying that violent games provide an outlet for the natural urge to kill. Dr. Bartha, imagery founder for SegaSoft, says, "We kill. It's OK. It's not our fault any more than breathing or urinating. The safe way to deal with that urge is to play video-games in cyberspace." Peter Loeb, a vice president at SegaSoft, says, "It's a marketing campaign, but there is some validity to the concept that you need an outlet for aggressive urges. If it becomes a movement, all the better. Starting a movement is a good way to market a product."[35]

There is widespread belief in the theory that viewing aggression or acting it out will relieve anger. But is it true? Not according to those who study it. Social psychologists say there is no research to support the catharsis theory. In fact, the research evidence indicates that aggression does not reduce anger but is likely to increase it.[36] Scholars report that people who participate in activities that are aggressive or focused on vengeance are likely to have further thoughts, emotions, and behaviors that focus on aggression and anger.

It is not clear how many people are seeking closure through mock vengeance and symbolic death. Studies on revenge in relationships uncover a range of activities employed to get even with an ex. Many of the payback activities that are reported in research studies are fairly mild although some acts are more serious, including kidnapping children and pets, getting someone fired, or attempting to poison an ex.[37] Research also indicates that although revenge may be sweet for a brief time, regret, fear of retaliation, and shame are some of the negative emotions that follow acts of revenge in the long term.[38]

Does venting anger by acting out mock vengeance or revenge toward another person lead to closure? Social psychologists have also tried answering this question. In a study on revenge, psychologists found that acts of vengeance cause people to continue thinking about their offender—the target of their revenge—longer, thus perpetuating the anger rather than ending it. The researchers argue, "People punish others, in part, to repair their negative mood and to provide psychological closure to the precipitating event, but the act of punishment yields precisely the opposite outcome."[39] If they are expecting revenge to help them heal and forget about the pain, they might actually experience the opposite. Or to quote Sir Francis Bacon, "A man that studieth revenge, keeps his own wounds green, which otherwise would heal, and do well."

Sometimes people encouraging closure through revenge do acknowledge the risks involved. In the article "How to Get Even with Your Ex-Wife: Are the Rewards Worth the Risks?" the risks listed include retaliation, self-loathing, fleeting satisfaction, and empty victory. The rewards, however, are listed as closure, satisfaction, and ability to move on.[40]

Advice for throwing a divorce party sometimes comes with warnings for whom not to invite, including the ex, coworkers, the ex's family and friends, and casual acquaintances. And almost always, people are warned not to let their children be present. In her article on divorce parties, Jennifer DeMeritt says, "A few enlightened folks actually invite their exes. If it's an amicable divorce, this lets your shared friends know they don't have to pick sides. But even if you're still friends with your ex, do not invite your children. Even well-adjusted kids will be angry or hurt to see Mom toasting her freedom from Dad, or vice versa."[41] In another warning against inviting children, Lisa Bower says, "Chances are children will need a long time to process and get over a divorce, and inviting or including them in a divorce party's festivities can open or worsen their wounds."[42]

The concern for children adds a layer of complication for those marketing divorce parties. It is hard to sell revenge-themed items while also reminding people (even if implicitly) that children could be hurt. Children will not go unscathed when the divorce of their parents is celebrated. Divorce "experts" who are not selling divorce party products are usually more explicit in their warnings about taking care of children during a divorce. Alternative non-vengeful narratives about divorce encourage those with children to pack away personal items such as rings, photographs, and other things in order to give the items to children when they grow up.

A more extreme warning about divorce parties appeared in news coverage following a murder in Great Britain. In November 2009, Brian Jones showed up at his ex-wife's house as she prepared for her divorce party. He claims that seeing banners that said "Free at Last" and his picture on the Pin the Tail on the Ex game was too much to handle. He proceeded to fatally stab his ex-wife, Katrina, twelve times in the chest and arm.[43] I am not claiming the game caused Jones to kill his wife, but that was exactly what he argued in his legal defense. The judge said he thought there was some provocation but not enough to excuse murder and sentenced him to a minimum of ten years. As divorce parties continue to grow in the United States and other countries, it will be interesting to see if more people use parties and mock vengeance as legal defenses for any retaliation or further violence.

So What's the Problem?

The promise of closure after a painful breakup can be appealing. Seeking closure allows a new motivation for acting out revenge or mock vengeance. Focusing on the goal of closure or healing may overcome personal inhibitions about hurting others. Closure as a psychological goal might trump other concerns.

The appeal of party gifts and products that have themes of vengeance and death may lie in the hope that making light of the situation will make the pain go away. People want to "be over" the pain without grieving the relationship. They want to find closure. Keeping the rhetoric versed in celebration may make people think it is harmless fun. Some people may have inhibitions against acting out revenge and may not see themselves as the "type" that would send dead fish or make anonymous reports about their ex online. However, they may be more easily convinced to humiliate their ex if it is "just for fun." One way people rationalize the use of mock vengeance is to think, "If it is all in good fun, then it cannot be harmful."

While funeral industry rhetoric uses closure as something people need after a death, businesses selling symbolic death for bad relationships focus on death as that which provides closure. The mock vengeance and symbolic death approach to the end of a relationship uses death as an opportunity for humor and humiliation rather than actual grieving for the loss that any divorce or breakup brings. Grieving the death of a relationship might be therapeutic, but making fun of the death might just mask the grief.

This industry not only markets closure to sell services and products, but the business of divorce parties and mock vengeance helps shape feeling rules for how we should feel about the end of a relationship. Celebrate the end and make fun of your ex. The rhetoric shapes expectations that mock vengeance, symbolic death, and celebrations will bring closure and healing.

Vengeance is not the only option for responding to those who hurt us. Even in the most violent cases, not everyone responds with revenge. This is the case when tragedy struck the quiet Amish community in Nickel Mines, Pennsylvania, on October 2, 2006. An outsider invaded their country schoolhouse, lining up and killing five girls ages six to thirteen and injuring five others. The country was shocked by the violence. Perhaps many were even more stunned by the forgiveness the Amish community offered the killer and his family. Some people could not understand how the Amish could offer this undeserved gift to the killer's family. How could they do that?

We should not be surprised when people have a hard time understanding forgiveness as a response. Certainly, our mass media entertainment promotes violence and payback more readily than forgiveness as a means to justice and healing. Revenge is often considered more dramatic and provides a better storyline for those producing television shows and movies. But in real life vengeance has not proven very effective for healing.

In the next chapter, we explore themes about vengeance versus forgiveness as discussed in cases of homicide and death penalty politics. Family members travel a rocky terrain of grief when mourning a loved one who has been killed. Along their journey, advocates try to tell them how to find closure. Some say executions; others say forgiveness. But does either of them provide closure?

7. Should You Watch an Execution or Forgive a Murderer?

Closure Talk and Death Penalty Politics

Nothing could have prepared sixteen-year-old Brooks Douglass for the future that lay before him. Brooks grew up in a loving family in a rural home near Oklahoma City. His father, Richard Douglass, was pastor of Putnam City Baptist Church, which had more than 3,000 members in its congregation. Brooks's mother, Marilyn, devoted her time to her children, who, in addition to Brooks, included twelve-year-old Leslie. Tragically, both of their parents were murdered, and Brooks and Leslie were left to pick up the pieces.

This chapter may be hard to read. Although it is impossible to fully explain the difficult recovery that loved ones go through after a murder, I attempt to give a sense of why the trauma can continue and how the court process can play a role in dragging out the pain. Some readers might feel I am dwelling too much on painful details of the murder case. It is important, though, to contrast the easy answers often given in the name of closure with the reality of the long-term pain and trauma that many individuals face.

So far in this book, I have discussed people coping with difficult issues, but most are less traumatic than cases of homicide. Many deaths and divorces are expected and familiar from watching others cope with similar circumstances. But Brooks's case is especially traumatic—sudden, unexpected, and severe. Furthermore, his story becomes intertwined with legal and political processes. In this chapter, we follow Brooks Douglass's life as he tries to move on from this tragedy. Along the way, we explore death penalty politics, the use of closure, and the implications for victims' families.

A Night of Tragic Loss

On October 15, 1979, while Marilyn finished cooking the family's meal and Richard studied Scripture, Leslie went outside to see why the dogs were barking. She found a stranger asking about a neighbor. The man asked to use the phone, and Brooks let him in. Then a second man burst into the home. Once inside, Glen Ake and Steven Hatch both drew guns and told the family of four they would "blow their heads off" if they did not do as told. After taking the family's $43 and wedding rings, Ake and Hatch forced Brooks and his parents into the living room. All three were bound and gagged and told to lie on the floor. After the two men raped Leslie, they bound and gagged her as well. Official records would later only state that the men were charged with "attempted rape." Relatives raised concern that making the rapes public would be too difficult for Leslie. Officials agreed to hide the rapes and only reported "attempted rapes."[1] This decision would later complicate Leslie's recovery and the trials.

As they ate the family's dinner, Ake and Hatch tormented the family with threats before they prepared to leave. Hatch covered the heads of all four family members. Then Ake told Hatch to go outside and start the car. First, Ake shot Brooks in the back, injuring his lung and grazing his heart. Then he shot Marilyn in the back. Next he shot Richard twice. Brooks later recalled, "I looked up and saw a bullet hit my dad, and I saw blood splatter all over the windows and the curtains."[2] Finally, Ake shot Leslie twice in the back, piercing a lung, kidney, and her intestines. Then the two men were gone.

Brooks called to his parents: "I told them both I loved them. The only thing I remember my dad saying is, 'Take care of your mother, get your mother untied.' I scooted over to her on my stomach and I untied her with my teeth. I said, 'Mom, you're okay. Can you untie me?' Her arms just collapsed at her side. I saw the life go out of her. I said, 'Dad, Mom is dead.' He never said another word."[3]

"Leslie remembers Brooks calling to her as she lay bleeding. Hog-tied, blood pouring from wounds in her abdomen and chest where the bullets had exited, she walked on her knees to the kitchen for a knife to cut her brother loose."[4]

Brooks later recalled that, before fleeing the scene, he took a long last look at his mother and father. "'I knew he would be dead before I got help,' Douglass recalls. Only later when reviewing crime scene photos for the first time, did Douglass see that his father had summoned enough strength for one final gesture: 'My dad had somehow made his way over to my mother and put his head on her shoulder.'"[5]

Brooks and Leslie, although seriously injured, managed to drive to a neighbor's house where they summoned help. The tragedy was far from over for Brooks and Leslie. They spent weeks in intensive care after their near-fatal attacks. In fact, both were still in the hospital when their parents were buried. Leslie spent her thirteenth birthday in the hospital. After their physical recovery, they were separated and raised by different families.

In November, thirty-seven days after the murders, authorities apprehended Ake and Hatch in Colorado. At the time of the arrest, Hatch was wearing Richard's wedding ring.[6] Marilyn's ring was also recovered, and it was discovered that Ake had been using her credit card.[7]

What Happens Next?

What do survivors like Brooks and Leslie need in order to heal? What advice do others give those who are grieving for a murdered loved one? Some say that killing the murderer will bring closure to the families of homicide victims. Others argue that only forgiveness will bring closure. And many families of murder victims believe that there is no such thing as closure and disdain the word.

The promise of closure for crime victims and their families has become a prominent narrative for defining not only victims' needs but also the broader concept of justice. Politicians and advocates use closure to talk about grief, victimization, justice, and healing.[8] Abolitionists and death penalty advocates use the promise of closure when they argue for their political agendas.

In pro–death penalty rhetoric, execution is recommended in order to achieve closure. These advocates argue that the death of the killer will provide closure for victims' families who cannot move on until the offender is dead. Furthermore, they claim that it is right and therapeutic for families of victims to want the killer to suffer; some even argue that only watching the offender's execution can provide closure.

The narratives offered by anti–death penalty advocates tell a different story. Abolitionists claim that closure can only come through means other than capital punishment, such as life without parole, forgiveness, or meeting the offender. They argue that life in prison is a better option because the death penalty prolongs suffering by forcing families to wait years while offenders appeal their sentences.

As we follow the story of Brooks Douglass, we will consider these questions: Does the notion of closure begin to capture what he has endured? How do advocates try to shape feeling rules for people like Brooks? And what does Brooks have to say as he reflects on the crime and trials more than thirty years later?

The Sentence, Testimonies, and Ongoing Appeals

In separate trials, Ake and Hatch were both sentenced to die. After a complicated series of court decisions and psychiatric reviews, Ake, the triggerman, was granted a new trial. Hatch also gained another hearing based on his argument that he did not intend to kill anyone as he was the one who sat in the car while Ake shot the family. These additional hearings would go on for years and continue to haunt Brooks and Leslie.

Brooks dropped out of several colleges and wandered around the Midwest. He moved from job to job, basically homeless, living out of his car. "After my parents died I was like the Bubble Boy, watching the world go by and not being a part of it. I couldn't feel anything." The one constant in his life was the testimony he had to give over and over.[9] For the next seventeen years, Brooks and Leslie could not escape the tragedy but rather had to relive it through the trials, appeals, and hearings.

In 1981, Brooks finally got some traction in his life. With the help of an uncle, he enrolled at Baylor University. But less than two years later, Brooks had to return to Oklahoma to testify at a new sentencing hearing for Hatch. A U.S. Supreme Court ruling set a different standard regarding a defendant's intent to commit murder. Hatch had long argued that he did not intend for the family to be shot as he was in the car when Ake shot everyone. Still, Hatch was sentenced to death once again.

In 1985—shortly before Brooks's college graduation—the court ruled that Ake should have been provided a state-paid psychiatrist to assist in an insanity defense. He received a new trial. In order to be close for the trial, Brooks enrolled at the Oklahoma City University School of Law. Ake was convicted in the second trial, but his sentence was reduced to life in prison. Brooks was stunned by the sentence. "I was walking out one door of the courtroom and they brought him out right in front of me," he recalled. "There was a sheriff's deputy standing right next to me and his gun was right by my hand, and I stood there and thought about reaching for that gun. I know I could have. I remember stopping myself and thinking, 'Is it worth it?'"[10]

Devastated by the ruling, Brooks quit law school, married, moved to Atlanta, and got a new job. Once again, though, in 1987, he learned that Hatch would get yet another sentencing hearing. "I was livid. You want to go forward, not to have to talk about what happened when you were 16. I had to leave my job for two weeks within a month after I started it. Finally we just picked up, quit our jobs and moved back to Oklahoma City. We realized those things weren't over."[11] Frustrated by the court system, he entered law school again in 1988 and earned his law degree in 1990.

A few years later, after some rough times, including a divorce, a *Washington Post* reporter asked Brooks if it would have been better to have the two men sentenced to life without parole. He replied:

> No. They threatened, they tortured, they raped. They sat down and ate our dinner, they murdered. It was an emotionally detached action that can only be met with the death penalty. Why? Just because it is right. Just because that is what they deserve. When I was in college, I never got to go home on holidays. I spent them alone in a dorm. And when I sat through a graduation this spring, when all these fathers were cheering their sons and daughters graduating from med school, I got sick to my stomach. You go on with your life. But don't tell me because in some way I have moved forward that they should get off the hook. They have given up the right to their own life. Now I want mine back.[12]

From Personal to Political: Changing Laws

In 1990, at age twenty-six, Brooks Douglass became the youngest state senator in Oklahoma history. Brooks said he did not set out to champion crime victims' rights. However, after his election, he continued to hear the hauntingly familiar pain from other crime victims. He decided it was time that victims had rights and a role in the justice system, so Brooks committed to writing and passing victims' rights legislation during his twelve years as a state senator. He was not the only advocate working for crime victims' rights.[13] A broader victims' rights movement influenced a key Supreme Court decision. After two cases in the prior two years that were viewed as setbacks for victims' rights,[14] the Supreme Court reversed its position on victim impact statements for capital cases. In *Payne v. Tennessee* (1991), the Court ruled that the Eighth Amendment does not prohibit a capital sentencing jury from considering victim impact evidence.[15] The belief that allowing victims to give their testimonies will help reduce the harm done was one of the reasons offered for the decision.[16]

In 1992, Senator Brooks Douglass sponsored a victims' rights bill that allowed families of murder victims to tell juries how the murders of their loved ones had changed their lives. A particularly powerful result of the crime victims' movement has been the emergence of victim impact statements.[17] Victims' rights advocates argue that because the prosecution represents the state and not the individual victim, the state does not serve the interests or memory of the victim. Therefore, victim testimony is necessary to show victims respect and to remind the court of victims' suffering and harm. For Brooks, the legislation that helped give victims a voice in the courtroom was important—and personal. He said that he always wanted to tell the court that he lost much more than his parents that night, but never had a chance. He explained those losses further: "Things like I never, ever, went home for the holidays, and I never, ever, got to hear my parents say they were proud of me or that they loved me. Or the fact that I don't like taking my shirt off when I'm working out because I've got all these scars all over my body and I'm reminded of that every morning when I get in the shower."[18]

Brooks also helped write and pass a pivotal right-to-view statute that allows families of murder victims to watch the execution of their family member's killer. However, Brooks said it was not just his own experience that initiated this process, but rather he was inspired to write the bill because of another family's tragedy. In 1978, Roger Dale Stafford killed nine people in two different incidents. First, Stafford, his wife, and his brother killed a family of three along Interstate 35 near Purcell, Oklahoma. Three weeks later, they killed six employees at a Sirloin Stockade in Oklahoma City. Brooks had an early connection to this tragedy as his father, Richard, counseled a family of one of the murder victims before his own tragic death just over a year later.

Stafford was sentenced to death in 1980 and was executed July 1, 1995. After the execution, a member of one of the families called Brooks and asked why they were forced to stand outside with protestors during the execution rather than have the chance to be inside as witnesses when it happened. Brooks said he thought it was wrong that the victims' family, who has suffered more than anyone, was not allowed to be present when it came time for the punishment. He believes that for some people, being present for the execution may be part of the healing process. However, he is quick to say that it is not for everyone. "In the bill that I authored, it in no way tells anybody that they have to or that they should go. I completely respect anybody who says, 'You know what, I have no desire to go.' And they shouldn't go. But if they think it is part of their process to heal and find closure, if you will, then the State of Oklahoma shouldn't be telling them you shan't and you're forbidden from going."[19]

Texas, in 1995, and Oklahoma, in 1996, became the first states to pass right-to-view legislation. Even as he worked on this legislation, Brooks thought that the execution of his tormentor would be years away. Suddenly, after the U.S. Supreme Court rejected Hatch's appeal, his execution was set shortly after Brooks's sponsored bill was passed.

The Execution

In 1996, Brooks and his sister became the first family members allowed to watch an execution inside the death chamber.[20] On August 9, Brooks and Leslie sat in the Oklahoma State Penitentiary less than twelve feet away from the man who helped murder their parents. They wore their parents' wedding rings, including Richard's ring, which Hatch had been wearing at the time of his arrest. Only a glass partition physically separated them from Hatch, but emotionally they were forever linked. Minutes after being strapped to the gurney, Hatch took his last breath.

Attending the execution raised concerns. The siblings told a *Dallas Morning News* reporter that they had doubts. Although Leslie said she debated about going in part because the idea upset her children, she said that the clemency hearing in July helped her decide to attend the execution.[21] Sheila Weller interviewed Leslie about this experience for a 1997 article:

> Leslie had a speech prepared—she was going to describe what this man had taken from her, how the pain and loss would never end. But then Hatch made his case, claiming, Leslie says, that he did not try to rape her, that Ake tried to and that he had attempted to stop it. "That lie," Leslie says, "just made me so sick!" When it was her time to speak, she got out only a small part. Then she faced the parole board and—in an emotional rush of words—broke years of silence. "He did too rape me!" Leslie angrily declared, deciding, right then and there, to attend the execution. "I don't know how he can deny it! I was there! I want to say to him: 'Look me in the eye and I'll tell you what you really said and did!'"[22]

Brooks said that he would probably go to the execution but that it was not something to which he looked forward. "None of my choices are good. I know there will be emotional scars from watching the execution. But if he's executed and I'm not there, that will have repercussions, too." What it boils down to as much as anything, he said, is that "I've ridden this horse for 17 years; why not see it through to the end?"[23]

Brooks wrote an article for *USA Today* titled "Why I Want to Watch a Killer Die." He opens it by saying, "It is not retaliation or retribution that I seek in witnessing the execution of the man who killed my parents. It is closure. Closure on an era of my life into which I never chose to enter. Closure of years of anger and hate."[24]

In an extensive interview two days before Hatch's execution, a reporter summarized Brooks's reflections on his family's tragedy and life ever since.

One recent scorching summer day, he stopped his car on the isolated dirt road leading to the farmhouse where his family once laughed. He recounted the seven times he has testified at trials and hearings, and how his anger and sense of loss have only intensified. He spoke of the relief that he and his sister felt long ago when Glen Burton Ake and Steven Keith Hatch were sentenced to death in 1980. And he recalled his rage six years later, when Ake, the trigger man, was resentenced to life in prison. For Douglass, now 32 and a conservative Republican state senator, and his sister, Leslie Frizzell, 29, a grade-school teacher, their encounter with the death penalty has been an agonizing odyssey of legalisms, lost hopes, and a never-ending search for justice, vengeance and closure.[25]

About two weeks before Hatch's scheduled execution, Brooks and Leslie testified at Hatch's clemency hearing. Hatch told them he was sorry. "I am not the monster I have been portrayed to be," he began. "I am sorry beyond words for the pain I caused the Douglasses."[26] But on the day of his execution, seventeen years after the murder, he offered no apology or remorse. Allegedly bitter after learning about possible book deals that Brooks was working on, Hatch just left an angry note saying those who sit in judgment are evil and barbaric.

A *Washington Post* reporter summarized an interview with the Douglass siblings: "They have spent their entire adult lives dealing with this tragedy. They had high expectations that this execution would afford them the peace and closure they have long sought."[27] Leslie said, "It was appalling—we were just horrified. But he has allowed me to never doubt what he is. He had no remorse. I just sat there watching him die and feeling so much anger that he was able to go peacefully. All I kept thinking about was how I laid hog-tied, with my face buried in a carpet, praying that I would live."[28] The "peaceful" death that Hatch experienced was one of the most difficult things for Leslie in witnessing the execution.

We were sitting there saying, "I just can't believe it. This is it?" she recalls. We waited 17 years for him to go to sleep as peacefully as everybody else wishes they could die? There we were, listening to my mom vomit blood, and knowing how much pain they were in, and the worst pain he ever felt was the needle going into his arm. If he could have felt 10 percent of the pain that we felt, I would have at least felt better. It was just too easy.[29]

Her brother Brooks said, "I'll let others draw their own conclusions about his final message. All I can do is deal with my own feelings. I will say that I wished he had surprised me in some way."[30] The day after the execution, the Douglass siblings shared their feelings with a reporter:

> "I do believe that it's the end of a very long ordeal that's dominated our lives," said Douglass this afternoon, having not slept at all. "I'm just glad that I hadn't ignored the rest of my life all these years because I would be very disappointed today. He's gone, it's over. I can get back to my law practice, my family." Leslie said that the outpouring of support from friends and family this week has helped her to overcome her lingering feelings of isolation since her parents' deaths. "I don't know if it will last, but I feel great today," she said. "I feel people care and I feel my parents are at peace. . . . I can move on. I can focus on my children."[31]

Fourteen years after the execution, Brooks told me, "The greatest relief I got from the Hatch execution was just the knowledge that I wasn't going to testify against him one more time. And here we were seventeen years later. That is the legal part of moving on."[32]

Face to Face, Again, with His Attacker

There is more to the story of Brooks Douglass. Not only did he witness the execution of one of his parents' killers but he also met face to face with the other offender. This meeting actually happened before Hatch's execution.

In 1994, as a state senator, Brooks took a tour of the prison where both Ake and Hatch were being held. For reasons he said he did not understand, Brooks "suddenly had a strong urge to meet them."[33] While walking around during the tour, he spotted Ake in the prison yard and asked the warden if he could meet with Ake.

When asked if he knew ahead of time that he wanted to meet with Ake, Brooks replied: "I think it is something that had been in the back of my mind and in some ways something I'd been preparing myself for. But certainly forgiving him was not at all what was on my mind as far as a direction to go with it." Brooks explained that his motivation to meet Ake did not originate with forgiveness but that it evolved during the meeting.

The fact that Ake was given the death sentence and then the court turned around and reversed it to life in prison was almost like being revictimized. What it all came down to was that there is nothing I can ever do to this guy other than physically harming him. There is just nothing that can be done. That is something I can assure you comes up in every victim's mind: "If I ever get my hands on this person. . . ." Ultimately I was in a position to be able to do that. That's where I had to make a decision: do I want to move on or do I want to keep this going and continue to suffer the consequences of it. I made the decision that what I needed to do was forgive him and let it go.[34]

For two to three hours, Brooks sat face to face with only a glass partition separating him from the man who critically injured him, raped his sister, and killed his parents. Reporting it as "an out-of-body experience," Brooks told a reporter, "It turned out, luckily for me, to be one of the best things I've ever done in my life."[35] Ake was remorseful, and they both cried through the conversation. Ake said, "I want you to know that I am so, so sorry about what I did to you and your family." Ake wept as he told Brooks that he had accepted Christ eight years earlier.[36]

In an interview fifteen years later, Brooks said that it is impossible to depict what happened during that meeting. "Literally, it was as if God laid his hand on me. The air was so thick I could almost taste it. I could feel God's presence as if He was telling me, 'I'm not going to let you get angry, I'm not going to let you blow this.' The only way to describe it was this very intense and powerful sense of love. It was so thick around me that I was unable to do what I thought I was there to do."[37] As mentioned earlier, Brooks indicated that his initial desire was to harm Ake rather than to forgive him. He explained further:

> As I unloaded on him about Leslie, who suffered far more than me, I felt as if my body was full of water and my head full of poison. Then as I got up and put my hand on the door, I turned around and looked back at him and thought, "There's more to this." I went back to the table, as if pulled by a magnet, and after an eternity of silence, something completely unexpected came out of my mouth. "I forgive you." It was not at all what I was there to do. I had told Ake, "My father was a minister and he taught me that I was always to forgive. I can't. It's not in me to do that." But when those words "I forgive you" were spoken, I just fell back in the chair, suddenly feeling as if the bottoms of my feet opened up and the water and hatred were pouring out over

the floor. I could almost see it. At the same time, it felt like a clamp was taken off my chest and I could breathe again for the first time in 15 years. I remember walking out the doors of the prison and feeling like the sky was bluer, the trees were greener. All my senses were just extraordinarily heightened. It was a life-changing experience.[38]

Brooks sought a meeting with Hatch, too: "I tried to meet with Steven Hatch and he wouldn't meet with me. So there was never an opportunity to sit and talk with him and discuss anything with him. I wish I had but it was never there."

A few years after Hatch's execution, Brooks shared his views on forgiving murderers. When comparing his meeting to Ake with Hatch's execution, Brooks said that while witnessing the death was useful in putting the bad memories behind him, his feelings about it contained none of the euphoria of his meeting with Ake. "I was just happy it was over with and got the heck out of there," he said.[39] Still, Brooks continues to say that Hatch's execution was important in helping him end that part of the legal process. He told a committee in Massachusetts that was considering reinstating the death penalty that "he met and forgave one of the men, but that forgiveness is a personal thing, not something he can ask other victims to do, and that he does not believe it means absolution."[40]

Timothy McVeigh's Execution

In the middle of Brooks's ongoing experiences dealing with his own tragedy, his state endured a terrorist attack. On April 19, 1995, just two months after Brooks had his remarkable meeting with Ake, Timothy McVeigh bombed the Alfred P. Murrah Federal Building in Oklahoma City. In the eighteen months following the bombing, Brooks finished the right-to-view legislation and witnessed the execution of Hatch.

In the spring of 2001, McVeigh was scheduled to die in the federal prison in Terre Haute, Indiana.[41] Death penalty advocates used McVeigh's case to push for allowing families to view the execution. Because 168 people were killed in the Oklahoma City bombing, the number of family members affected dwarfed most murder cases. Politicians called for a televised execution in order to provide closure for the families.

During the media blitz surrounding McVeigh's execution, reporters flocked to Brooks since he was author of Oklahoma's right-to-view statute and witness to the execution of his parents' murderer. Standing in the shadow of the memorial for the Oklahoma City bombing victims, a reporter asked Brooks why he wanted to be there for his parents' killer's execution. He replied: "It wasn't a matter of hating him or revenge. The biggest issue for me was that it was over. I'm never going to have to testify against this guy again."[42] Another response reflects his pain: "As I was watching him dying in the background, on top of that I was seeing the events of that night happening all over again. Going to an execution is like having cancer: You know you're going to have to have surgery and the cure's not any fun, but you've still got to go through with it or you're not going to live."[43]

In another interview, Brooks warns about what comes after the execution:

> Tonight, these people are all going to go home, they're going to lay down in bed and—and then it's just them. There's no cameras, no media, no other survivors around them. And that's when I think that the reality of what's happened begins to set in. And—and I think it's—it's—it can be depressing. It was for me. You've witnessed a death. You've—you've finally gotten to a point where, you know, it's time to begin to let go of some of that emotion. You still love your loved one, but it's time to move on.[44]

Brooks warned family members of McVeigh's victims that the execution may not provide the satisfaction they want. "If a victim's family member thinks they're suddenly going to have euphoric feelings and everything's going to be wonderful immediately, they're going to be disappointed."[45]

Closure Politics, Feeling Rules, and Murder

Death penalty advocates construct rules for family members and the public regarding how we should feel about executions. Arguing that victims' families will not find closure until the offender is dead constructs three main feeling rules about grief management in the case of murder. First, after an execution, victims' families will be relieved and have a sense of closure. Second, the pain felt when a loved one is murdered is so great that only the same suffering on the part of the offender can bring healing. And, finally, supporting the death penalty is a proper way to show support and sympathy for victims of crime and their families.

For some victims' families, the death penalty and/or witnessing executions leave them with an emotional disconnection—they do not feel the closure promised. A common response from families of homicide victims after viewing an execution is that it still hurts, or there was not the closure I was expecting, or I'm even angrier. Pro–death penalty feeling rules prepare family members to expect peace or a sense of relief, but some instead feel worse. In an article for the *Christian Science Monitor*, staff writers Dante Chinni and Peter Grier describe how executions are not the end of grief for families. Their article gives many examples of people expressing emotive dissonance, as in this quote:

> As she watched Ricky McGinn lying in front of her in the death chamber, Mozelle Hamm could not find it in herself to forgive him. He had murdered her granddaughter, Christi Jo, and now the state of Texas was going to give him his own back. Finally, after the waiting, the trial, the appeals, she would at least know—for certain this time—that McGinn would never hurt anyone again. But then, as the execution spooled out in front of her last Sept. 27, something happened. Or rather, it didn't happen. Ms. Hamm felt . . . less than one might suppose. There was no flood of relief. There was no lifting of weight, no sense of turning a personal page. And today, months later, that is the message Mozelle Hamm has for the Oklahoma City bombing survivors and victim relatives who were to watch Timothy McVeigh's execution: Remember, closure is for doors.[46]

The method of execution is one reason that family members who witness executions describe an emotional disconnect between what they expected to feel and what they felt. Methods of execution have evolved in an effort to make them more humane, which, interestingly, has complicated the rhetoric of retribution. An increasing objection to capital punishment is that it is "too easy," "too quick," and without enough pain. These objections are usually tied to executions by lethal injection.[47]

Using the victims' families' claim that the execution of the offender did not provide enough satisfaction, some death penalty opponents argue that executions fail to provide the closure victims hope for (and death penalty advocates promise) because the executions themselves are too serene to provide a sense of justice. Judy Busch of Oklahoma City witnessed the execution of Floyd Medlock, who had killed her seven-year-old granddaughter. After the execution, Judy said that she did not leave fully satisfied: "It was so quick and so sterile and so serene," she says. "It left me feeling angry, I guess."[48]

Research has found little evidence that people "find closure" through executions or victim impact statements.[49] Defense attorney Michael Goodwin argues that the right-to-view statutes intended to help families may actually make things worse. He claims that after viewing executions, some families have felt disappointment and a desire for more vengeance rather than closure.[50] This may be in part because they think the offender died too easily or they wish they could watch him be tortured and in more pain. Marilyn Armour and Mark Umbreit have talked to many family members grieving for those who were murdered. These scholars state, "The notion of closure is rarely advanced by the survivors themselves. Many, if not most, vehemently deny that there is closure or that closure will ever be possible for them; they abhor the word because it implies 'getting over it.' Many survivors also insist there can be no justice because nothing will bring their loved ones back."[51] In their book *Who Owns Death?* Robert Lifton and Greg Mitchell argue that closure is at best elusive but more likely nonexistent.

A large and vocal group of families oppose the death penalty and fight against others using their names to politicize and mobilize support for executions. Marie Deans founded Murder Victims' Families for Reconciliation (MVFR) in 1976 after Penny, her mother-in-law, was murdered. MVFR is a national organization of people who have lost a family member to murder and who are opposed to the death penalty. Marie shares her view on closure: "The death penalty is a false God promising to bring justice and closure to victims' families. We did not seek closure. We sought healing, a way to get beyond the 'legal case' and back to the memories that honored Penny."[52]

Jeanne Bishop also knows the pain and horror of losing a family member to murder. Her sister, Nancy Bishop Langert, was twenty-five and pregnant when she and her husband were murdered in 1990. Since her sister's death, Jeanne has argued against the death penalty and against closure. She says, "'Closure,' a neatly wrapped-up end to the horror and grief of murder, simply doesn't exist—nor perhaps should it." She says that the "most blatant perpetrators of this lie" are advocates of the death penalty who promise peace and resolution after an execution. She continues,

> It doesn't happen this way. Grief, the culmination of sweet memories and the bitter loss of possibilities, lives on—and it should. The grief I felt after my sister's murder is not closed. It lives in me today, but differently. At first it was a grief that numbed, that paralyzed. Now it is a grief that energizes me to love more passionately, to share more generously, to live more fearlessly, to work to prevent the violence which could inflict on another family the suffering mine has endured.[53]

Robert "Renny" Cushing Jr. did not run away from his father's murder. His father, Robert Cushing Sr., a retired teacher and father of seven, was murdered in the hallway of what is now Renny's house, which he shares with his wife and three daughters.

> "After my father was killed, it seemed real important not to lose this house," Cushing explains. He is a slim man with a long melancholy face and a strong New England accent. "My dad and my grandfather built it. The killer may have taken my dad from us, but he wasn't going to take my roots, too. Staying here was one way of regaining control over my life. Besides, with time, the house has become something else. The floors that were once stained with my father's blood are also where my daughters learned how to walk.[54]

Instead of focusing on retribution, Renny became a leader in the fight against capital punishment. He is the founder and executive director of Murder Victims' Families for Human Rights. He has written and lectured extensively on his opposition to the death penalty. He also served two terms in the New Hampshire House of Representatives where, in 1998, he urged his colleagues to abolish the death penalty. He told his fellow legislators, "I favor abolition . . . not so much because I want murderers to live as because, if the state kills them, that forever forecloses the possibility that those of us who are victims might figure out how to forgive. We've lost enough already. Don't take that option for healing away, please."[55]

In 1999, Renny gave a presentation to the Human Rights Initiative at Harvard University. In response to a question about homicide survivors who do not have closure, he said:

> I wouldn't presume to dictate how an individual should heal, I just know that they need to. I respect the people who feel the need for an execution; I just don't think that it works. The whole criminal justice system reinforces the notion that people need an execution to heal. And there's this notion that goes along with that, that if you don't want an execution, then you obviously don't love your family. We need to publicly affirm that it is ok to not want an execution, that ultimately we'll be better off without it.[56]

Renny continues to speak on behalf of homicide survivors who oppose the death penalty.

Carol Duncanson and Sally Peck also speak out against the death penalty and the myth of closure. Carol and Sally's mother, Bernice O'Connor, died a victim of rape and murder at the age of eighty-two. The two sisters celebrate their mother's life by seeking alternatives to the death penalty.

> Where the death penalty is an option, the victim's family is apt to be drawn into the spirit of vengeance with the promise that an execution will give them closure. This prolongs their grief and pain through the years of court proceedings. We are grateful that Michigan does not have the death penalty and did not give us a sentence of prolonged grief or hold out a false promise that an execution would make it all better. Holding on to hate and vengeance will not help us heal. We are thankful that our mother raised us to believe in forgiveness, because if hatred had been added to our burden of pain, loss, and grief after her brutal murder, it would have destroyed us.[57]

A particularly valuable testimony for abolitionists comes from converts: those who used to favor the death penalty but changed their view after a loved one was killed. Tom Mauser's son Daniel was a fifteen-year-old sophomore who was among those killed at Columbine High School in Littleton, Colorado, in 1999. On a memorial website honoring his son, Tom answers the question "Now that you've had a child murdered, has your opinion on the death penalty changed in any way?"

> Yes. Prior to Columbine, I considered myself a mild supporter of the death penalty—not liking it, but seeing it as somewhat as a deterrent. My reservations about the death penalty were mostly practical ones—for example, the fact that death sentence appeals cost taxpayers so much. Since Columbine, I have come to strongly oppose the death penalty. I have come to learn, based on talking with a few other parents of murdered children, that there is little closure in seeing a murderer put to death. I believe that a victim's parent gains revenge with an execution, but not closure. I recognize that some parents say they do reach closure, but I question that, wondering if they merely feel societal pressure to acknowledge they have found closure. I say that because I have observed some in this community who want very much to hear no more about Columbine and to hear us say we're finding closure. I believe that closure comes with reconciliation, with

honoring one's child in a positive way, and with making a closer spiritual connection with God.[58]

These stories reflect just a few of the voices that cry "do not kill others in
my name." Many families who live with murder do not seek closure and certainly do not want others promising them closure through death.

Prosecutor Kelly Siegler is an advocate of the death penalty. Successfully
prosecuting high-profile cases in Texas has earned her a reputation as a "giant
killer."[59] She is known for her courtroom theatrics, such as bringing in a
full-size bed to reenact a stabbing. Siegler also touched off a firestorm of controversy when she referred to members of Joel Osteen's Lakewood Church
as "screwballs and nuts" as part of her explanation for turning down a man
for a jury. She tried to explain that she was only trying to seat a tough jury,
arguing that the church member was too forgiving.[60] Her record backs up
her reputation as unforgiving and partial to capital punishment. She has tried
over 150 jury trials and is considered a national expert on capital punishment
litigation and an advocate for victims of crime. Although eighteen of her
nineteen capital cases resulted in the death penalty, she is not one to argue
that closure exists. In fact, she argues the opposite:

> The truth is that there is no closure. Sure, you hear it all of the time.
> You hear that closure is what we should be seeking on behalf of vic-
> tims everywhere. You hear experts and psychologists and even law
> enforcement officials all over the country talking about closure as if it
> is some "state of mind" that we can help a mommy and a daddy, who
> have learned they will never see their baby again, obtain. But when
> you ask those same victims if any of that—the arrest, the conviction,
> the sentencing, the execution—ever truly help them gain "closure,"
> you know what they all say? They all say no. They all say there is no
> such thing. They all say they are glad that phase of the process of the
> criminal justice system is complete. They all say thank you, and then
> they go back to having to figure out how to get up again the next
> morning and live another day in a world that no longer has the same
> color and light and joy in it that it did "before."[61]

One of the reasons so few death penalty supporters acknowledge that there
is no closure is the potential political backlash that could follow. It is significant that a top prosecutor who has successfully litigated death penalty cases
argues that closure does *not* exist. Mark Bennett, a Houston area criminal
defense lawyer, picked up on Kelly Siegler's post about no closure:

A successful death penalty prosecutor concedes that, where closure is concerned, the emperor has no clothes: it's astounding not because of the novelty of the idea, for it isn't novel—anyone not steeped in overwrought victimology can *intuit* that there can be no "closure" for the death of a child—but because it weakens the justification for a penalty of which the prosecutor is unabashedly in favor.[62]

Although fear of political backlash is always part of the game, there are other reasons that closure remains a big part of death penalty politics.

Death Penalty Politics and Closure

In order to appreciate how closure has influenced death penalty politics, it is helpful to briefly summarize the capital punishment debate.[63] Historically, two key rationales in favor of the death penalty have been deterrence and retribution. Expressive values associated with the death penalty center around the idea of retribution—allowing societal expressions of moral outrage, giving the offender his or her just desserts, and reinforcing a shared sense of community norms.[64]

The abolitionist movement struggled to find an argument that appealed to a mainstream majority because so many of its reasons for opposing the death penalty put it on the side of murderers. For example, the sanctity of life argument holds that human life has infinite value and must be protected at all costs. Abolitionists argue against the death penalty for even "the worst murderers" because "even murderers must be treated in light of the value of their lives, a value not erased by the harm and injustice their lethal violence has caused the innocent."[65] Related arguments include the violation of the Eighth Amendment, which forbids cruel and unusual punishment, and the immorality for the state to be killing people. It is difficult to gather widespread public support for a movement when critics can easily charge it with siding with "evil offenders" over "innocent victims."

Abolitionists developed a new argument for opposing capital punishment that had mass appeal: innocent people may be executed. The larger scope of this argument includes fairness, constitutional issues of practice, and racial/class discrimination. Probably the most effective part, though, has been the fear of convicting and executing innocent people. Rather than just defending the value of a murderer's life, this shift in focus allows abolitionists to be on the side of innocent people—a strategy that appeals to a larger section of society.[66] Abolitionists were able to expand their arguments to include compassion for innocent people rather than just compassion for murderers. The growing evidence that innocent people are being convicted and placed on death row has been the linchpin in the new abolitionism. This development led to several key political events.

In the 1994 *Callins* case, Justice Harry Blackmun dramatically reversed his position on the death penalty, using the now famous line "From this day forward, I will no longer tinker with the machinery of death."[67] Other notable judges and political figures began to speak out against the death penalty because of their concern for the process and the mounting evidence that innocent people were at risk. These voices aided the new abolitionism and gave political power to the moratorium movement. In 1997, the American Bar Association passed a resolution calling for a moratorium on executions.

By 2004, 3,500 groups had called for a moratorium on executions.[68] Perhaps the most dramatic response to the call for a moratorium came from Illinois. The discovery that thirteen defendants on death row in Illinois had been wrongly convicted led then governor George Ryan to order a moratorium on executions in that state. Not yet done, before he left office in 2003, Ryan commuted the death sentences of all 167 prisoners on death row in Illinois. There has been debate about Ryan's motivation. Some argue that he took these actions to distract from his own political problems and criminal investigations into his conduct while he was Illinois secretary of state. No matter why he acted, Ryan's moratorium on the death penalty made significant waves in the capital punishment debate. And, incidentally, if the moratorium was politically motivated, it did not keep him out of trouble as Ryan received a six-year prison sentence in 2006 and started his prison time a year later in Terre Haute, Indiana—at the same prison that carried out the execution of Timothy McVeigh.

With the success of new abolitionism, presumed benefits of capital punishment in terms of deterrence had to compete with concerns about the by-products of implementing the death penalty, including lack of due process, executing the innocent, high costs, and racial discrimination. Furthermore, with an expanding body of literature questioning the effects of deterrence and the public's growing awareness of the death penalty's economic costs, the argument for the death penalty started to face stiff challenges.[69] With dramatic stories and solid evidence of innocent people on death row, the expressive value of retribution can be argued as not worth the risk. Death penalty advocates have countered the innocence argument by denying that any innocent person has been executed and arguing that safeguards are in place to prevent wrongful conviction. However, a more effective counterargument to the new abolitionism is the pro–death penalty advocates' rhetorical shift to focusing on closure for victims' families.

The argument that the death penalty is needed to provide closure for victims' families takes the focus away from the offender—and thus away from issues of due process and fairness—and places it on victims' families. Focusing on closure shifts attention away from the public's growing concern about executing innocent people and embraces even more fully a desire for retribution—only this time retribution is cast in the context of sympathy for victims' families. Advocates reconstructed their claims about capital punishment to include a new type of retribution, which focuses on closure for victims' families.

Two practices related to capital cases are victim impact statements and right-to-view statutes. These practices embed closure within the criminal justice system as well as normalize and establish closure as part of "justice." They institutionalize closure. The institutionalization of closure refers to the establishment of opportunities for victims to achieve closure within the legal system. The institutionalization makes closure seem "real" rather than a socially constructed concept.[70]

For the families of murder victims, the stakes are high since the feeling rules surrounding closure promise not just success in the legal system but relief from the terrible pain of having a loved one murdered.[71] However, the organization of our death penalty system makes this result unlikely for most family members of homicide victims. The majority of homicide cases do not involve capital punishment. Not only is "closure through execution" unavailable to these families, but they may be left blaming the criminal justice system for denying them this relief. This type of closure is also unavailable for families of victims whose killers were not caught.

Also denied "closure through execution" are those family members who do not support the death penalty. Not only do they oppose the mechanism that is supposed to give them relief but the justice system may also deny them the opportunity to tell their story and whatever satisfaction that may bring. In addition, others may believe that their opposition to an execution suggests a lack of real grief for the murder victim.[72] Even for those few family members who embrace these feeling rules, and see a loved one's murderer executed, many report not experiencing the closure predicted.

Brooks Douglass defends victims' right to say they do not want the offender to be executed: "There are some victims who say, 'I absolutely don't think this person should be given the death penalty.' They ought to be able to say that in their victim impact testimony. That can be part of the victim's healing process."

Victim impact statements and right-to-view legislation support pro–death penalty claims more than abolitionist rhetoric. Those victims' families who oppose the death penalty are not given the same space and time in court as those who favor the death penalty.[73] Critics of victim impact statements voice concern over the state's discrimination regarding which victims get to talk. Courts have barred victims from giving their testimony because they oppose the death penalty.[74] In a 2002 report, Renny Cushing, then the executive director of MVFR, argues, "family members who oppose the death penalty are silenced, marginalized, and abandoned, even by the people who are theoretically charged with helping them."[75] Renny said that they published the *Dignity Denied* report to push for policies in victim services agencies "to develop a protocol that recognizes opposition to the death penalty as a valid response to the trauma of murder."[76]

As illustrated in this chapter, abolitionists also use closure in their politics. There could be institutional practices that favor abolitionist claims about closure. For example, we could have a "right to keep the offender alive" so that victims' families can find answers about the murder and possibly forgive the offenders, or a "right to avoid the appeals process" because it drags out the legal trials, or a "right not to have my name used in killing someone else." There are a few prosecutors who listen to victims' families who oppose the death penalty and seek a plea bargain for life in prison, and there are advocates who try to use victim impact statements as a way to voice compassion for defendants and opposition to the death penalty. But these exceptions do not carry the weight of institutionalized practices like the right-to-view legislation. Closure talk has favored pro–death penalty politics, although that is different from saying it has favored all family members of the victims.

In the debate over the death penalty, closure has become a dominant political and rhetorical tool. As part of the political debate, advocates tell grieving individuals "we know how you can find closure." "Executions," says one side. Yet others say "Life without parole." These answers are for people who are grieving, but they originate from long-standing interests of advocates who have reframed the debate to tap into the hunt for closure. Not only has closure discourse dramatically shifted death penalty rhetoric from the offender to the victims' families, but closure has also become something people may be desperate to find through a variety of methods even though it is not at all clear that one can "close" the unbearable pain of having a loved one murdered.

Reflections on Executions, Forgiveness, and Healing

Brooks Douglass's story reflects the complexity involved with surviving a crime and grieving the murder of loved ones and represents an important contrast to the simplified answers that some people give for what they think will help family members. Fortunately, we also see his resilience as he walks through this process.

Over thirty years after that tragic night, Brooks told me that forgiveness was an important part of his journey.

> Forgiveness is one of the things I needed to do to move on with my life which is part of what I think is this thing people refer to as closure. Getting to a point where they can process what has happened to them and be able to look forward in their lives instead of backwards. Not forgetting their loved ones and not in any way dishonoring them but in fact maybe honoring them by living their lives more fully. I looked at what my parents would have wanted for me and it would have been to live a full life and have a family and move on beyond what happened as much as possible and not allow Glen Ake and Steven Hatch to dominate or even control my life any more than they already had.[77]

When I asked if his perspective on families viewing an execution has changed since he authored the right-to-view statute, Brooks said that he still believes in the right of family members to be at an execution if they choose so. However, he is not a staunch defender of capital punishment. Brooks explains:

> I can't say I care that much whether there is a death penalty or not. Personally I think there is a place for it. I think there are some people who have committed crimes that are so absolutely atrocious that they've given up their right to continue to breathe air with the rest of us. I think that is a very, very rare instance. It bothers me a lot that there are prosecutors that have a knee jerk reaction, any killing and we're going to go with the death penalty. That is just not appropriate.[78]

Today, Brooks is likely to tell those who will listen that more victims should have the opportunity to talk with their offenders. He was one of the keynote speakers at the 2010 conference of the National District Attorneys Association. He told the prosecutors there that they should encourage programs that allow victims to talk with offenders. He knows there are risks involved and that the people should be properly prepared and vetted before meetings happen.

Brooks agrees that there is no one answer: "It is tough for either side [of the death penalty debate] to say, 'gee we have the answer for this' because they don't. Closure, or moving on, is something that will be different for every human being." He believes that every victim's journey is going to be different but emphasizes that there is a way to heal.

> What I tell people is that healing is a process and it takes a long time. I think the biggest thing that you have to start with is the desire to live your life. There is a reason why I got up off the floor that night. Just the decision to get up off the floor doesn't mean I was going to survive. But the decision to just lay down is something I could have easily done. To decide, "hey, I want to get up and I want to live my life" sort of implicitly says, "I want it to be a good one. And I don't want to spend the rest of my life suffering or having it dominated by what these other people did to me. I want it to be meaningful." So it starts there. From there it is the search we all have, the search for a meaningful life. It's just that you start off with a great big hole where you say I've got to deal with all this other stuff first and some of it is the legal side and the rest is the emotions of it. And unfortunately both of those can take a long, long time.[79]

Brooks is not the only person who says that healing is a long process. After a decade, the families grieving for those killed on September 11, 2001, continue to be inundated with talk about closure. The debates intensified following the death of Osama bin Laden—long considered the mastermind behind the 9/11 attacks. These debates reflect feeling rules found in death penalty rhetoric.

Immediately following Osama bin Laden's death on May 1, 2011, many claimed we could now have closure. This perspective follows the feeling rule that once an offender is dead, the case can be closed and the victim's family can finally move on. However, many grieving family members say that bin Laden's death did not bring closure because the pain of losing a loved one does not end. Many of these individuals might say that bin Laden's death brought justice, but they distinguish that from closure. His death also raised debates about forgiveness—whether forgiveness in the case of bin Laden is possible, acceptable, or needed for people's healing.

Just hours after bin Laden's death, the U.S. military disposed of his body in a burial at sea. A few days later, President Obama decided not to release official pictures of bin Laden's dead body. Many people argued that they would not be able to find closure unless they were allowed to see the pictures.

This argument reflects the expectation that seeing the execution of someone will help with closure, except this case is about viewing pictures of a dead body. This taps into the belief that seeing someone else suffer will provide closure to one's own pain—the "getting even" type of closure talk. This is also another example of how closure is used as a political tool. The argument that President Obama denied people closure because he declined to release the photos has more to do with politics than concern for healing. Unfortunately, this rhetoric also helps to shape feeling rules about grief in ways that are not useful to those who are grieving.

Brooks Douglass continues to write his story. Literally. Now living in California with his wife and two young children, Brooks has cowritten and produced a film based on his family's story. He even played the role of his father, and his sister Leslie had a short scene as a singer. Called *Heaven's Rain*, the film is described as a "powerful family drama telling a true story of love, loss, anger, redemption and ultimately forgiveness."[80] "Hopefully, it's a story that will touch people," Brooks says. "It's a story about love. It's a story about forgiveness. The biggest thing I hope is that it can show people a way to forgive."[81]

Brooks says that after production ended, people kept asking if he found closure by making the film. He replies that he is not sure about finding closure but that his faith has helped him find peace: "I don't know if you ever get over something like this. I doubt there's a day that goes by that I don't think about it, but I also think I've tried to deal with it in a way that my faith has taught me, in a way that my parents taught me. Ultimately, we have to move on—not forgetting our loved ones or forgetting what happened—and live our lives to the fullest. This is what I had to do."[82]

Heaven's Rain will also serve as a memorial to Brooks and Leslie's parents. Not everyone has a chance to write and produce a film honoring his or her loved ones, but, nonetheless, many want memorials to remember those who died. Unfortunately, there can be roadblocks along the way when establishing public memorials. In the next chapter, we look at the politics of mourning, sacred space, and public memory as we examine how closure plays a role in debates about memorials.

8. Forgetting versus Remembering

Politics of Mourning, Sacred Space, and Public Memory

On September 11, 2008, seven years after the 9/11 attacks, the first major public memorial for 9/11 was dedicated in front of the Pentagon. The words on the memorial frame the invitation: "Remember, Reflect, Renew." The day after the memorial opened, the *Washington Post* ran a story titled "A Long-Awaited Opening, Bringing Closure to Many." Marcellia Potler said she feels closure at the memorial since her father's remains were never recovered after he died at the site. She knows he is there at the memorial. Marcellia tattooed her shoulder with an outline of the Pentagon around the date 9-11-01 to remind her of her father.[1] Thomas Heidenberger visited the memorial to honor his wife who was the head flight attendant on the plane that crashed into the Pentagon. Thomas said, "You get a sense that this is hallowed ground. This is in many respects almost sacred ground." He agreed with his son, who said, "Dad, it gives us a sense of closure."[2] Thomas worried about those in New York who do not yet have a memorial. They have "no place to go, have no closure."[3]

Barbara Boykin finds comfort in a different type of memorial. In January 2003, her son died while driving to a friend's home when he lost control of his car and hit some trees. There is now a marker decorated with flowers that quietly marks that spot—a roadside memorial. Barbara says the memorial reminds her of the crash but also helps her remember her son: "It gives me comfort when I pass by there. At the cemetery, I know that was the final goodbye there." However, she describes the marker as where she finds closure: "I know that's the last place he was alive. It does something to me."[4]

From national public memorials to private roadside markers, people seek ways to help remember their loved ones. There are others, though, who disagree over the legal right to establish such memorials as well as what is included in their design and content. Some want to remember, but others want to forget. As with other issues, people who argue about memorials have different interpretations of how to find closure. The previous chapter highlighted closure and death penalty politics. Here I explain how closure plays a role in debates about public memorials and collective memory.

Struggles over public memorials represent contests over what should be remembered following a tragedy and who has the right to decide. By defining a tragedy, we can influence how others view what issues matter. By influencing what others remember, we can shape what happened; what lessons we are supposed to have learned. We help decide whose life is worthy of memory and how. The concept of closure shows up in the politics of remembrance and mourning. People's definitions of closure and their perspectives on how to find it frequently collide. These collisions can lead to arguments and heated political rhetoric. The debates help shape feeling rules for how people are supposed to grieve.

Closure as Remembering and Closure as Forgetting

In debates about public memorials, one of the main collisions is "closure as forgetting" versus "closure as remembering." Within this larger discussion, people disagree on *who* is worthy of remembrance, and how much, if at all, public mourning should be regulated. Advocates for different types of public memorials use the importance of remembrance as a key political argument. The cultural concept of closure is used to support their claims, which can be effective given the success of closure talk in other politics, including the crime victims' movement and the death penalty debate.

"Remembering" may seem like an unlikely type of closure. However, as discussed in chapter 2, people seeking closure through remembrance are trying to end the fear of forgetting. Or the fear that others will forget. Closing the fear of forgetting means feeling assured that you have figured out how to remember. You can assure yourself that you have memories and rituals to show respect to your loved one. Those who grieve sometimes want others to remember, too. Some seek closure by participating in public rituals of remembrance.

The desire to have others remember your loved one can upset people who may want to forget the pain and grief in order to move on with their own lives. In these cases, a struggle transpires between those who want to remember and those who want to forget. Sometimes it is a matter of what details people want to remember (or that others want to forget) regarding a public tragedy as reflected in the design and content of a memorial.

The dominant theories on grief during the twentieth century focused on "letting go," or "detaching from the deceased" and "moving on."[5] People were advised to detach themselves from their grief, to get on with their lives. During the 1990s and into the twenty-first century, detachment theory began to fade. Many contemporary bereavement scholars have moved in a different direction, often referring to continuing bonds theory, which emphasizes that people do not just let go and move on but hang on to bonds with the deceased by transforming the relationship.[6] Thinking of closure as forgetting supports the detachment theories of grief. However, the continuing bonds theory supports remembrance as a type of closure.[7]

So how do you continue the memory of a loved one? There are two types of bonds: public and private. Private bonds include rituals, memories, and artifacts that help someone remain attached to a loved one who has died. This might include establishing private memorial rituals, talking to the deceased, visiting a grave, looking at photographs, and so on. There are hundreds and hundreds of memorial products available, and closure through remembrance is a major marketing strategy used to sell them.

Public bonds require the help of others to secure the memory of someone in a public setting. Many are comforted by the knowledge that others remember their loved one. Some people will do advocacy work on behalf of a loved one. Others might place an ad in the paper recognizing the anniversary of a loved one's death with a poem or picture.

Rituals involving memorialization vary depending on the cause of death, who died, and where. Not everyone feels a need to have a public memorial for a loved one. And, obviously, not everyone can have a national memorial recognizing a loved one's death. Although there are many ways to memorialize someone, this chapter focuses on the politics of public memorials and, more specifically, advocates' strategic use of the term "closure" regarding those memorials.

Why is it that establishing a public memorial for a loved one needs to be political? Why would anyone oppose another person for trying to remember a loved one who died? There are several reasons why people disagree on the importance of public memorials or the appropriateness of them. Disagreements about memorials hinge on issues such as property rights, separation of church and state, public safety, collective purpose of a national memorial, and the right of others not to be reminded of grief. One way that advocates for public memorials fight these arguments is through closure. In many cases, loved ones who are trying to establish a memorial do not have a legal claim, but they use their grief as an emotion claim. One of the key arguments for public memorials is the need to preserve sacred space and allow access to it for loved ones who need healing and closure.

To explore the role of closure in debates about public memorials, we turn first to debates about 9/11. Then we discuss individual memorials that generate similar arguments with a focus on roadside memorials.

9/11 and Ground Zero: Whose Space Is It?

Debates about 9/11 include arguments over what to do with the space that is commonly referred to as Ground Zero (the area where both World Trade Center towers collapsed after being struck by airplanes). Ground Zero is a site of sacred space for many family members of those who died there. They consider it sacred not only because that is where their loved ones died but also because many believe human remains are still part of the site. However, Ground Zero is on some highly valued commercial real estate, which complicates debates about what to do with that space. The family members do not have a legal claim to the site, so they make an emotion claim to it. We consider a few of the debates regarding 9/11 and what to do with the space.

What is the proper way to treat space and the debris where large numbers of people have died? The answer has not been straightforward. After almost a decade, controversy continues to plague the search for remains from the 9/11 attacks in New York City. After the attacks, debris from the site was taken to Staten Island's Fresh Kills landfill, which reportedly holds over one million tons of material from the World Trade Center in addition to common household garbage. Families argue that the unsifted debris from the World Trade Center contains human remains. Families of 9/11 victims wanted to have a formal resting place for the remaining debris from the site of the attacks. Because so many of them had no remains to bury, they wanted to have a formal place to go to remember their loved ones. They set up an advocacy group called WTC Families for a Proper Burial. The chaplain for the group writes, "As a Christian clergyperson, my concern is also regarding the need for some closure and the grieving process surviving family members and friends of the deceased WTC victims."[8]

Referring to the Fresh Kills landfill as a national disgrace, families have called for the remains of their loved ones to be removed from the landfill and given a proper burial. They expressed outrage over having to visit a garbage dump to pay respects to their loved ones. Sergeant Michael Ryan of the New York Police Department said that the search for victims at Fresh Kills was incomplete: "We drove our cars right up to the landfill. We didn't know then, nobody knew, that they were dumping truckfuls of debris from the World Trade Center. I was just handed a rake and told, 'There's your pile, see what you can find.'"[9] Rose Foti's son Robert, a firefighter, died while responding to the 9/11 attacks. Rose said she was coping with her loss until she learned about the possibility of remains being dumped in the landfill: "There is no such thing as closure. It's really hard to explain what this has done to me, but all I know is I was fine until I found out about Fresh Kills." She asked the city to let families bury their dead so that they can move on a little bit.[10]

In August 2005, families of the victims sued the city in an effort to get officials to separate the debris from the World Trade Center from the rest of the garbage at the landfill and put it in a separate burial place. In 2007, further evidence for their lawsuit was filed, including a letter from the city's chief medical examiner, Charles Hirsch, who admits that he is certain at least some human tissue and remains are part of the dirt in the landfill. The new evidence also contained an affidavit from a recycling supervisor who says he watched officials take debris that likely contained human remains and used it to fill potholes. The families' lawyer said, "You can't even consider the issue of closure for 9/11 families until this issue has been resolved."[11]

In July 2008, federal judge Alvin Hellerstein threw out the lawsuit, ruling that the families did not have a legal standing to sue the city. He said that over 1,100 victims "perished without leaving a trace, utterly consumed into incorporeality by the intense, raging fires or pulverized into dust by the massive tons of collapsing concrete and steel." He said the families had no property rights because the dirt in the landfill was "an undifferentiated mass of dirt." The judge's comments upset victims' families as he failed to understand the sacredness of their loved ones' remains.[12] The families' lawyer, Norman Siegel, responded: "We are not prepared to have hundreds of human remains from victims of the 9/11 attacks have their final resting place on top of a garbage dump."[13] In his ruling, the judge urged the city to build a memorial at the Fresh Kills landfill site. The families appealed the ruling but lost that decision in December 2009. They asked the Supreme Court to hear their case, but in October 2010, the Court declined to review it.

In light of the concerns about human remains left at Fresh Kills, it was decided in January 2010 that a new three-month search for remains would resume at the landfill. In a memo to Mayor Michael Bloomberg, Edward Skyler, the deputy mayor for operations, said the expanded search would cover material excavated from the World Trade Center site since 2007.[14] So, in April 2010, officials resumed the search for remains of the victims of the 9/11 attacks in New York. Under the supervision of the Office of the Chief Medical Examiner, people searched for traces of 1,123 victims whose remains have never been identified. The new search yielded over seventy-two new identifications of human remains.

Not all family members think that the identification of remains will bring closure, but some do use that term to describe what they want. Talat Dalani, whose twenty-six-year-old son died in the attacks, reflected on the meaning of having a part of her son to bury: "Instead of believing in the twilight zone—is he dead, is he alive?—we could move on. There's a place he is buried. A sense of closure."[15]

In describing the recent search for remains, one reporter said, "It's estimated that the operation will cost $1.4 million and provide the equivalent of closure."[16] In another story, a reporter states that New York City officials are looking to give the families of victims "a little bit more closure as they prepare for another search for remains."[17] Staten Island borough president James Molinar said he thought the examination of the material could help bring closure to victims' families.

Also on September 11, 2001, United Airlines Flight 93 crashed in Somerset County, Pennsylvania—on land owned by Tim Lambert. In the years since the crash, debate over who has the right to that land has produced emotional turmoil and political tension. The U.S. National Park Service, families of the Flight 93 victims, and property owners have been engaged in a long and messy debate. At the heart of this conflict: Does the public good for honoring a plane full of heroes whose remains are part of private land outweigh private property rights? Is it now sacred space in a way that trumps private property rights?

Officials with the National Park Service wanted to establish a public memorial at the crash site by the tenth anniversary. In 2008, they knew they were running out of time. That same year, Congress changed the Flight 93 National Memorial Act to allow for eminent domain. The U.S. government was now attempting to seize Tim Lambert's land through eminent domain, along with property from six other landowners.

Patrick White, whose cousin was killed on the flight, is vice president of Families of Flight 93. He agrees that eminent domain is necessary in this case and argues that the land became public when private citizens' lives and remains merged with the land.[18] Patrick says that no individual should stand in the way of the National Park Service securing land where lost loved one's remains are.[19] He said, "While it is true that the property is needed for construction of the memorial, that isn't the main factor in the possibility of going with eminent domain. The driving force is the need to protect the sacred ground. The sacred ground is to be part of Phase 1A, with construction to begin by 2010."[20] "For us, and I believe for the president and the first lady, it is a sense of closure and a degree of healing to get this done," said Patrick.[21]

In June 2009, the government backed down from its attempt to seize the land through eminent domain. The National Park Service negotiated the purchase of property from the multiple owners throughout the end of 2009 and into early 2010. On November 7, 2009, ground was broken in Somerset County for the $58 million memorial for Flight 93. The entire memorial will cover over 2,200 acres.

For many people who are grieving for loved ones, public space transforms into sacred space, and they argue that the rights of those grieving should trump other rights such as those of property owners. We see this not only in cases of national memorials but also in debates about roadside memorials.

Roadside Memorials: Is the Space Sacred or Public?

Roadside memorials have been used in Mexico and in regions of the southwestern United States for over 200 years.[22] In Hispanic culture, these memorials are called *descansos*, or "resting places," which refer to a tradition of marking the places where a funeral procession stopped to rest on the journey between the church and the cemetery. With the introduction of automobiles, and thus more roadside accidents, *descansos* have come to mark the actual spot of death, not just the resting spot between church and cemetery but the place of departure from life.

In the past two decades, roadside memorials have appeared in all fifty states and have led to heated policy debates. Many roadside memorials consist of crosses with flowers around them and often include a name and date. In most states, officials have been unsure about whether to allow them. Do they represent closure for the families of those victims, or are they road hazards? Are they, as some claim, improper state-sanctioned religious symbols?

Family members claim privilege to the sacred space where their loved one died in an auto accident even if it is public property (state owned) or private property (someone else's front yard). In this context, similarly to Ground Zero, sacred space refers to the place where a loved one died and may actually contain some human remains (e.g., bone fragments, blood, hair, etc.). Some argue that one can find closure by having access to the sacred space. The right to sacred space is an emotion claim that is then used to challenge legal claims such as those of the property owners. Sacred space is also used to explain why people cannot just put a memorial in their home or in the cemetery. Those who build and care for memorials frequently say that they want to mark the last place their loved one was alive and may even try to find that spot based on blood stains.[23] As with arguments from families of 9/11 victims, the logic for them is that public space has been transformed into sacred space because their loved one died there.

Closure is used as a central argument for the right to roadside memorials. Photographer C. H. Paquette captures poignant images of roadside memorials and posts them online. In his introduction to the memorial gallery, Paquette says that artistic expression is valuable to the grieving process and "may represent the fullest source of healing and closure for those without traditional spiritual or religious connections."[24] Psychology professor Todd McCallum says, "People in mourning can find closure in seeing the place where their loved one died."[25]

Those in favor of roadside memorials explain that they help remember a loved one. Erika Doss, a scholar in American studies, explains that spontaneous memorials are memory aids: "They specifically function to remember the recently, suddenly dead: they make their loss visible and public, and they make their deaths memorable within the realm of social responsibility— hence, cards and signs reading 'we will never forget' and 'we remember' at various spontaneous memorials."[26]

This type of closure represents an end to the fear of forgetting. Perhaps easing that fear is what helps Thomas Crellin, whose daughter died in a car accident on Interstate 90 in Ohio. He says, "Sometimes, when I drive past, I'll give it a thumbs-up, just an acknowledgment that Amanda was there. It's sad, but I look for the memorial every day."[27]

Many say they need the memorial to be at the place where their loved one died—the sacred space—not some other location. In 1995, Lynn Saatchi's daughter Shelley died in a car crash on County Road 20 in Ontario, Canada. Lynn initially could not bring herself to visit the site of her daughter's death. But now, several years later, she describes that place as a sacred refuge: "Going there gives me peace of mind, talking to Shelley there. I still feel that I get closure there, because that's where the accident was." Alvin Burgos would agree. He placed a cross at the intersection where his best friend was killed. He says, "Putting the cross out there was a bit of closure for me."[28]

Family members face barriers because in most cases it is illegal to erect private roadside memorials. Because they do not have a legal right to the property, grieving family members often face challenges to their memorials. Dawn Thompson broke the law when she placed a four-foot cross along a highway where her husband died. She knew that it was illegal at the time, but there was a higher call—honoring her husband and staying close to the sacred place where he was last alive. She was horrified, then, the day she went to visit the roadside memorial only to find that the California Department of Transportation had rolled the heavy cross off the road and threw it down a ravine. Dawn said, "It was very hurtful to see that it had been thrown over the edge like a piece of trash."[29] Like Dawn, other family members become emotionally tied to the sacred space and the memorial and therefore go through pain when others take down the memorials.

Why do people remove someone else's memorial? Public policy debates on roadside memorials feature struggles over freedom of expression and whether religious symbols are allowed on public property. The argument for sacred space clearly does not convince all. In April 2000, in Colorado, Rodney Scott removed a roadside memorial that was made out of crosses and flowers. Rodney was not related to the family maintaining this memorial, but he had driven past the memorial each day for several years on his way to work. As he explained, "I had gone through a lot of personal turmoil myself. I didn't appreciate somebody else throwing their hurt and sorrow out for the public view, as if it was more important than someone else's hurt or losses."[30]

The state of Colorado charged Rodney with "desecration of a venerated object." However, after his attorney challenged the legal right of allowing religious symbols on public land, the charge was dropped. Later Colorado banned private roadside memorials and moved to "nondenominational blue and white markers of the state's Roadside Memorial Signing Program."[31]

Most states either prohibit memorials or place restrictions on them. Still, officials often overlook the policy or at least try to be compassionate about how and when they remove the memorials in order to be sensitive to family members. Some states have moved to official, but generic, roadside memorials that the state erects at a place of death in an effort to mark the sacred space while prohibiting religious symbols and private memorials.

In January 2010, officials in West Virginia placed the first "legal" roadside memorial in their state. The first sign is in memory of Tennille Davis, an emergency medical technician who was killed by an impaired driver. A reporter on this story said that her family would now find closure thanks to the memorial. Her husband said he thought the sign would help his children: "I felt honored for them that they could have some place at least they could drive by and see where their mom died."[32] Each sign costs a family $200 plus a three-year renewable fee of $200 for maintenance. The state says that the official signs offer a safer alternative to homemade memorials. However, the official markers have not generated a high level of interest. Only twenty-five families applied for an official roadside memorial in the first year since the state started accepting applications.[33] Many families will likely continue to put up their homemade memorials.

The use of official markers has not set well with many grieving family members. Virginia delegate Robert G. Marshall's son was killed in a car accident in 2001. Referring to the move to prohibit personalized memorials, Robert says, "This is the bureaucratization of love. I don't like it one bit. I intend to put a cross up for my son. Period."[34] Victims' rights advocates argue that memorials are important for healing and that the government should not regulate grief. Robert agrees, saying that the government should not be "interfering with the grieving of a family."[35]

Public officials are not the only ones debating how to limit or remove roadside markers. Atheist groups are now educating others on how to tear down roadside memorials. One atheist activist website provides instructions on how to get rid of the memorials, including information about specific tools needed to cut through the steel crosses that are erected. The site then provides a link to what it calls "the funniest site yet on roadside crosses."[36] Clicking on that link takes you to porkjerky.com, where you can find commentary and pictures making fun of not only specific roadside memorials but also the people who died.

Those who protest religion on public property are not the only ones who want to see the roadside memorials disappear. Others protest the memorials because they interfere with the ability to forget. Sometimes people who use the argument of closure through remembrance run up against those who argue for closure through forgetting.

Whether one wants to remember a tragedy—or forget it—is subjective and contextual. Emotions and memories you might want to forget include other people's pain, your pain, anger, and guilt. Whereas some family members say that the memorials are good because they provide warnings to drivers (someone died here, you could, too, so drive carefully), others say they do not want to be constantly reminded of their own potential death.

Sometimes people involved in an accident do not want to be reminded so visually by a marker. For example, a woman drove her car onto the railroad tracks to commit suicide. Randy Meek was driving the train that struck and killed her. In discussing whether a memorial should be allowed to mark that spot, Randy says he could not stop the train that killed her and felt so helpless. "It is not something that I want to remember every day of my life. It's almost vindictive."[37]

Other passers-by do not want to be reminded of accidents even if they were not involved in them. They are asking for closure, but of a different type—they want to forget other people's pain. Or maybe they seek closure by getting rid of reminders that trigger their own pain and memories. They would rather avoid thinking about pain and sorrow while driving down the road. They do not want to be reminded of death every time they drive to work or to the grocery store.

Roadside memorials highlight some of the difficulties that emerge when private mourning happens in public places. Disagreements over the appropriateness of roadside memorials include political issues such as freedom of religion and property rights. Closure is put forward as a reason grieving families should be given access to public space.

Space to Grieve: Closure and Unborn Memorials

Debate over physical space is not the only struggle that occurs during efforts to acknowledge life and remember a loss. Sometimes people fight for *social* space to allow for grief and the acknowledgment of life as in the case of unborn memorials. Grieving an aborted child is an example of disenfranchised grief. Generally, those experiencing grief that others may not acknowledge have little social support or resources for helping them through the grieving process. When experiencing disenfranchised grief, it is difficult to talk to others about your pain. For instance, there is social stigma attached to grieving for an aborted baby. Women who grieve over an abortion may find it difficult to talk about their grief. In order to grieve and heal, some may feel a need to acknowledge the life lost. Advocates of unborn memorials highlight closure in their rhetoric.

Not all women who choose to have an abortion seek closure or report experiencing grief. In analyzing rhetoric about unborn memorials, I focus specifically on those who use the concept of closure to help explain the need for the memorials.

Memorials for the unborn open up rhetorical and physical space for abortion grief. In some cases, that space is virtual, such as a place online to post a letter in memory of an aborted baby:

> *Joshua, I am so sorry for killing you. For letting others pressure me and not having the strength needed to say "NO." Truly I am sorry, but also for waiting so long to remember what I did. You would be 18 now. A full grown man. You were my only pregnancy. You are precious to me. I know the Lord is holding you and I cannot wait to be reunited with you. The void in my heart has never ever been filled. I don't know if anyone else thinks of you, but know I do, I love you . . . please forgive me. Signed, Never a Mom*[38]

This woman, like others who regret an abortion, can post a letter on a memorial website that gives grieving family members of aborted babies a place to acknowledge a life and a loss. Advocates of these memorials say that those who grieve abortions have no grave to visit and no way to formally grieve. Therefore, a memorial offers a place to find closure.

Advocates creating memorials for unborn children frame the problem as an unrelenting pain that needs relief and closure. The website of the National Memorial for the Unborn claims that a memorial is a place of healing that can lift the burden of the pain: "A place where the unborn can be honored and remembered in a tangible way . . . a place of closure."[39]

The National Memorial for the Unborn houses the Wall of Names in a former abortion clinic in Tennessee. In 1975, two years after the legalization of abortion, the Chattanooga Women's Clinic opened and served as the only abortion clinic in the city. In 1993, the owner of the clinic decided to sell the building. A pro-life group bought it and opened the National Memorial for the Unborn in one half of the building. The other half contains services that allow for alternatives to abortion. The description on its website says that anyone who lost a baby to abortion can find forgiveness, hope, and healing at the Wall of Names. And "by way of placing a brass plate on the Wall in honor of aborted children . . . finally . . . closure."[40]

The Kentucky Memorial for the Unborn website explains that the memorial was started because of one woman's search for closure. That woman, Kathy Rutledge, started the drive to establish Kentucky's memorial in honor of her son whom she aborted when she was eighteen. Kathy told a reporter that working on the memorial project gave her a sense of closure and self-forgiveness. Her story is reflected in the description of the memorial: "A healing and living garden is being established in historic Frankfort Cemetery as a unique place of closure for those who have lost unborn children."[41]

The claim that naming a baby and acknowledging life helps with closure is a key argument for unborn memorials. The introduction to the Florida Memorial for the Unborn tells grieving parents that "many times meaningful closure can be reached by giving the child a name, finding a place and way to memorialize him or her and allowing yourself to grieve your loss."[42] The founders of UnbornMemorials.com tell parents: "The most important thing you can do for your unborn child is to acknowledge him or her as a real person that actually existed. This will help you develop a real relationship with your child and help you find closure."[43] Advocates for a public memorial claim it is helpful because it provides a place to remember the child and also an outlet to tell the world about the loss.

Politics of Memorials for the Unborn

As with the death penalty debate, in which pro–death penalty advocates shifted the debate by focusing on closure for victims' families, pro-life advocates use closure to change conventional abortion politics. In the late 1980s, pro-life groups began exploring postabortion counseling as a way not only to help women but also to raise concerns about abortion.[44] Dana Goldstein argues that the pro-life movement has "become more sophisticated in recent years, co-opting themes of female empowerment to argue that women are abortion's central victims."[45] Even today, most postabortion counseling services are connected directly or indirectly with pro-life perspectives.

Pro-choice groups have tried to counter pro-life rhetoric by arguing that the most common reaction to an abortion is relief. Therefore, people who experienced abortion would likely not seek closure because there is no pain or regret. One strategy from pro-choice advocates was to sell T-shirts with the slogan "I Had an Abortion" to encourage women not to stay silent about having abortions. Planned Parenthood sold the T-shirts. Julie Redman, president of Planned Parenthood of Louisiana and the Mississippi Delta, said that the T-shirts are meant to show women that abortions are not shameful.[46] In a similar effort, women who have had an abortion can sign up on the website I'mNotSorry.net to share their experiences.

In 2006, Pro-Choice Resources started Emerge, a six-week secular support group for women who have had an abortion. Emerge is described as "an alternative to politically motivated counseling agencies."[47] Claiming that its services empower women, the Emerge tagline reads, "Sharing Our Voices, Supporting Our Choices." Emerge encourages women to "share and discuss their individual experiences." The concept of closure does not work as well in pro-choice rhetoric. To say that someone needs closure could imply that an abortion led to trauma, grief, or regret, which complicates pro-choice arguments.

Some prominent pro-choice feminists have acknowledged that abortion is a complicated, moral experience that cannot be brushed over. In 2005, Hillary Clinton said that abortion is "a sad, even tragic choice to many, many women."[48] Ten years earlier, Naomi Wolf, though also pro-choice, argued that pro-choice feminists needed to be more honest about the life and death issues of abortion. She said:

> If we fail to treat abortion with grief and reverence, we risk forgetting that, when it comes to the children we choose to bear, we are here

to serve them—whomever they are; they are not here to serve us . . . those footprints are in fact the footprints of a 10-week-old fetus, the pro-life slogan, 'Abortion stops a beating heart,' is incontrovertibly true. While images of violent fetal death work significantly for pro-lifers as political polemic, the pictures are not polemical in themselves: they are biological facts. We know this.[49]

Closure is a prominent part of pro-life postabortion rhetoric. In the case of abortion grief, pro-life advocates use closure as part of their larger argument for founding memorials and opening public space for parents and other family members to share their pain. Advocates argue that the physical space of memorials is necessary for parents to process grief and have a place to visit and memorialize their children. However, the physical space is also important for establishing collective memory, not just an individual's memory. Katharyne Mitchell, a scholar of memory politics, argues that "memory is sustained through the interplay between collective recollection and repetition."[50] Establishing collective memorials for the unborn and repeating memorial services and news stories about them help to build a collective memory about the pain and regret of abortion. Mitchell points out that "the capacity for those remembrances to be sustained is vastly dependent on the socioeconomic power of the groups who produce and maintain them."[51] Whether memorials for the unborn can continue to build momentum and maintain collective memories of abortion grief depends on their political and cultural power. The concept of closure helps them to maintain this power.

Unborn memorials provide a physical and social space for private mourning, but they also help shape collective memory about abortion and contribute to public debate about the politics involved. The same process is happening with other types of public memorials.

Public Memorials and Private Mourning

Public memorials recognize national tragedies such as those honoring victims of the Oklahoma City bombing, the 9/11 attacks, and the Columbine shootings. However, the design of the memorials, one might argue, privileges the private. A critical look at public memorials poses several questions: What is the purpose of a national memorial? Is it to remember the political context? Are we to learn particular lessons when visiting the memorial? Or is the main reason to provide a place for victims' families to seek healing?

Contemporary memorial designs highlight the effort to recognize the individual lives lost as a primary design feature. The precedent for this design style is the Vietnam Veterans Memorial in Washington, D.C., which features individuals' names on the walls. Maya Lin, at age twenty-one, designed the Vietnam Veterans Memorial to highlight the loss of individual lives in the war. She described the purpose of her design as a place for individuals to come to terms with death and loss. Art historian Kirk Savage explains that contemporary memorial spaces have new psychological demands as places of healing and that the Vietnam Veterans Memorial was the first therapeutic memorial. Savage argues that Lin's design of the Vietnam Veterans Memorial reflects a cultural turn away from political activism and toward self-exploration and awareness of loss.[52]

The design of the Vietnam Veterans Memorial drew criticism from some, including President Ronald Reagan, who refused to attend the 1982 dedication of the memorial. Scholar Erika Doss argues that Reagan and others were angered that the design featured the large numbers of soldiers who died, which questioned the value of the war.[53] Savage explains that critics of the Vietnam Veterans Memorial recognized that it was a "victim monument, not meant to glorify the deeds of the soldiers but to console and reconcile the survivors who had experienced the tragedy of their loss."[54]

Time has shown that people intimately connect to this design, and the Vietnam Veterans Memorial has become one of the most visited memorials. Doss reports: "Every day, thousands of people come to the site, many leaving flowers, flags, letters, poems, photographs, teddy bears, dog (identity) tags, wedding rings, high school yearbooks and other offerings; many others tracing the names that are inscribed on the monument's black walls."[55] These tributes and offerings left by people are collected by National Park Service employees and stored in a warehouse in Maryland.[56]

At the time, Lin's design was considered countercultural, but now a focus on the individuals who died is typical for public memorials. The main architectural feature of the Oklahoma City National Memorial and Museum's Outdoor Symbolic Memorial consists of 168 empty chairs in a field. Nineteen of those chairs are small to represent the children who died. Each chair has a victim's name etched in the base and three unborn children are listed with their mothers. The Pentagon Memorial, honoring victims of the 9/11 attack on the Pentagon, has 184 individual benches, each with the name of a victim. The benches face different directions depending on whether the victim died in the plane or in the Pentagon.

The focus on closure for victims' families has not escaped architectural critic Catesby Leigh. In a 2006 article, discussing the Pentagon Memorial, he writes, "The main idea behind design seems to be that the memorial units, with the names of their loved ones inscribed on the benches' front ends, will help the bereaved reach closure."[57] Leigh argues that the "therapeutic culture's dominion over memorial design" has suppressed any symbolic expression of public tragedy and civil idealism.

Although individual loss is now highlighted in public memorials, family members of those who died are not the only people giving input on the specific content or design. Because of other stakeholders, including designers, politicians, and landowners, family members sometimes have to fight hard to have significant input on the design and content of a memorial. We only have to look at the design process of the National September 11 Memorial in New York City for an issue that might on the surface seem simple—how to display victims' names. For loved ones who are grieving, a name is critical. The contemporary national public memorials emphasize individual victims' stories as a main design feature. The question of how to display the names of victims for the memorial in New York City has been one of the most difficult features of the design.

At first, the designers of the memorial wanted to display victims' names in a random order to reflect the randomness of who was killed. Mayor Bloomberg endorsed the idea.[58] Families of the victims protested, however, saying that it was "just a cold random list of names," and they even created ads to protest Bloomberg's proposal. Cantor Fitzgerald CEO Howard Lutnick, who lost his brother in the attack along with 657 other coworkers, offered $25 million to go toward the memorial if the designers dropped the idea of displaying names randomly. Although the memorial designers did not accept Howard's money, the families eventually won the debate.

Representatives of the families proposed a display of names listed by the location at which the victims worked or the rescue unit to which they belonged. People wanted to keep coworkers and family members together in the display of names. They requested details such as the age of victims and the rank of rescue workers. Another factor was where the names would be placed. In one version, some names would have been near the ground, which, many argued, would show disrespect. Families also wanted to make art rubbings of the names, which led designers to use raised lettering.

The revised plan for placement of names is described on the official National September 11 Memorial and Museum website. Victims' names will be grouped with those they were with at the time of their deaths. "Next-of-kin were invited to request the names of specific individuals next to whom they would like their loved ones' names inscribed." Relatives were also allowed to indicate if a victim was pregnant so that the words "and her unborn child" could follow her name. The explanation about the display of names includes this wish: "We hope that by arranging the names of those who knew each other in their lives next to one another in their deaths, their loved ones will have a deeper and more significant Memorial experience."[59]

The content of memorials is often quite important to grieving loved ones, who have to work hard to secure particular details. Sometimes, however, these personal details cause conflict for others. We see this conflict in several situations involving the memorialization efforts following the 1999 shootings at Columbine High School near Littleton, Colorado. A central character in this conflict is Brian Rohrbough.

On April 20, 1999, Brian's son Daniel was murdered when Eric Harris and Dylan Klebold opened fire at Columbine High School, killing twelve students and one teacher before committing suicide. In the years following this tragedy, Brian has used the news media as an outlet to fight for what he views as the proper way to memorialize the Columbine shootings. Brian was not seeking closure, arguing that closure was an "insult and hoax" to parents of those who died.[60] Instead, he wanted people to remember what happened and learn some particular lessons. Although Brian was not seeking closure, others involved were and they found themselves at odds with Brian's memorial activities.

After Columbine, people around the nation followed the story and offered ways to help those grieving. Greg Zanis went further than some in offering his support. In 1996, Greg, a self-identified born-again Christian from Illinois, began making crosses for victims of various tragedies because of his own experience with his father-in-law's murder. He views the cross making as a ministry in which he hand carves crosses and personally delivers them to places where tragedies occur. A week after the Columbine shooting, Greg made fifteen crosses: thirteen for the shooting victims and two for the shooters. He said he thought the Columbine shooters were victims of society. Each eight-foot cross was eventually surrounded by offerings from visitors, including signs on the young shooters' crosses ranging from "May God Forgive You" to "evil bastard."[61] Two days after the crosses were put up, Brian Rohrbough destroyed the two crosses that represented the shooters.

Greg Zanis was not the only one to memorialize the shooters. A group of youth from West Bowles Community Church designed and planted a memorial of trees in a prayer park on the church's own property to remember those who died in the Columbine school shooting, including the two young shooters. During a worship service, a group of angry parents carried signs that said "unrepentant murderers buried here" and "no peace for the wicked." They used saws to cut down the two trees that represented the shooters. Again, Brian Rohrbough was one of the leaders of the group.[62]

Political controversy surrounded official Columbine memorials as well. After the shootings at Columbine, the school district invited people to paint ceramic tiles that would be placed above the school lockers. Although the project was supposed to help the community heal, the school denied that the tiles were memorials, going so far as to prohibit any religious symbols or mention of the shootings. These guidelines set off a firestorm of controversy. Some community members, including parents of the slain, challenged the restrictions as a violation of free speech and freedom of religion. An initial decision favored the parents. The U.S. Court of Appeals for the Tenth Circuit overturned that decision, however, saying that friends and family of shooting victims do not have a right to display tiles bearing religious symbols.

Sue Petrone, the mother of Daniel Rohrbough, spent hours designing a tile that had a cross over a heart with the name of her son. School officials refused to include her tile. "When they told her no, they wouldn't put her tile up, she just cried," said Rich Petrone, Sue's husband and Daniel's stepfather. "They were basically telling us, 'We want you to express your feelings, but they have to agree with our feelings.'"[63] The Supreme Court refused to hear the case.[64] Brian Rohrbough argued that by refusing to hear the case, the Supreme Court was allowing censorship. He also said that no one had the right to tell him what he could say as a memorial to his son.[65]

School officials argued that they did not want the tiles as a memorial because they did not want students reminded of the tragedy. What, then, was the purpose of the tiles? Were they hoping the activity would provide closure? A seventeen-year-old student at Columbine High School, Jennifer, referred to the tiles when discussing her experience: "Most people have already had some kind of closure at the school. We went back a couple of times for renovation, registration, to paint tiles. Now, we're just ready to move on."[66]

The school tiles and spontaneous memorials consisting of crosses and trees were not the only places where the content of the memorials was contested. The design and construction of the official public memorial in the community also led to debates about content and who had ownership over it and what content would best help people heal.

A community group labored for years designing and constructing a public memorial honoring the victims of Columbine. Finally, on September 21, 2007, the committee dedicated the public memorial. It cost $1.5 million to construct and will require an estimated $10,000 to 15,000 per year for maintenance.[67] Eight years after the shootings, construction of the Columbine Memorial was heralded by a reporter as the "latest attempt at closure in this community."[68] Columbine's music director agreed, "The memorial is part of closure on an important event in our lives, although you don't totally close the door on it."[69] Yet memorial committee member Paul Rufien said, "We're going out of our way to avoid the word closure, because closure sounds like we mean forgetting. This place is about remembrance."[70] The principal of Columbine High School, Frank DeAngelis, agreed, saying the memorial does not bring closure: "It just allows us to live on with the memories of the students who died that day, the memories of the students who were injured, and everyone so deeply impacted."[71]

Parents were allowed to inscribe messages on the memorial to remember their loved ones. In his memorial message, Brian Rohrbough tied the shootings to abortion, moral decline, and accusations of lies and local cover-ups. His inscription follows in full:

> "Dad, I have a question." Why?
> My son in a Nation that legalized the killing of innocent children in the womb; in a County where authorities would lie and cover up what they knew and what they did; in a Godless school system your life was taken. . . . Dan I'm sorry.
> "I love you dad. I'll see you tomorrow."
> 7:00 p.m., April 19, 1999.
> "There is no peace," says the Lord, "for the wicked." Isaiah 48:22[72]

The memorial committee asked Brian to soften the tone of the message, but he refused. They decided to allow his message as he wanted.[73]

Terri Perello told a reporter that even though she agreed with Brian's position on abortion, she thought "politics should be put aside so the community can find closure."[74] Brian would likely disagree. Earlier in the year, he commented on the potential memorial: "One thing the memorial will not bring is closure. I think all the families know there is no point at which this ends."[75] Brian is making it his life work to make sure people do not forget what he sees as the political and moral failures that led to his son's death. He not only disagrees with the concept of closure, but he does not want others to have it, or at least he does not want people to forget what he sees as the reasons for the shootings.

Public Memorials and Feeling Rules

To have control over a public memorial is to shape history. Those who control public memorials do not limit their decisions to location or appearance; in fact, they control who or what should be remembered, and how. As part of this process, people judge whose life is worthy of memory. In the midst of public tragedy, individuals have different definitions of closure and perspectives on how to find it, which leads to heated debates and shapes feeling rules for how people are supposed to grieve.

Facilitating the healing process is increasingly becoming one of the most important purposes for public memorials, a trend that strongly influences both how they are designed and who has a say in their design. Increasingly, we hear people argue that grieving loved ones need access to the sacred space where their loved ones died in order to find healing. Closure is often used as an argument for why victims' families need ownership over content of memorials or access to sacred space. As an emotion claim, closure is used to challenge claims such as property rights and other legal matters. Use of closure as a "right" in debates about memorials builds on the success of closure as a quasi-legal concept in crime victims' rights and the death penalty. The use of a psychological or emotional claim makes it more complicated to balance the needs of those grieving with other concerns, such as property owners' rights or the debate of religious symbols on state property.

The rhetoric of closure influences memorial design and content to highlight individual losses but ignores or marginalizes discussion of social, cultural, and political causes for the particular tragedy. Similarly, media coverage of national tragedies frequently focuses on individual loss and the public drama of victimization rather than larger social and political issues.[76] The culture of public memorials continues to shape our efforts at remembering individual victims and healing those who come to the memorial—both goals benefit from the closure argument. However, these goals frequently shift the discourse of the tragedy away from the roots of the violence.[77]

Arguments about memorials and closure build feeling rules for people who are grieving. Although the aim of public memorials is usually to help people heal, there are problems with the expectations that are constructed through these claims. Here are three to consider.

First, it is problematic to build feeling rules around the notion that you need access to sacred space in order to heal and find closure. Not everyone has access to the place where a loved one died. Or they will not have ongoing access to it. Although it is a precious place for many people, it is not feasible to allow everyone to establish a public memorial at the site of a death. If we continue to build large public memorials for various tragedies and allow private memorials on public land, we may soon have more sacred space than public space.[78]

Second, when loved ones become attached to the memorials as an extension of a loved one, removal or destruction of the memorials can cause significant emotional trauma. Even when loved ones do maintain a memorial, such as on the roadside, they cannot guarantee that it will be permanent. In some cases, individual citizens remove memorials because they are tired of looking at them. In other cases, officials remove them because they are difficult to maintain or because they are enforcing the law against the memorials. Even in cases of state-erected memorials, some officials remove them after a certain amount of time. Tying closure and healing to a particular place and memorial also adds a risk to one's grieving process. A loved one may be traumatized if his or her roadside memorial gets sawed down or if another person steals the artifacts.

Finally, when a common narrative suggests that people need to erect memorials at the site of a tragedy, what happens when people cannot afford the memorial (in the case of state-sanctioned memorials that have to be purchased) or live in a different state and cannot make it to the place? In the rhetoric of closure, memorialization is becoming increasingly professionalized as people are told how to "properly" remember their loved ones in "dignified ways" worthy of their love. How do people feel when they cannot have a memorial that they have come to believe is an important part of closure?

Concerns about the feeling rules that accompany closure talk go beyond public memorials. We turn next to the concluding chapter to reflect on what our society's quest for closure might be costing us and how it shapes our social world. Is there another way to frame what we need after a loss besides the notion of closure?

9. Framing Grief beyond Closure

Walking up to the podium, I was still struggling with what to say to a group of mourners who had gathered to say good-bye to Fred at his memorial service.[1] Fred had been a student at the college where I teach. Many students were grieving and searching for comfort. I was also thinking about his parents. What do you say to parents whose child had taken his life earlier that week? There are few words that ever sound right at these times. Two phrases I think are most helpful when talking to someone who is awash with grief are "I don't know what to say" and "I'm sorry." So I started there: "I have no idea what it is like to lose a young adult son. It is unimaginable pain, and I am sorry for your loss." Beyond these sentiments, I wanted to frame grief in a way that respected the pain while offering hope. I encouraged family and friends at the memorial service to be patient with each other as each finds his or her way through the grief. I wanted them to know that they could remember Fred with joy as they carried him forward in their hearts even as they continued to grieve. We have the capacity to carry grief and joy together. We do not have to "close" the pain before we start to heal. I wanted to frame grief beyond the notion of closure.

The compassion and hope I attempted to share with those at this memorial service are connected to my concerns with the popular quest for closure. The closure frame limits the possibilities for how we think about grief and fails to capture the experience of many who face death or some other loss.

I did not want to frame grief in a way that led people to believe that they had a limited amount of time to find "closure."

The concept of closure taps into a desire to have things ordered and simple, but experiences with loss and grief are typically messy, complicated, and not easily resolved. Still, we long for peace, order, and resolution. The appeal of closure rests in large part on the hope that pain will lessen and healing will come. Yes, of course we long for healing and we should seek it. But healing can come without closure. Even if you do not want to give up the concept of closure, at least know that it is subjective and may take a long time to "find" and that no one particular ritual, product, service, or politician's promise can guarantee closure.

Shaped through social interactions in arenas such as politics, law, media, self-help, and the funeral industry, closure has emerged as a dominant narrative in our everyday talk about grief and loss. How people use the word "closure" varies widely as explained throughout this book. Closure is socially constructed and carries multiple definitions and interpretations. Rhetoric about closure reflects six types: closing a chapter, remembering, forgetting, getting even, knowing, and confessing or forgiving. In spite of the differences among these six visions of closure, they all assume that closure is possible, good, desired, and necessary.

It is not the mere presence of closure as a concept that is a problem. The concern comes when people believe closure has to be achieved in order for them to move forward. This has led to all sorts of people promising closure as a way to sell products, services, and politics. Closure has become a central part of marketing for funeral, grief, relationship advice, and memorialization industries as well as a strategic political argument. Although Myth Slayers warn others about the misleading promises embedded in closure talk, many people continue to believe that closure is an emotional state that exists and can be found—and, in some cases, purchased from businesses or secured through political movements. Closure has emerged as a "need" that people are told they can fulfill through services such as executions, autopsies, funerals, private cremations, ash scatterings, wrongful death lawsuits, and memorials, to say nothing of psychic readings, private investigations, and divorce parties.

When people have cultural, religious, or family traditions that guide them in how to respond when someone dies, they may be less likely to turn to those selling the promise of closure for advice on grief. Increasingly, however, there are more people looking to the consumer market for rituals and customs for how to respond to death and loss. Why are people searching for rituals? In less diverse cultures, there has typically been a shared authoritative perspective on what to do after a death. For example, in a culture dominated by one religion, there is a prevailing set of rituals to follow. However, in a more diverse, more secular, and more individualized world, we no longer share one vision of appropriate rituals for responding to death, loss, and grief. In premodern Western cultures, clergy had the authoritative voice on death. With the rise of modernity, medical doctors began rivaling clergy as death experts. In a postmodern world, clergy and doctors no longer dominate guidelines for grief and death—although some people will still heavily rely on them. Others, though, may turn to a consumer culture for choosing rituals and meanings related to death and loss.

When we lack a common authority for ritualizing loss, a marketplace with competing solutions on how to grieve takes its place. Those using closure to sell products and politics claim to be "grief experts" and are a potential resource for people trying to navigate grief and loss. I am not suggesting we go back to one authoritative perspective on death and grief rituals. My point is that we should be cautious and intentional about whose narratives we choose to follow. Since many self-proclaimed grief experts are selling the products and services that they promise will bring closure, we should pay attention to the motives and implications for feeling rules underlying the scripts for grieving.

Closure is one way to frame what we need after a loss—but it is not the only way. The emphasis on closure that has come to dominate marketing campaigns, political rhetoric, and grief counseling not only reinforces the assumption that closure is a real and necessary thing but also prevents people from thinking about loss and trauma in any other way. You can find other ways to heal without seeking closure. The social construction of closure has formed a narrow view of how we should respond to loss. When I say that closure is socially constructed or that we can choose how to frame grief, I am not suggesting that the pain following a loss is made up. The pain is real. What we construct is the frame used to understand and respond to the pain. Frames provide a way for people to make sense of a situation. In this conclusion, I further examine the closure frame and then reflect on how to frame grief beyond closure.

Selling Closure—the Sizzle

Closure has been transformed into something that people believe can be bought and sold—the commodification of closure. But closure is not something concrete that can be sold. It is a subjective, constructed concept that varies in interpretation depending on the context and audience. To understand closure's role in sales, let's return to the sales cliché "Sell the sizzle, not the steak." Closure is the sizzle. It is emotionally laden marketing that often targets people's fear, pain, and hope. The "steak" that is actually being sold does not guarantee the sizzle. Whether one experiences closure is not something a business can control. People who are promising closure as part of their service or product do not have the ability to deliver on this promise.

Closure is an appealing frame for businesses. Selling closure is a nicer, more comfortable idea than selling services or products such as autopsies, expensive caskets, cremation, private investigations, and DNA profile kits. Closure is the sizzle that makes these other products emotionally appealing. Those selling services and products related to grief, death, and other types of loss do not need to sell closure; they can sell the actual purposes of the services and products. But marketing the products and services without the sizzle of closure would not have the same emotional connection with potential consumers. If you have experienced a loss and are wondering about closure, you will encounter this rhetoric. As a consumer you need to see behind and beyond the promise of closure to get a look at what is really being sold. Then make a decision about whether you want the particular product or service without buying into the promise of closure.

You might argue that one can simply choose not to buy the services or products so there is little concern about how closure is used by various industries. However, closure in the marketplace does affect your social world even if you are not aware of it. Not every technique for finding closure works well in the marketplace. Only certain profitable strategies for "finding closure" are marketed. For example, writing letters to someone who has died does not sell many products. It is not hard to find pen and paper to write your letter. Burying your beloved pet in the backyard in a shoebox with a lovely handcrafted tombstone does not sell fancy caskets, private cremations with expensive urns, or perpetual burial plots in a pet cemetery. Planting a tree in memory of a loved one or creating a special memory scrapbook might help with healing, but those rituals do not sell custom-made memorial products. Alternative ways of grieving are marginalized if they do not require buying products or services. Industries profit from people's emotions and grief while shaping how people are supposed to feel and respond to death. The commodification of closure implies that you need money to grieve "properly."

Even if you are not one of the people buying products because of closure marketing, your social world is still affected by the commodification of the concept. Feeling rules for grief are shaped by the marketing rhetoric, and those around you may use the closure frame in responding to others' grief or yours. Increasingly, the word closure is applied to diverse situations because it has become a popular commodity for so many businesses. Closure sizzles.

Politicizing Closure—the Trump Card

Closure has become a political trump card for politicians and advocates. The subjective and fluid meanings attached to closure allow the concept to be used in a range of political arguments. More importantly, the closure frame allows politicians to advocate for victims and healing, a position that is difficult and politically risky to oppose. Closure has emerged as a powerful political tool for talking about social problems, including grief, victimization, the criminal justice system, capital punishment, DNA collection, abortion, terrorism, and public memorials.

Closure acts as a trump card because it can shift attention away from more politically cumbersome issues and onto victims and healing. For example, the case for collecting DNA samples includes a perceived need for victims' families to find closure, which shifts attention away from issues such as privacy and due process. Similarly, death penalty advocates can use the more uplifting rhetoric of closure for victims in order to mask particularly difficult problems of capital punishment, such as racial and class discrimination, questions of innocence, and incompetent legal counsel.

Politicians and advocates use the concept of closure to further their agendas. As with concern about the commodification of closure, you should look behind the promise of closure to see what political argument is attached. Although politicians would like you to assume that closure is a need—even a right—it should not be forgotten that the concept is constructed and subjective. This is why you see contradictory messages about how to find closure from opposing political groups.

The politicization of closure reinforces the notion that it is an emotional state that can be measured and orchestrated. You are led to believe that certain public policies or legal rights will bring closure to those who have been hurt or wronged. The use of this argument in politics has led to the institutionalization of closure, which is the establishment of opportunities for victims to achieve closure within institutions such as the legal system. For example, closure rhetoric has helped advocates establish victim impact statements and family members' right-to-view executions legislation. Closure is also used to argue that family members should have the right to maintain a roadside memorial on state property—or even other people's private property—and that states should collect DNA samples from all who are arrested so future victims will have closure. Practices such as these embed closure within the criminal justice system as well as normalize and establish it as part of justice. The institutionalization of closure furthers its impact beyond a mere rhetorical tool as it becomes something that people try to achieve within the legal system. Closure is made more "real" through institutional practices. After all, why would we have these policies if closure did not exist?

The politics and policies connected to closure further reinforce feeling rules for grief. Once a concept has become institutionalized, you are less likely to examine how it emerged as a belief or imagine alternative views that might be better in understanding your world. With less questioning, the closure frame continues to gain value as a trump card.

Public Closure and Private Disclosure

Not everyone's journey through grief and loss will be the same. Our culture's dominant narratives about loss lead us to believe that there is a universal road map through grief. Grief is often conceptualized as a process that needs to be completed in a particular way. Closure frequently becomes a one-word description of what we are supposed to find at the end of this process—as if there is a box you receive when someone dies and you are to fit all your feelings into that box—nice and tidy—in order to put it on a shelf. Closure. Different rituals are offered as strategies for packing the box. But many people's grieving experiences and feelings do not fit into that box. There are those who grieve outside the box. And some do not want to pack up all the hurt and memories as quickly as others would like them to—if ever. There may be memories and emotions they never want to pack away.

The closure frame presents a plan to navigate and contain grief—not just your own, but others' grief, too. This frame may be appealing since it keeps grief and loss tidy and short-lived, but it is a poor reflection of what many people experience when grieving a deep loss. Although the closure frame shapes feeling rules for grieving, people often do not experience grief in the way these rules predict. Frequently, people's own experiences with grief do not match social expectations for grieving. At times, those grieving are giving others what they expect—a sense of closure. However, privately they continue to grieve and experience *disclosure*—the absence of closure. Therefore, people may have public closure but private disclosure.

Disclosure has a secondary meaning reflecting the word's more traditional definition: to reveal information that was previously kept hidden. Therefore, *private disclosure* also reflects the point that people are more likely to express their actual feelings about grief in a private circle rather than in public. In larger public circles, a grieving person may put on a face of having achieved closure even if it does not reflect his or her private feelings.

The pervasiveness of closure rhetoric pressures people who are grieving to achieve it in a timely manner. Some people may spend a lot of energy trying to meet social expectations for closure when privately they resent the idea of closure or, worse, they may wonder if something is wrong with them because they do not have it.

This disconnect between public closure and private disclosure further distorts our understanding of grief and can affect people's ability to find support beyond the immediate time following a loss. Once the public rituals of funerals or memorial services are over, the disclosure of grief is more likely to occur in private. The private circle of people aware of an individual's ongoing grief varies in size and continues to get smaller over time. In my own experience after our son's death, when others appeared uncomfortable with my grief, I "closed" the subject with them. I realized that they would not be someone with whom I could talk about grief. I suppose this gave an impression of closure to them. There was a small circle of people in my life with whom I opened up about my grief. Initially, that circle was bigger: Through the first few days after our son's funeral, people were willing to acknowledge his death. Not long after the funeral, the circle of people open to talking about my pain became smaller. As time went on, the circle became smaller and smaller. Because I talked about it less, if at all, it is likely that many assumed I had "closure" to the grief.

Many who are grieving give others what they expect—a sense of closure—but privately continue to grieve and experience disclosure. Occasionally, private mourning does return to the public. For example, specific days may be set aside to honor the dead, such as Memorial Day, Mexico's *Día de los Muertos* (Day of the Dead), or public memorial services on the anniversary of a national tragedy such as 9/11. Others may from time to time place a poem in the newspaper or give a donation to a charity in memory of a loved one. However, most activities that nurture continuing bonds with those who have died or express one's ongoing grief happen in private.

The Victorian era is well known for its public and long-term mourning rituals. For example, a woman whose husband died was expected to wear black for over a year. After the first year, she entered a secondary mourning period that allowed for some flexibility in clothing but still marked her as bereaved. Of course, there are many concerns with such strict grieving rituals and expectations, and I would never advocate a return to this type of rigorous protocol. However, it would be nice to return to an understanding that grief typically lasts longer than a few weeks.

I am not arguing that we should announce our grief to everyone we encounter. It is reasonable and understandable that we may quite soon in the grieving process share our pain with only a few people. My concern lies in the possibility that the paradoxical combination of public closure and private disclosure leaves too many people uneducated about the realities of grieving. We need people to understand that closure does not neatly follow a funeral, divorce party, or other ritual. Those facing a deep loss need support from at least a few people for a long time.

When people are grieving for loved ones who were killed in a high-profile case, they likely encounter public commentary about when or how they should find closure. In the case of 9/11, certain events, such as the opening of the Pentagon Memorial or an anniversary memorial service, would prompt some to argue, "There can now be closure." Of course, Osama bin Laden's death was a historic and momentous event that intensified the use of "closure" regarding 9/11. While a vast number of news stories reported that bin Laden's death brought closure, many of those grieving for loved ones who died on 9/11 tried to counter these claims. They explained that though there may be justice or relief, there is no such thing as closure.

One of the concerns with the rush to proclaim closure after the death of Osama bin Laden (or any other event) is that it fails to reflect the grief and loss that many feel because of the 9/11 attacks. People do not want others implying that his death was that final box in which they can pack away the rest of their pain and finally be able to put it behind them. They want people to understand that the loss in their lives will continue, but they may feel pressure to accept a form of "public closure" to 9/11. It is likely that many who lost loved ones on 9/11 will continue to feel private disclosure rather than what others describe as closure.

Navigating Closure Rhetoric

When you face a deep loss, you are confronted with choices about how to respond. In the case of death, decisions might include funeral arrangements, final dispositions, and memorials. Some people face tragic deaths that may force decisions about autopsies, wrongful death lawsuits, private investigations, and, in rare cases, whether to witness an execution. In situations of divorce, missing people, adoption, abortion, school shootings, terrorism, and other times of loss, people face competing political arguments and sales marketing that try to influence responses. How do you navigate the competing narratives about grief when encountering these traumatic times? How do you guard hope for healing while making decisions about rituals, death care, memorials, and so on? Here are three strategies to consider.

Imagine Frames beyond Closure

Closure rhetoric echoes finality. Closing a door. Bringing something to an end. Finishing a process. When grieving loved ones hear the word "closure," many interpret it as the ending of a life, love, and relationship. From this perspective, it is easier to see why some say, "I hate closure" or "I do not want closure." They want to remember their loved one and continue a relationship. Although "closure as remembering" could allow for this meaning, the underlying assumptions about closure as "an ending" limit the understanding for continuing a relationship.

The language of closure may help some people. However, if it does not, and people cannot find closure or do not want to try, there are other ways to think about grief. You do not need to attain "closure" to heal. I am not attempting to just replace the closure frame with another frame for grief. Let it be clear that I am not proposing that any change in how we frame grief or the language we use to describe it will make grief simple or loss easy to absorb. I do not want people to think that proposing we move beyond closure is one more attempt at a shortcut through grief and loss. The pain is real and the grief can be overwhelming. Rather, I want to open up the dialogue about grieving and emphasize that people experience loss differently and their journeys through grief are unique.

Theories and frameworks for understanding grief that challenge the concept of closure include redefining relationships, continuing bonds, and making meanings. These concepts do not need to be the only ones we consider, but they are a good start for imagining language beyond closure. Redefining one's relationship with a loved one who has died takes on many forms. Taking care of a grave continues a nurturing role. Other parents work for causes in the name of their children. Continuing bonds is part of a theory that explains how those who grieve often search for ways to stay connected with their deceased loved ones. This concept challenges other popular notions that you have to find ways to completely "let go" of those bonds. Finding ways to keep someone's life meaningful after he or she is dead may lead people to create a diversity of memorials or to dedicate their lives in new directions in honor of a loved one. People who grieve are often interested in rituals that help them privately—and often publicly—uphold their loved one's memory. These are specific points, but the larger picture is that it is all right if you cannot find closure; it is a constructed concept anyway. You can use other language to talk about what you feel and what you need.

Choose "Grief Experts" Carefully, and Talk about Death with Loved Ones

Who do you want guiding you through grief? The answer will not be the same for everyone. Some people will prefer their pastor, priest, or rabbi to guide them through death rituals and grief. Others will choose a counselor or a grief support group, and some people will find enough help among family and friends. Many will reach out to more than one of these resources. It is not that you need to have anyone in particular as a guide, but not having someone you trust with whom you can discuss your feelings may make you more susceptible to consumer marketing that targets your grief.

If you give up the guidance of a particular tradition (religion, culture, family), then you have to find your own way. This opens up possibilities, which can be good. It is fine and often necessary to create your own sense of meaning after the death of a loved one. However, any doubt that creeps in about what you are doing can leave you searching for assurance in vulnerable times. You may question if you have done enough and may be tempted by marketing that tells you to do X, Y, or Z in order to find closure.

You will be more prepared for navigating marketing and political arguments that sell closure if you are secure in the frame you want to use for responding to grief. Now, of course, I am oversimplifying the process here. Obviously, we cannot prepare for every possible tragedy and set of circumstances that might befall us. My point is that opening up dialogue about grief and death and hearing people's stories and experiences will hopefully provide more scripts to choose from other than just the closure frame.

Talking to family about funerals, memorial services, and other rituals before a death occurs can help in making decisions when the time comes. If you have rituals and beliefs, you are less likely to be looking to the consumer market for guidance on grieving. If you and a loved one are comfortable with the funeral arrangements discussed ahead of time, then you are better equipped to handle the marketing at a funeral home. For example, if you already know your loved one wants a simple pine casket, you are less vulnerable to the pressure to buy the really expensive one.

You will never avoid the construction of feeling rules for grieving. The point is to expand the variety of scripts showing the diversity in how people experience grief. The hope is that you can learn to avoid guilt and anxiety when feeling rules fail. For example, you ought not to feel guilty for buying a less expensive casket, or for opposing the death penalty for the person who murdered your loved one, or for opting not to pursue a lawsuit.

I teach a class called Death and Society. Most of my college students are initially nervous about the topic and report having few opportunities to talk about death. They want to talk about it, but they are also afraid to do so. Shared conversations about death, funerals, loss, grief, and other related topics are important. Parents are encouraged to have the "drug and sex talks" with their children; perhaps we should add the "death talk," too. We need to demystify the experience of grief and open up the diversity in how people choose death care rituals and traverse grief's road.

Know You Can Carry Grief and Joy Together

The hope for healing after a loss keeps people searching for answers. The rush to reach closure may limit your ability to find your own way through grief. Releasing one's grip on the notion of closure may grant the freedom to grieve and process loss differently. When I speak of freedom from closure, I refer to the ability to grieve openly as needed. You need freedom to grieve individually—to discover your own path through the terrain without the constraints of a universal road map. Not being entrenched in a "need for closure" will give you a measure of freedom from the political and marketing rhetoric about what you need to believe or buy in order to achieve closure.

The closure frame implies that "moving on" cannot happen until the messiness of grief is wrapped up. Framing grief beyond closure offers a different opportunity—the ability to integrate grief into one's life without having to pretend all is fine. For example, for some bereaved parents, freedom may come in no longer being afraid to embrace one's role as a grieving mother or father. Losing a child changes your world. It will never go back to "normal." That does not mean you cannot find growth and joy even as you carry some degree of pain and grief the rest of your life. It is important to know that people's abilities and time lines for finding joy again after a loss will vary. Having at least some people who will support you and acknowledge the pain through long-term grief is helpful.

You do not need to "close" pain in order to live life again. It would be scary if you believed that joy would not come again until the grief is over. You would want to do whatever it takes to find "closure." Framing grief beyond closure requires language, rituals, and public understanding that it is possible to hold joy and grief together. You do not need to rush through grief in order to have joy again. Until people learn to carry both grief and joy at the same time, we will continue to support cultural narratives that shorten the expected grieving period.

Hope beyond Closure

As might be expected in a book that questions closure, I am not proposing that this conclusion should close our discussion about grief. Rather, I hope it is the start of many conversations about what we need after a loss. This book untangles the topic of closure, which emerged as a new way of talking about loss and has led to specific expectations for those who are grieving. By understanding the social construction of this idea, we can see behind and beyond the commercial interests and political agendas of those selling the promise of closure.

There are many ways to grieve and healing does not require closure. If you still like the language of closure, then I hope this book helps you sort out the contradictory interpretations and some of the motives behind those who construct the concept. And may the information here also help you to be sensitive when suggesting that others need closure or assuming that they have found it.

The concept of closure resonates with a desire to have things ordered and simple. But life is messy and our future unknown. Our hope comes in knowing we can carry complicated combinations of emotions as we journey through grief and loss. We can still grieve the loss of a loved one while learning how to once again engage in joyful events. The language of closure does not easily capture this complexity. We can survive a loss even when there are questions or grief that remain. We do not have to find an emotional state of closure to make progress in transcending a loss or in integrating a loss into our lives. By recognizing the tangled web of closure and the reasons behind the rhetoric, we can help ourselves and others navigate the emotions and feeling rules that come with grief and loss. Closure is best considered subjective, elusive, and optional. However, progress toward healing is possible. Hope remains intact even as we untangle the story of closure.

Notes

CHAPTER 1

1. "University Project: Your Tattoos and Their Meaning," Specktra.net, http://specktra.net/f179/university-project-your-tattoos-their-meaning-please-help-70288/ (accessed April 3, 2008).

2. Suma Varughese, "Finishing Touches Life Positive," http://www.lifepositive.com/Mind/Personal_Growth/Finishing_Touches122004.asp (accessed August 22, 2008).

3. Wedding Ring Coffin, http://www.weddingringcoffin.com/ (accessed October 23, 2008).

4. Kylie Mendonca, "The Business of the Beyond," *San Luis Obispo County's News and Entertainment Weekly*, October 24, 2007, http://www.newtimesslo.com/archives/ (accessed June 15, 2008).

5. At Peace: Pet Urn and Pet Memorial website, http://www.atpeace.com/ (accessed April 21, 2007).

6. Other scholars have used various terms to describe new discourses used to talk about social problems, such as cultural resources (e.g., Joel Best, *Random Violence: How We Talk about New Crimes and New Victims*, Berkeley: University of California Press, 1999), cultural narrations (e.g., David A. Snow and Robert D. Benford, "Ideology, Frame Resonance, and Participant Mobilization," in *From Structure to Action: Social Movement Participation across Cultures*, ed. Bert Klandermans, Hanspeter Kriesi, and Sidney Tarrow, Greenwich, CT: JAI, 1988, 197–217), moral vocabularies (e.g., Peter R. Ibarra and John I. Kitsuse, "Vernacular Constituents of Moral Discourse," in *Reconsidering Social Constructionism*, ed. James A. Holstein and Gale Miller, Hawthorne, NY: Aldine de Gruyter, 1993, 25–58), emotional discourses (e.g., Donileen R. Loseke, "Ethos, Pathos, and Social Problems: Reflections on Formula Narratives," in *Perspectives on Social Problems*, ed. James A. Holstein and Gale Miller, Greenwich, CT: JAI,

2000, 12:41–54), or cultural themes (e.g., William A. Gamson, *Talking Politics*, Cambridge: Cambridge University Press, 1992; Stephen Hilgartner and Charles L. Bosk, "The Rise and Fall of Social Problems," *American Journal of Sociology* 94 [1988]: 53–78).

7. Arlie Hochschild defines feeling rules as "standards used in emotional conversation to determine what is rightly owed and owing in the currency of feeling." See Arlie Hochschild, *The Managed Heart: The Commercialization of Human Feeling*, Berkeley: University of California Press, 1983, 18.

8. A large body of research on social problems uses social constructionism to study the claims-making activities of advocates, officials, media, and others who shape social problems. See, for example, Joel Best, "Rhetoric in Claims-Making," *Social Problems* 34 (1987): 101–121; Joel Best, *Threatened Children: Rhetoric and Concern about Child-Victims*, Chicago: University of Chicago Press, 1990; James A. Holstein and Gale Miller, *Reconsidering Social Constructionism*, Hawthorne, NY: Aldine de Gruyter, 1993; Donileen R. Loseke, "Constructing Conditions, People, Morality, and Emotion: Expanding the Agenda of Constructionism," in *Constructionist Controversies: Issues in Social Problems Theory*, ed. Gale Miller and James A. Holstein, Hawthorne, NY: Aldine de Gruyter, 1993, 207–216; Malcolm Spector and John I. Kitsuse, *Constructing Social Problems*, Hawthorne, NY: Aldine de Gruyter, 1987. Framing analysis in the social movement literature shares some of these theoretical ideas. For example, David Snow and Robert Benford specified three types of framing as necessary for successful rhetoric: diagnostic, prognostic, and motivational. See Snow and Benford, "Ideology, Frame Resonance, and Participant Mobilization."

9. Erving Goffman, *Frame Analysis: An Essay on the Organization of Experience*, New York: Harper and Row, 1974.

10. The data collection was guided by theoretical sampling; that is, the sample is not intended to be representative of the entire population of closure rhetoric. Instead, sampling was organized on the basis of the concepts and connections developed during the analysis. Selective coding was used to connect the concepts of feeling rules, emotion-domain expansion, and emotive dissonance to other relevant concepts and to validate these relationships. The analysis involved constant comparison between the developing theory and the data. While conducting the analysis, I continued theoretical sampling until I reached theoretical saturation. For a discussion of sampling techniques, see Anselm Strauss and Juliet Corbin, *Basics of Qualitative Research*, 2nd ed., Thousand Oaks, CA: Sage, 1998.

11. Tony Clark, "Judge Mulls Moving Bomb Trial," CNN.com, http://www.cnn.com/US/OKC/daily/9512/12-12/index.html (accessed June 20, 2008).

12. "Four Months Later, Columbine Re-Opens," *USA Today*, http://www.usatoday.com/news/index/colo/colo177.htm (accessed June 21, 2008).

13. Andrew Goldstein, "The Victims: Never Again," Time.com, http://www.time.com/time/magazine/article/0,9171,992874,00.html?promoid=googlep (accessed June 21, 2008).

14. Matthew Pearl, "Dante and the Death Penalty: How Capital Punishment Fails Its Audience," *Legal Affairs* (January 2003), http://www.legalaffairs.org/issues/January-February-2003/review_pearl_janfeb2003.msp (accessed February 24, 2011).

15. Frank Rich, "It's Closure Mongering Time," *New York Times*, April 28, 2001, A23.

16. Pearl, "Dante and the Death Penalty."

17. James H. Bennett, "Pastoral Statement on Capital Punishment," http://www
.dontkillinmynamect.org/pastoralstatement.html (accessed June 7, 2005).

18. David Spiegel, "Closure? The Execution Was Just the Start," *Washington Post*,
April 29, 2001, http://www.deathpenaltyinfo.org/article.php?did=401&scid= (accessed June 21, 2008).

19. Ed Lavandera and Ann Kellan, "Relatives Express Mixed Feelings after Execution," CNN.com, http://archives.cnn.com/2001/LAW/06/11/victims.reax/ (accessed June 20, 2008).

20. Linda J. Skitka, Christopher W. Bauman, and Elizabeth Mullen, "Political
Tolerance and Coming to Psychological Closure Following the September 11, 2001,
Terrorist Attacks: An Integrative Approach," *Personality and Social Psychology Bulletin*
30, no. 6 (2004): 743–756.

21. Sewell Chan, "Man Confronts Giuliani at Ground Zero Ceremony," *New
York Times*, September 11, 2007, http://cityroom.blogs.nytimes.com/2007/09/11/man-
confronts-giuliani-at-ground-zero-ceremony/ (accessed December 16, 2008).

22. International Association of Fire Fighters, "Firefighters Union Letter on Rudy
Guiliani," March 14, 2007, http://firefightingnews.com/articleUS.cfm?articleID
=27125 (accessed January 10, 2008).

23. Psychology professor Denise Beike claims that people who can talk about
something that happened, and not become emotional while discussing it, have closure.
When people think of an event frequently, there is less closure. See Denise Beike and
Erin Wirth-Beaumont, "Psychological Closure as a Memory Phenomenon," *Memory*
13, no. 6 (2005): 574–593.

24. Donna M. Webster and Arie W. Kruglanski, "Individual Differences in Need
for Cognitive Closure," *Journal of Personality and Social Psychology* 67, no. 6 (1994):
1049–1062.

25. Skitka, Bauman, and Mullen, "Political Tolerance and Coming to Psychological Closure Following the September 11, 2001, Terrorist Attacks."

26. Closure has been used in the social construction of technology studies to
describe the point where technological artifacts are no longer under the process of
social construction. Max Weber used the term "social closure" to describe a process whereby a dominant group keeps power by controlling resources for one group
and denying them for another through exclusion. In philosophy, Hilary Lawson
describes closure as "the imposition of fixity on openness." See Hilary Lawson, *Closure: A Story of Everything*, New York: Routledge, 2001. In mathematics, the closure
axiom is used to describe a set of real numbers that is closed under the operations
of addition and multiplication. In the 1960s, computer science developed its own
concept of closure to describe a function that closes free variables, which is used in
programming language.

27. Best, *Random Violence*.

28. Bruce J. Winick, "The Jurisprudence of Therapeutic Jurisprudence," *Psychology, Public Policy, and Law* 3, no. 1 (1997): 184–206.

29. Vik Kanwar, "Capital Punishment as 'Closure': The Limits of a Victim-
Centered Jurisprudence," *New York University Review of Law and Social Change* 27,
no. 2–3 (2001): 215–255.

30. Jody Lynee Madeira, "'Why Rebottle the Genie?' Capitalizing on Closure in Death Penalty Proceedings," Indiana Legal Studies Research Paper 127 (2009), http://ssrn.com/abstract=1347844.

31. *State v. Richmond*, 886 P.2d 1329, 1333 (Ariz. 1994).

32. *Patterson v. State*, 660 So. 2d 966, 969 (Miss. 1995).

33. *United States v. Chong*, 181 F. Supp. 2d 1135, 1137 (D. Haw. 2001).

34. *State v. Rimmer*, 2001 WL 567960, 13 (Tenn. Crim. App. 2001).

35. *State v. Watts*, 835 So. 2d 441, 453 (La. 2003).

36. *Winkles v. State*, 894 So. 2d 842, 848 (Fla. 2005).

37. See *People v. Garvin*, 847 N.E.2d 82 (Ill. 2006).

38. For an extensive view on our therapeutic culture, see Eva Illouz, *Saving the Modern Soul: Therapy, Emotions, and the Culture of Self-Help*, Berkeley: University of California Press, 2008.

39. For an extended look at how television talk shows connect to the self-help movement, see Kathleen S. Lowney, *Baring Our Souls: TV Talk Shows and the Religion of Recovery*, Hawthorne, NY: Aldine de Gruyter, 1999.

40. Elayne Rapping, "Television, Melodrama, and the Rise of the Victims' Rights Movement," *New York Law School Legal Review* 43 (2000): 678.

41. For more information on how magazine editors shape stories about social problems, see Nancy Berns, *Framing the Victim: Domestic Violence, Media and Social Problems*, Hawthorne, NY: Aldine de Gruyter, 2004.

CHAPTER 2

1. "DNA Confirms Skeletal Remains Are Caylee," CBS News, http://www.cbsnews.com/stories/2008/12/19/national/main4677980.shtml (accessed March 13, 2009).

2. Holly Bristow, "George Anthony: There Is a Hole in My Heart," Fox 35 News, http://www.myfoxgj.com/myfox (accessed February 11, 2009).

3. Walter Pacheco, "Caylee Anthony Memorial Service Draws Crowd," *Orlando Sentinel*, February 10, 2009, http://www.newsday.com/news/nationworld/ny-uscaylee0211,0,6767581.story (accessed February 11, 2009).

4. Keren Tenenboim Weinblatt, "Fighting for the Story's Life: Nonclosure in Journalistic Narrative," paper presented at the annual meeting of the International Communication Association, Dresden, Germany, June 16, 2006.

5. Robert Fulford, "Robert Fulford's Column about the Word 'Closure,'" *National Post*, November 10, 2001, available at http://www.robertfulford.com/Closure.html (accessed February 17, 2011).

6. Earlier dictionary entries of closure have included "means of enclosing," "the property that a number system or a set has when it is mathematically closed under an operation," and "a set that consists of a given set together with all the limit points of that set." Another earlier dictionary entry of closure is "a procedure by which a debate may be stopped and an immediate vote taken."

7. "Closure," *Collins English Dictionary*, 5th ed., New York: HarperCollins, 2000.

8. "Closure," Merriam-Webster.com, http://www.merriam-webster.com/dictionary/closure (accessed June 30, 2008).

9. "Human Emotions," Answerbag, http://www.answerbag.co.uk/q_view/733055 (accessed June 12, 2008).

10. Denise Beike and Erin Wirth-Beaumont, "Psychological Closure as a Memory Phenomenon," *Memory* 13, no. 6 (2005): 574–593.

11. Arie Kruglanski and Donna Webster, "Motivated Closing of the Mind: Seizing and Freezing," *Psychological Review* 103 (1996): 264.

12. Donna Webster and Arie W. Kruglanski. "Individual Differences in Need for Cognitive Closure," *Journal of Personality and Social Psychology* 67 no. 6 (1994): 1049–1062.

13. J. T. Jost, J. Glaser, A. W. Kruglanski, and F. Sulloway, "Political Conservatism as Motivated Social Cognition," *Psychological Bulletin* 129 (2003): 339–375.

14. Linda J. Skitka, Christopher W. Bauman, and Elizabeth Mullen, "Political Tolerance and Coming to Psychological Closure Following the September 11, 2001, Terrorist Attacks: An Integrative Approach," *Personality and Social Psychology Bulletin* 30, no. 6 (2004): 743–756.

15. L. A. King and K. N. Miner, "Writing about the Perceived Benefits of Traumatic Events: Implications for Physical Health," *Personality and Social Psychology Bulletin* 26 (2000): 220–230; J. L. Pals, "Narrative Identity Processing of Difficult Life Experiences: Pathways of Personality Development and Positive Self-Transformation in Adulthood," *Journal of Personality* 74 (2006): 1079–1110.

16. Jonathan M. Adler and Michael J. Poulin, "The Political Is Personal: Narrating 9/11 and Psychological Well-Being," *Journal of Personality* 77, no. 4 (2009): 903–932.

17. John W. Moles, "A Personal Pre-Planning Funeral Guide," Moles Family Services, Inc.

18. "Clinton Escapes Lewinsky Scandal," BBC News, http://news.bbc.co.uk/2/hi/americas/1126591.stm (accessed April 26, 2008).

19. Allen G. Breed "As Much as They Hate to Admit It, Some Americans Are Tired of Being Reminded," Boston.com news, http://www.boston.com/news/packages/sept11/anniversary/wire_stories/0908_fatigue.htm (accessed March 19, 2009).

20. "Should the Death Penalty Be Banned as a Form of Punishment?" Balanced Politics.org, http://www.balancedpolitics.org/death_penalty.htm (accessed August 17, 2007).

21. Stephen Sultan, "Case for Death Penalty," *New York Times*, August 18, 1997, http://query.nytimes.com/gst/fullpage.html (accessed August 17, 2007).

22. Adam Russ, *The Revenge Seeker's Handbook: Everything You Need to Know about Getting Even*, http://www.amazon.com/Revenge-Seekers-Handbook-Adam-Russ/dp/186105775X (accessed November 11, 2008).

23. Kathy Farren and Matt Schury, "NIU Tragedy Hits Close to Home," *Oswego Ledger-Sentinel*, February 21, 2008, http://www.ledgersentinel.com/article.asp?a=7021 (accessed June 21, 2008).

24. "Forensic Pathologist," Expertwitness.com, http://www.expertwitness.com/prof/second/private/autopsy.html (accessed October 21, 2008).

25. New Mexico Coalition to Repeal the Death Penalty, "Frequently Asked Questions," http://nmrepeal.org/FAQ2.htm#b (accessed May 3, 2006).

26. David Herman, "Last Statement," Texas Department of Criminal Justice, http://www.tdcj.state.tx.us/stat/hermandavidlast.htm (accessed August 15, 2008).

27. Sociologist Arlie Hochschild defines feeling rules as "standards used in emotional conversation to determine what is rightly owed and owing in the currency of feeling." See Arlie Hochschild, *The Managed Heart: The Commercialization of Human Feeling*, Berkeley: University of California Press, 1983.

CHAPTER 3

1. eHow.com, http://ehow.qwapi.com/site?t=4t2CciEYlhuclwyljoESGA (accessed May 31, 2008).

2. Some examples of factors that shape one's grief include "the circumstances of the death, such as whether or not the death was anticipated, violent, able to be prevented, or followed a lengthy illness; the relationship to the deceased, with closer relationships between the deceased and the bereaved usually yielding a potentially more distressing grief experience; the characteristics of the bereaved individual, including one's age, cognitive style, coping strategies, gender, spirituality/religiosity, previous life history, and concurrent crises; the availability, type, and extent of interpersonal support received by the bereaved, and whether or not the support is perceived as helpful by the bereaved; and an assortment of sociocultural factors that include the presence and perceived relevance of mourning rituals, customs, and traditions." Lauren Breen and Moira O'Conner, "The Fundamental Paradox in the Grief Literature: A Critical Reflection," *Omega* 55, no. 3 (2007), 200.

3. Catherine Foote and Arthur Frank critique the stages as part of the larger medicalization of grief perspective: "Grief is expected to be an ordered, limited process that moves by identifiable steps toward 'recovery': restored happiness, adaptation to the absence of the deceased, reestablished engagement with the everyday world." See C. Foote and A. Frank, "Foucault and Therapy: The Discipline of Grief," in *Reading Foucault for Social Work*, ed. A. Chambon, A. Irving, and L. Epstein, New York: Columbia University Press, 1999, 165.

4. Elisabeth Kübler-Ross, *On Death and Dying*, London: Routledge, 1973.

5. William Worden, *Grief Counseling and Grief Therapy*, 3rd ed., New York: Springer, 1983, 26.

6. George Bonanno, *The Other Side of Sadness: What the New Science of Bereavement Tells Us about Life after a Loss*, New York: Basic Books, 2009, 6.

7. For more information on the medicalization of social problems, see Peter Conrad, *The Medicalization of Society: On the Transformation of Human Conditions into Treatable Disorders*, Baltimore: Johns Hopkins University Press; Peter Conrad and Joseph W. Schneider, *Deviance and Medicalization: From Badness to Sickness*, Philadelphia: Temple University Press, 1992.

8. M. J. Horowitz, B. Siegel, A. Holen, G. Bonanno, C. Milbrath, and C. Stinson, "Diagnostic Criteria for Complicated Grief Disorders," *American Journal of Psychiatry* 154, no. 7 (1997): 904–911.

9. Tony Walter, "What Is Complicated Grief? A Social Constructionist Perspective," *Omega* 52, no. 1 (2006): 74.

10. For more information on the relationship between the *DSM* and insurance companies, see Herb Kutchins and Stuart Kirk, *Making Us Crazy: DSM: The Psychiatric Bible and the Creation of Mental Disorder*, New York: Simon and Schuster, 1997.

11. A. V. Horwitz, "Transforming Normality into Pathology: The *DSM* and the Outcomes of Stressful Social Arrangements," *Journal of Health and Social Behavior* 48 (2007): 211–222.

12. Psychiatrists Ronald Pies and Sidney Zisook are two of the biggest advocates for allowing a diagnosis of major depression for those who are grieving an immediate loss. Pies and Zisook argue "that continuing the bereavement exclusion in DSM5 would be a serious error. It would encourage bereaved individuals, their families, and health care providers to ignore signs and symptoms of a potentially debilitating, life-threatening, yet treatable disorder. Extending this exclusion to still other loss events could create a public health disaster." Ronald Pies and Sidney Zisook, Letter (response to Wakefield and Horwitz), *Psychiatric Times*, http://www.psychiatrictimes.com/display/article/10168/1413394 (accessed February 20, 2011). Here we can see them use language such as "disorder" and "public health disaster" to describe what we have for a long time considered normal reactions to the loss of a loved one.

13. Allen Frances, "DSM-V: Medicalization of Grief," *Psychiatric Times*, March 16, 2010, http://www.mha-ne.org/2010/03/-dsmv-medicalization-of-grief.html (accessed April 16, 2010).

14. Dr. Frances has been trying to warn people about the increasing tendency to widen the net of those who are diagnosed with some syndrome or disorder. One concern is that once a "psychiatric fad" becomes "official" in the *DSM*, pharmaceutical companies, advocacy groups, and media will push the diagnosis. More and more people will be diagnosed with some syndrome who in the past would have been considered "normal" under earlier, more restrictive, categories of psychiatric syndromes. Frances argues there are practical concerns with expanding who is "abnormal": "There are unpredictable costs attached to having an inappropriate diagnosis. It can affect how you see yourself and how others see you; result in reduced ambitions and sense of personal control and responsibility, and difficulty getting insurance." Allen Frances, "A Few DSM-5 Updates and Commentaries," Integral-options.blogspot.com, http://integral-options.blogspot.com/2010/04/allen-frances-few-dsm-5-updates-and.html (accessed February 20, 2011).

15. Allen Frances, "The DSM5 Subthreshold Disorders: Not Ready for Prime Time," *Psychology Today*, April 15, 2010, http://www.psychologytoday.com/blog/dsm5-in-distress/201004/the-dsm5-subthreshold-disorders-not-ready-prime-time (accessed April 16, 2010).

16. Walter, "What Is Complicated Grief?"

17. Robert V. Kail and John C. Cavanaugh, *Human Development: A Life-Span View*, Belmont, CA: Wadsworth, 2008, 619.

18. John D. Canine, "Funeral Directors' Understanding of Complicated Grief," AuroraCasket.com, http://www.auroracasket.com/newweb/web.nsf/DocID/8A0C8CBB3221D5688525715C006CCCD9?OpenDocument (accessed April 15, 2010).

19. Ibid.

20. Walter, "What Is Complicated Grief?"

21. Kenneth J. Doka, "Evaluating Advice and Information in Grief," Hospice and Caregiving blog, http://www.hospicefoundation.org/blog/labels/grief.html (accessed September 11, 2008).

22. Richard Kaplan, "9–11 Anniversary Reactions: An Interview with Dr. Frank Ochberg," http://www.giftfromwithin.org/html/9–11.html (accessed January 10, 2008).

23. Jane E. Brody, "Often, Time Beats Therapy for Treating Grief," The Kaiser Papers, January 27, 2004, http://behavioral.kaiserpapers.org/timegrief.html (accessed January 10, 2008).

24. For more discussion on the concept of policing grief, see Tony Walter, *On Bereavement: The Culture of Grief*, Maidenhead, UK: Open University Press, 1999.

25. Pauline Boss, personal website, http://www.ambiguousloss.com/ (accessed August 15, 2010).

26. Pauline Boss, *Loss, Trauma, and Resilience: Therapeutic Work with Ambiguous Loss*, New York: Norton, 2006, 7.

27. John Baker, "Portsmouth Talk to Judges," Families Need Fathers, http://www.fnf.org.uk/news-and-events/campaigns/submissions-and-consultation-responses/portsmouth-talk-to-judges-john-baker (accessed April 21, 2009).

28. Barb Hepperle, "How to Heal from a Broken Heart," http://www.google.com/search?q=%22there+is+no+closure%22+and+bad+relationships&hl=en&start=80&sa=N (accessed April 19, 2009).

29. http://www.midsummerseve.com/thread/116035/1/death_or_divorce.

30. Breakups and Divorce Support Group, http://www.dailystrength.org/c/Breakups_Divorce/forum/975564-pretending-hes-dead (accessed September 10, 2010).

31. Exiled Mothers, http://www.exiledmothers.com/ index.html (accessed April 21, 2009).

32. Karen Wilson Buterbaugh, "Domestic Infant Adoption: Setting the Record Straight," http://www.adoptioncrossroads.org/STRS.html (accessed September 10, 2010).

33. David Kirschner, "Sometimes a Fatal Quest . . . Losses in Adoption," Pound Pup Legacy, http://poundpuplegacy.org/node/19853 (accessed April 23, 2009).

34. Susan Solomon Yem, "Life after Adoption," http://www.babyzone.com/preconception/adoption/article/adoption-issues-challenges-pg4 (accessed April 23, 2009).

35. "No Closure for Family of Missing 11-Year-Old," *Stabroek News*, March 27, 2007, http://www.stabroeknews.com/2007/news/local/03/26/no-closure-for-family-of-missing-11-year-old/ (accessed April 23, 2009).

36. "Family Still Awaiting Results in Missing Person Case," WWAY News Channel 3, July 30, 2008, https://www.wwaytv3.com/node/9334/print (accessed September 14, 2010).

37. Rick Hampson and Martha T. Moore, "Closure from 9/11 Elusive for Many," http://www.usatoday.com/news/nation/2003–09-03-sept-11-son_x.htm (accessed January 10, 2008).

38. Pauline Boss, "Ambiguous Loss Research, Theory, and Practice: Reflections after 9/11," *Journal of Marriage and Family* 66, no. 3 (2004): 561.

39. Sarah Hass, "Jon Lacina's Body Found," *Iowa State Daily*, April 15, 2010, http://www.iowastatedaily.com/articles/2010/04/15/news/local_news/doc4bc7e 89182b62236107833.txt (accessed April 26, 2010).

40. Michael MacLeod, "Wounded Warriors Return to Iraq," Department of Defense, http://www.defense.gov/news/newsarticle.aspx?id=57335 (accessed April 12, 2010).

41. Tom Sileo, "USO, Troops First Foundation Bring Peace to Aching Heart," The Unknown Soldiers, http://www.unknownsoldiersblog.com/2010/02/uso-troops-first-foundation-bring-peace.html (accessed April 12, 2010).

42. Rod Nordland, "Wounded Soldiers Return to Iraq, Seeking Solace," *New York Times*, http://www.nytimes.com/2009/10/15/world/middleeast/15exit.html (accessed April 12, 2010).

43. Chelsea J. Carter, "Wounded U.S. Troops Return to Iraq to Find Closure," ABC.News.com, http://abcnews.go.com/International/wireStory?id=8856571 (accessed April 10, 2010).

44. Sharee Posey, "The USO and Troops First Foundation Launch Fourth 'Operation Proper Exit' Tour to the Persian Gulf," USO.com, http://uso.mediaroom.com/index.php?s=press_releases&item=875 (accessed April 12, 2010).

45. "Operation Proper Exit," Real American Stories.com, http://www.realameri canstories.com/operation-proper-exit/?curpage=3 (accessed April 12, 2010).

46. Wilbert "Shorty" Estabrook, "Purple Hearts for POW's Who Die in Captivity," Korean War Project, http://www.koreanwar.org/html/newsletter_march_10_ 2004.html (accessed November 5, 2010).

47. Harold Fencl, "Purple Heart Rules Need Changing," HomerNews.com, http://homernews.com/stories/120105/letters_20051201017.shtml (accessed November 5, 2010).

48. Matt Vande Bunte, "Lowell Man Surprised by Purple Heart Award for Korean War Injury," *Grand Rapids Press*, August 8, 2010, http://www.mlive.com/news/grand-rapids/index.ssf/2010/08/lowell_man_surprised_by_purple.html (accessed November 5, 2010).

49. Linda Wertheimer, "Purple Hearts Elusive for Traumatic Brain Injuries," National Public Radio, http://www.npr.org/templates/transcript/transcript.php?storyId =129606127 (accessed November 5, 2010).

50. Gordon Livingston, *Too Soon Old, Too Late Smart: Thirty True Things You Need to Know Now*, New York: Marlowe, 2004, 116.

51. Gordon Livingston, "Grave Situation: Don't Landfill the Tsunami Bodies," The Hook, http://www.readthehook.com/Stories/2005/01/06/essayGraveSituation DontLan.html (accessed September 11, 2008).

52. Amy Florian, "Chasing after Closure," Atlanta's Compassionate Friends website, http://www.tcfatlanta.org/daily090207.html (accessed January 16, 2009).

53. Kevin Caruso, "Suicide Survivors: There Is No Closure after a Suicide," Sui cide.org, http://www.suicide.org/suicide-survivors-there-is-no-closure.html (accessed April 28, 2007).

54. Joseph M. Dougherty, "There Is No Closure," http://www.tommydoc.net/pencil/stuff/wakeaddress.html (accessed April 28, 2007).

55. Sherry Russell, "Sorrow and Closure," The Bright Side, http://www.the-bright-side.org/site/thebrightside/content.php?type=1&section_id=337&id=800 (accessed January 16, 2009).

56. Darcie Sims, "Changing the Language of Grief: A New Century's Challenge," Life Files, http://www.lifefiles.com/libraryArticle.php?i_messageid=146 (accessed January 16, 2009).

57. Robert Jay Lifton and Greg Mitchell, *Who Owns Death? Capital Punishment, the American Conscience, and the End of Executions*, New York: William Morrow, 2000, 204.

58. Jonathan Wallace, "Memory. Fear. Hope. Closure," Year Zero, http://www.spectacle.org/yearzero/memory.html (accessed May 30, 2007).

59. Dana Williamson, "No Closure for Victims, Families, Rescue Workers," *Baptist Press*, http://bpnews.net/BPnews.asp?ID=5693 (accessed August 26, 2008).

60. "How You Can Help," Northside Hospital Perinatal Loss Office, http://www.northsidepnl.com/for-family-friends.html (accessed March 1, 2011).

61. Ibid.

62. Gerry J. Gilmore, "Gates, Pace Vow to Pursue, Defeat 9/11 Perpetrators," http://www.defense.gov/news/newsarticle.aspx?id=47396 (accessed January 11, 2008).

63. Nina Bennett's poem from *Forgotten Tears: A Grandmother's Journey through Grief*, available at http://www.griefhealing.com/grievinghearts.htm (accessed February 18, 2011).

64. Al Miles, "When Do Grieving Parents Reach Closure?" *Clergy Journal*, January 2001, 17.

65. Russell, "Sorrow and Closure."

66. Robert Sadamu Shimabukuro, *Born in Seattle: The Campaign for Japanese American*, Seattle: University of Washington Press, 2001, 116.

67. Florian, "Chasing after Closure."

68. Wallace, "Memory. Fear. Hope. Closure."

69. Anna Quindlen, "Public and Private: Life after Death," *New York Times*, May 4, 1994.

70. Quinn McDonald, "Is There Closure?" http://quinncreative.wordpress.com/2007/03/31/is-there-closure/ (accessed April 28 2007).

71. Dougherty, "There Is No Closure."

72. Thomas Attig, *The Heart of Grief*, New York: Oxford University Press, 2002, 115.

CHAPTER 4

1. Gary M. Laderman, "Funeral Industry," *Encyclopedia of Death and Dying*, Deathreference.com, http://www.deathreference.com/En-Gh/Funeral-Industry.html (accessed June 5, 2009).

2. Gary M. Laderman, *Rest in Peace: A Cultural History of Death and the Funeral Home in Twentieth-Century America*, New York: Oxford University Press, 2003.

3. Bryant Mortuary, http://www.bryantmortuary.com/traditional.shtml (accessed November 13, 2008).

4. DeVoe Funeral Service, Inc., http://www.devoefuneral.com/faq.htm (accessed November 13, 2008).

5. "Embracing Life by Confronting Death," Chicago Teamsters, http://www .chicagoteamsters.org/news/2005/0602_funeral.html (accessed November 13, 2008).

6. "Consumer Resource Guide," International Cemetery, Cremation and Funeral Association, http://consumer.iccfa.com/ (accessed June 20, 2009).

7. Jared Solis, "Mortuary Science Students, Professionals See Embalming of Head Trauma Victims," *The Ranger*, http://media.www.theranger.org/media/storage/ paper1010/news/2007/04/20/News/Mortuary.Science.Students.Professionals.See .Embalming.Of.Head.Trauma.Victims-2869599.shtml (accessed June 12, 2009).

8. Ibid.

9. In order to protect the identity of this family, I have removed their names and am not posting the specific funeral home.

10. State laws vary regarding refrigeration and specific circumstances that might require embalming.

11. Springfield Funeral Home, http://www.springfieldfuneralhome.com/ answers.php (accessed November 13, 2008).

12. Kohut Funeral Home, Inc., http://www.kohutfuneralhome.com/faq/ (accessed November 13, 2008).

13. Ralph J. Wittich-Riley-Freers Funeral Home, http://www.wittichfuneral home.com/faq.htm (accessed November 13, 2008).

14. "Funeral Planning Frequently Asked Questions," Bliley's Funeral Homes, http://www.blileyfuneralhomes.com/_mgxroot/page_10796.php (accessed June 13, 2009).

15. Hugeback Funeral Home, http://www.hugebackfuneralhome.com/cremation questions.htm (accessed November 29, 2008).

16. Ibid.

17. Benedict-Rettey Mortuary & Crematory, http://www.benedictretteymortuary .com/cremation.htm (accessed November 13, 2008).

18. "Cremation Options," Iles Funeral Homes, http://www.ilesfuneralhomes .com/_mgxroot/page_10752.php (accessed June 13, 2009).

19. "Services," Atchley Funeral Home, http://www.atchleyfuneralhome.com/ services.html (accessed June 13, 2009).

20. Hugeback Funeral Home.

21. Cynthia Dizikes, "Death Midwives Tap a Growing Market," *Seattle Times*, December 27, 2008, http://seattletimes.nwsource.com/html/nationworld/2008563478_ funerals27.html (accessed June 7, 2009).

22. "Green and Loving Family–Directed Home Funerals," Final Passages, http:// www.finalpassages.org/ (accessed June 1, 2009).

23. Christina Leimer, "Interview with Jerri Lyons of Final Passages," Home Funeral.info, http://homefuneral.info/archives/23 (accessed June 7, 2009).

24. Elizabeth Knox, "Crossings: Caring for Our Own at Death," http://www .crossings.net/story.html (accessed June 5, 2009).

25. Ken Picard, "Dead Wrong: Are Vermonters Getting Stiffed on the Facts about Home Funerals?" *Seven Days*, http://www.7dvt.com/2007/dead-wrong (accessed February 20, 2011).

26. Tim Matson, "The Last Thing You Want to Do," *Mother Earth News*, http:// www.glendalenaturepreserve.org/Mother.htm (accessed June 7, 2009).

27. Bob Doran, "After You're Dead," *Journal of Politics, People and Art*, http://www.northcoastjournal.com/issues/2008/04/10/after-youre-dead/ (accessed June 15, 2009).

28. "In Repose," International Scattering Society, http://inrepose.typepad.com/in_repose_blog/last_wishes/ (accessed January 7, 2009).

29. "Aerial Ash Scattering," Air Legacy, http://www.airlegacy.com/ (accessed January 6, 2009).

30. "Scattering Ashes by Air," Everlife Memorials, http://www.everlifememorials.com/v/urns/scattering-ashes-air.htm (accessed January 6, 2009).

31. "Why Choose Scatter by Airplane?" Scatterings, http://www.scatteringbyair.com/faq.htm (accessed January 6, 2009).

32. Ibid.

33. Homeward Bound Aerial Services, http://www.ashscattering.org/ (accessed January 7, 2009).

34. Final Flights, http://www.finalflights.com/index.html (accessed January 8, 2009).

35. Scatterings.

36. Final Flights.

37. "Why Choose to Scatter by Airplane?" Clearwater Flight Services, http://www.clearwaterflightservices.com/scattering.htm (accessed January 7, 2009).

38. "Our Services," Eternal Ascent, http://ashestotheheavens.com/Ashes_Into_Space.html (accessed January 8, 2009).

39. Ibid.

40. Heavens above Fireworks, http://www.heavensabovefireworks.com/ (accessed April 17, 2009).

41. "Celestis," Memorial Spaceflights, http://www.memorialspaceflights.com/ (accessed June 1, 2009).

42. "Why Nature's Passage? Sea Burials Are Earth Friendly and Priced Right!" Nature's Passage, http://www.naturespassage.com/why.php (accessed June 12, 2009).

43. "Ashes Scattering," Serenity at Sea, http://www.serenityatsea.com/ (accessed June 13, 2009).

44. "Yachts for Scattering of Ashes in San Diego," California Cruisin', http://www.californiacruisin.com/charter-yachts-boats-for-scattering-of-ashes-san-diego.php (accessed June 12, 2009).

45. "Burials at Sea," Island Bound Cruises, http://www.islandboundcruises.com/index.php?option=com_content&view=article&id=7&Itemid=11 (accessed June 12, 2009).

46. Gail Condrick, "Sea Reef Burial," *Natural Awakenings*, http://www.naturalawakeningsmag.com/natural-library/march-2009/sea-reef-burial (accessed June 15, 2009).

47. Eternal Reefs, http://www.eternalreefs.com/index.html (accessed June 13, 2009).

48. Sylvia Cochran, "Eternal Reefs' Eco-Friendly Burials at Sea Coming to a Coast Near You," Associated Content News, http://www.associatedcontent.com/article/1485994/eternal_reefs_ecofriendly_burials_at.html?singlepage=tru&cat=62 (accessed June 13, 2009).

49. "Airborne Scattering Gives Options When Choosing a Place of Final Rest," http://scatteringcrematedashes.com/ (accessed January 7, 2009).

50. Air Legacy, http://www.airlegacy.com/ (accessed January 7, 2009).

51. Kimi Yoshino, "A Ride to the Great Beyond at Disneyland—Secret Scattering of Remains at Parks, Golf Courses and Other Sites May Be Growing," *Los Angeles Times*, November 14, 2007, http://articles.latimes.com/2007/nov/14/business/fi-disney14 (accessed June 10, 2009).

52. Al Lutz, "Backstage, at a Price," Miceage.com, http://miceage.micechat.com/allutz/al111307d.htm (accessed April 17, 2009).

53. Brady MacDonald, "Dearly Departed on Disneyland Rides!" *Los Angeles Times*, http://travel.latimes.com/daily-deal-blog/index.php/disneyland's-999/ (accessed April 17, 2009).

54. Laura Castle, "Burial Costs Are on the Rise, Pushing Popularity of Cremation," http://www.mysuburbanlife.com/darien/news/x1157485515/Burial-costs-are-on-the-rise-pushing-popularity-of-cremation (accessed January 8, 2009).

55. "Consumer Resource Guide," International Cemetery, Cremation and Funeral Association, http://consumer.iccfa.com/faq/2 (accessed January 8, 2009).

56. "Cremation Services," Herman Meyer and Son, http://www.meyerfuneral.com/meyer%20cremation.htm (accessed June 15, 2008).

57. Phoenix Diamonds, http://www.phoenix-diamonds.com/ (accessed January 8, 2009).

58. Ibid.

59. Huggableurns.com, http://www.huggableurns.com/index.htm (accessed January 10, 2009).

60. "Testimonials," Huggable Urns, http://www.huggableurns.com/testimonials.htm (accessed January 10, 2009).

61. In order to protect this woman's privacy, I am not publishing her information.

62. Memorials.com, http://www.memorials.com/Reasons-to-Memorialize-your-Pet-information.php (accessed February 20, 2011).

63. Ibid.

64. Ibid.

CHAPTER 5

1. Sandy Cullen, "Unanswered Questions Haunt Mother of Brittany Zimmermann," *Wisconsin State Journal*, October 27, 2008, http://www.madison.com/wsj/home/local/309092 (accessed October 27, 2008).

2. Monica Gaza, "Heath Ledger Cause of Death Announced," Softpedia, February 6, 2008, http://news.softpedia.com/news/Breaking-Heath-Ledger-Cause-of-Death-Announced-78110.shtml (accessed October 27, 2008).

3. K. G. Shojania and E. C. Burton, "The Vanishing Nonforensic Autopsy," *New England Journal of Medicine* 358, no. 9 (2008): 873–875.

4. P. N. Nemetz, E. Tanglos, L. P. Sands, W. P. Fisher Jr., W. P. Newman III, and E. C. Burton, "Attitudes toward the Autopsy—An 8-State Survey," *Medscape General Medicine* 8, no. 3 (2006): 80.

5. Pathology Support Services, http://www.pssautopsy.com/funeral.html (accessed May 2, 2007).

6. "Autopsy," Medicinenet.com, http://www.medicinenet.com/autopsy/page4.htm (accessed May 2, 2007).

7. Memory and Aging Center, University of California, San Francisco, http://memory.ucsf.edu/Research/autopsy.html (accessed May 2, 2007).

8. American Autopsy Services Inc., http://www.americanautopsy.com/facts.html (accessed October 21, 2008).

9. Autopsy Pathology Services, http://www.apsautopsy.com/Autopsy%20Information.htm (accessed October 21, 2008).

10. Pathology Support Services, http://www.pssautopsy.com/funeral.html (accessed May 2, 2007).

11. American Autopsy, http://www.americanautopsy.com/for-insurance.html#FAQ (accessed October 20, 2010).

12. Dennis Nishi, "Demand Breathes Life into Private-Autopsy Companies," *Wall Street Journal*, October 14, 2010.

13. Marcia King, "Necropsy: Searching for Answers," TheHorse.com, http://www.thehorse.com/ViewArticle.aspx?ID=2327 (accessed October 21, 2008).

14. Sarah Probst, "Protect Your Herd—Find Out Why Your Horse Died," http://vetmed.illinois.edu/petcolumns/petcols_article_page.php?PETCOLID=45&URL=0 (accessed February 21, 2011).

15. Sandy Harrison and Bill Harrison, "My Bird Died: Preparing for a Necropsy," *Winged Wisdom*, http://www.birdsnways.com/wisdom/ww62eiii.htm (accessed October 21, 2008).

16. Nancy J. LaRoche, "Should I Get a Necropsy When My Bunny Dies?" Colorado House Rabbit Society, http://www.coloradohrs.com/articles/medical_necropsy.asp (accessed October 21, 2008).

17. Necropsy Services Group, http://necropsyservices.com/about (accessed October 21, 2008).

18. Larmoyeux & Bone Trial Lawyers PL, http://www.lb-law.com/PracticeAreas/Wrongful-Death.asp (accessed October 22, 2008).

19. William M. Hayner & Associates, http://www.haynerlaw.com/WrongfulDeath.shtml.

20. John J. Hopkins, http://www.jjhandassociates.com/Practice-Area-Overview/Wrongful-Death.shtml.

21. Johnston Martineau Attorneys at Law, http://www.anyinjuryanytime.com/Personal-Injury/Wrongful-Death.shtml.

22. Eley, Galloway and Trigg, LLP, http://www.egtlaw.com/PracticeAreas/Wrongful-Death.asp.

23. Ibid.

24. Reardon & Reardon Attorneys at Law, http://www.rrlaw.com/PracticeAreas/Wrongful-Death.asp.

25. Drivon, Turner & Waters, http://www.drivonlaw.com/html/wrongful-death.html (accessed October 21, 2008).

26. Larmoyeux & Bone Trial Lawyers.

27. Kearney, Freeman, Fogarty & Joshi, PLLC, http://www.kffjlaw.com/Practice
Areas/Wrongful-Death.asp (accessed October 22, 2008).
28. Klitsas & Vercher, P.C., http://www.kv-law.com/PracticeAreas/DWI-Acci
dents.asp (accessed October 22, 2008).
29. John Gehlhausen, http://www.ridingmoweraccident.com/html/mower-
wrongful-death.html#compensation (accessed October 21, 2008).
30. Wrongful Death Lawyer Direct, http://www.wrongfuldeathlawyerdirect
.com/autoaccidentswrongfuldeath.php (accessed October 22, 2008).
31. Kelly Professional Investigations, Inc., http://www.kellypi.com/index.html.
32. SRS Investigative Consulting, LLC, http://www.stevescan.com/divorce.html.
33. The Tyson Group Private Investigations, http://www.thetysongroup.com/
web/ (accessed October 21, 2008).
34. "Accident Reconstruction Investigations," PINow.com, http://www.pinow
.com/investigations/accident_reconstruction (accessed October 21, 2008).
35. 7 Day Detective, http://7daydetective.blogspot.com/.
36. Ibid.
37. TM Morgan, LLC, http://www.tmmorgan.com/.
38. Private Investigators, http://www.privateinvestigatorsnj.com/CheatingInfidel
ityInvestigationsNJ.html.
39. Affair Investigations, http://www.affairinvestigations.com/index.html.
40. Hawk Private Investigations, Inc., http://www.infidelityproof.com/.
41. Dean Cortez, "Hiring a Private Investigator to Catch a Cheating Husband,"
EzineArticles.com, http://ezinearticles.com/?Hiring-a-Private-Investigator-to-Catch-
a-Cheating-Husband&id=3439114 (accessed March 8, 2010).
42. Chase Investigations, Inc., http://www.chaseinvestigationsinc.com/products
_dk.html.
43. AccuTrace, http://accutracetesting.com/infidelity.html.
44. Closure 4U Investigations, http://www.closure4u.com/.
45. T. L. Nash, "Within the Light," http://www.withinthelight.com/pages/abouttl
.htm (accessed October 21, 2008).
46. Carole Obley, The Open Mind, http://www.theopenmind.com (accessed October 21, 2008).
47. Be Within, Bewithin.com, http://www.bewithin.com/ (accessed October 21,
2008).
48. "Psychic Impressions," Visionimpressions.com, http://www.visionimpressions
.com/psyimp.htm (accessed October 21, 2008).
49. Heavenly Visions by Lady Magdalena, http://www.heavenlyvisions.net/index
.html (accessed October 21, 2008).
50. Federal Bureau of Investigation, http://www2.fbi.gov/page2/mar10/wanted
_031510.html.
51. Karen Zautyk, "Light the Way Home Etan Patz," *Daily News*, June 27, 1999,
http://www.nydailynews.com/archives/news/1999/06/27/1999–06-27_light_the_
way_home_etan_patz.html (accessed October 20, 2008).
52. Effective Playing Cards & Publications, http://www.shop.effectiveplaying
cards.com (accessed October 27, 2008).

53. Julie Montanaro, "Cold Case Playing Cards," November 6, 2007, http://www.wctv.tv/home/headlines/11058881.html (accessed October 27, 2008).

54. Sandi Copes, "Attorney General Bill McCollum News Release," August 29, 2008, http://myfloridalegal.com/newsrel.nsf/pv/0DC06FEBBA0565C1852574B4005 201A8 (accessed October 27, 2008).

55. James Hawver, "Playing Cards Seek Inmates' Help in Solving Unsolved Crimes in New York," http://www.crimeandjustice.us/forums/index.php?showtopic=8466 (accessed October 27, 2008).

56. Kathryn Zunno, "*United States v. Kincade* and the Constitutionality of the Federal DNA Act: Why We'll Need a New Pair of Genes to Wear Down the Slippery Slope," *St. John's Law Review* 79 (2005): 769–821.

57. Christopher H. Asplen, "From Crime Scene to Courtroom—Integrating DNA Technology into the Criminal Justice System," *Judicature* (November–December 1999), http://www.ornl.gov/sci/techresources/HumanGenome/publicat/judicature/article9.html (accessed October 30, 2008).

58. The Combined DNA Index System, *www.justice.gov/oig/reports/FBI/a0126/final.pdf (accessed March 20, 2010).*

59. "Advancing Justice through Forensic DNA Technology," Hearing before the Subcommittee on Crime, Terrorism, and Homeland Security, http://commdocs.house .gov/committees/judiciary/hju88394.000/hju88394_0f.htm (accessed March 20, 2010).

60. *United States v. Kincade*, 379 F.3d 813 (9th Cir. 2004).

61. Michael Berry and Joan Berry, "DNA Bill Will Bring Justice to Killers," *Atlanta-Journal Constitution*, February 15, 2010, http://www.ajc.com/opinion/dna-bill-will-bring-307084.html (accessed March 20, 2010).

62. Ibid.

63. Jason Mumpower, "The Johnia Berry Act: State Representative Jason Mumpower's Words," The Tennessean.com, http://www.johniaberry.org/2007_04_ 01_jbarc.html (accessed March 20, 2010).

64. *State v. Bartylla*, 755 N.W.2d 8, 15 (Minn. 2008).

65. *People v. Lakisha M.*, 882 N.E.2d 570 (Ill. 2008).

66. Matt Canham, "Father of Elizabeth Smart Pushes for Law Collecting DNA from Arrestees," *Salt Lake Tribune*, March 4, 2010, http://www.sltrib.com/justice/ci_14514081 (accessed March 19, 2010).

67. "Harry Teague's National 'Katie's Law' Passes House of Representatives with Bipartisan Support," http://teague.house.gov/index.php?option=com_content&task= view&id=609&Itemid=72 (accessed October 23, 2010).

68. "Make DNA Profiling Compulsory!!" http://www.facebook.com/group .php?gid=108330116097#!/group.php?gid=108330116097&v=walll (accessed October 23, 2010).

69. Jenny Hazan, "Double-Check That DNA," http://www.israel21c.org/technology/double-check-that-dna (accessed October 23, 2010).

70. David Ray Papke, "The American Courtroom Trial: Pop Culture, Courthouse Realities, and the Dream World of Justice," *South Texas Law Review* 40, no.4 (1999): 919–933.

71. Tom R. Tyler, "Viewing CSI and the Threshold of Guilt: Managing Truth and Justice in Reality and Fiction," *Yale Law Journal* 115 (2006): 1051–1085.

72. Michael Mann, "The 'CSI Effect': Better Jurors through Television and Science?" *Buffalo Public Interest Law Journal* 24 (2005): 211.

73. Allison Waldman, "'Maury' Producer Pins Success on Povich," TVweek .com, http://www.tvweek.com/news/2007/09/maury_producer_pins_success_on.php (accessed March 20, 2010).

74. Paternity Express, http://www.paternityexpress.com/education_center.html (accessed October 23, 2010).

75. Advanced Paternity, http://www.advancedpaternity.com/dna-tests.htm (accessed October 23, 2010).

76. "DNA Forensics at Fairfax Identity Labs—Personal DNA Profiling," Genetics Info, http://www.geneticsinfo.com/dna/dnaprofiling/ (accessed February 22, 2011).

77. "Personal DNA Profile Services," Fairfax Identity Laboratories, https://www .fairfaxidlab.com/global/services/personal-dna-profiles.aspx (accessed February 22, 2011).

78. "Personal DNA Profiling," Genetics Info, http://www.geneticsinfo.com/dna/ dnaprofiling/ (accessed October 23, 2010).

79. "Health: Home Test DNA Profile Kits," http://www.essortment.com/ lifestyle/healthhometest_skdx.htm (accessed October 23, 2010).

80. ID-Secure, http://www.id-secure.net/ (accessed October 23, 2010).

81. Galina Espinoza, "DNA Testing: The Ultimate ID for Your Child," NY Metroparents.com, http://www.nymetroparents.com/newarticle.cfm?colid=6896 (accessed March 20, 2010).

82. Stefan Timmermans, *Postmortem*, Chicago: University of Chicago Press, 2007.

83. "Diana Death a 'Tragic Accident,'" BBC News, December 14, 2006, http:// news.bbc.co.uk/2/hi/uk_news/6179275.stm (accessed October 27, 2008).

84. Gordon Rayner and Andrew Pierce, "Diana Inquest: William and Harry Welcome Verdict after Jury Blames Paparazzi and Paul, *The Telegraph*, April 8, 2008, http://www.telegraph.co.uk/news/newstopics/diana/1584297/Diana-inquest-William-and-Harry-welcome-verdict-after-jury-blames-paparazzi-and-Paul.html (accessed May 9, 2001).

CHAPTER 6

1. Melvinder Singh, "Divorce and the Media," DivorceMagazine.com, http://www .divorcemag.com/articles/News_and_Views/divorceandmedia.html (accessed October 24, 2010).

2. Christina Rowe, "Three Reasons to Throw Yourself a Divorce Party," Divorce360.com, http://www.divorce360.com/blogs/2007/10/26/christina-rowe/three-reasons-to-throw-yourself-a-divorce-party-blog-424 (accessed October 24, 2010).

3. Karla Zimmerman, "Happy Ending . . . to a Marriage?" http://www.milk wood.org/karla/divorce.html (accessed October 24, 2010).

4. "Relationship Obituaries," SexReally.com, http://www.sexreally.com/the-show/relationship-obituaries (accessed October 24, 2010).

5. "Web Site Allows Lovelorn to Bury a Relationship Gone Sour with an Obituary," http://www.foxnews.com/story/0,2933,330691,00.html (accessed October 24, 2010).

6. "Relationship Obituaries," First 30 Days, http://www.first30days.com/breaking-up/articles/relationship-obituaries.html (accessed October 24, 2010).

7. Relationship Obituaries, http://relationshipobit.com/obituary/show/768 (accessed October 16, 2008).

8. "How to Select Divorce Party Invitations," eHow.com, http://www.ehow.com/how_2061381_select-divorce-party-invitations.html (accessed December 2, 2008).

9. "Getting Closure: Throw Yourself a Divorce Theme Party," Divorce-support-and-care.com, http://www.divorce-support-and-care.com/divorcethemeparty.html (accessed August 22, 2008).

10. Darn Divorce, http://www.darndivorce.com/how-to-throw-a-divorce-party/ (accessed October 16, 2008).

11. "Divorce Cake," Coolest-birthday-cakes.com, http://www.coolest-birthday-cakes.com/divorce-cake-1.html (accessed October 16, 2008).

12. Ibid.

13. "Divorce Cake," Slashfood, http://www.slashfood.com/photos/divorce-cakes/639484/ (accessed October 16, 2008).

14. Heather Murtagh, "Finding Humor in Breaking Up," *Daily Journal: San Mateo*, http://www.smdailyjournal.com/article_preview.php?id=98532 (accessed October 22, 2008).

15. "Divorce Party Ex-Wife Voodoo Doll," Bachelorette.com, http://www.bachelorette.us.com/shop/product_info.php?products_id=638&osCsid=59b8084e1f02096a207c7d96d46b04bb (accessed October 16, 2008).

16. Jennifer DeMeritt, "Ideas, Tips, and Advice: How to Throw the Perfect Divorce Party," DivorceCandy.com, http://www.divorcecandy.com/concierge-services/article.cfm/view/ideas-tips-and-advice-how-to-throw-the-perfect-divorce-party (accessed June 17, 2010).

17. Bury the Past, http://www.burythepast.com/?page_id=2 (accessed April 20, 2007).

18. Wedding Ring Coffin, http://www.weddingringcoffin.com/ (accessed October 23, 2008).

19. Alexi Friedman, "When Love Dies, Bury It . . . the Wedding Ring That Is," http://www.nola.com/living/tp/index.ssf?/base/living8/118024774981950.xml&coll=1&thispage=1 (accessed April 20, 2008).

20. Ibid.

21. Wedding Ring Coffin.

22. "Good Grief: Cyber Cemetery Created for People to Bury Relationships Virtually: Exmarkstheplot.com," *PRLog Free Press Release*, http://www.prlog.org/10076976-good-grief-cyber-cemetery-created-for-people-to-bury-relationships-virtually-exmarkstheplot-com.html (accessed February 22, 2011).

23. Ex Marks the Plot, http://exmarkstheplot.mmediaweb.com/home.html (accessed February 22, 2011).

24. AshHoles.com, http://ashholes.com/ (accessed April 20, 2008).

25. "Relationship Closure and Recovery," Burythejerk.com, http://www.burythejerk.com/about.htm (accessed April 13, 2008).

26. Ibid.

27. "E-closure: The Official Definition," E-closure.com, http://e-closure.blogspot.com/2005/08/e-closure-official-definition.html#114644477931130540 (accessed April 13, 2008).

28. Report Your Ex, http://reportyourex.com/home/tag/revenge-on-your-ex (accessed October 26, 2010).

29. Owen Clark, "How to Make Your Ex Mad," http://www.howtodothings.com/family-relationships/how-to-make-your-ex-mad (accessed October 26, 2010).

30. Adam Russ, *The Revenge Seeker's Handbook: Everything You Need to Know about Getting Even*, http://www.amazon.com/Revenge-Seekers-Handbook-Adam-Russ/dp/186105775X (accessed November 11, 2008).

31. Ibid.

32. Ibid.

33. "Dead Flowers, Fish and Other Paybacks," The Payback.com, http://www.thepayback.com/getrevenge.html (accessed October 26, 2010).

34. "Catharsis Theory and Media Effects," Encyclopedia of Communication, http://encyclopedia.jrank.org/articles/pages/6455/Catharsis-Theory-and-Media-Effects.html (accessed June 10, 2010).

35. Alice Z. Cuneo, "SegaSoft Online Games Tap into Cultlike Mind-Set: Fictional Cause Aims to Channel the Urge to Kill; Could Draw Fire," Adage.com, April 7, 1997, http://adage.com/article?article_id=68665 (accessed June 10, 2010).

36. See B. J. Bushman, "Does Venting Anger Feed or Extinguish the Flame? Catharsis, Rumination, Distraction, Anger, and Aggressive Responding," *Personality and Social Psychology Bulletin* 28 (2002): 724–731; L. Berkowitz, "Frustration-Aggression Hypothesis: Examination and Reformulation," *Psychological Bulletin* 106 (1989): 59–73; D. M. Tice and R. F. Baumeister, "Controlling Anger: Self-Induced Emotion Change," in *Handbook of Mental Control*, ed. D. M. Wegner and J. Pennebaker, Englewood Cliffs, NJ: Prentice-Hall, 1993, 393–409.

37. Susan D. Boon, Vicki L. Deveau, and Alishia M. Alibhai, "Payback: The Parameters of Revenge in Romantic Relationships," *Journal of Social and Personal Relationships* 26, no. 6–7 (2009): 747–768.

38. Stephen Yoshimura, "Goals and Emotional Outcomes of Revenge Activities in Interpersonal Relationships," *Journal of Social and Personal Relationships* 24, no. 1 (2007): 87–98.

39. Kevin M. Carlsmith, Timothy D. Wilson, and Daniel T. Gilbert, "What Do We Know about Revenge?" *Journal of Personality and Social Psychology* 95, no. 6 (2008): 1316–1324.

40. T Dub Jackson, "How to Get Even with Your Ex Wife: Are the Rewards Worth the Risks?" http://ezinearticles.com/?How-to-Get-Even-With-Your-Ex-Wife-Are-the-Rewards-Worth-the-Risks?&id=2811117 (accessed June 10, 2010).

41. Jennifer DeMeritt, "How to Throw the Perfect Divorce Party," DivorceCandy.com, http://www.divorcecandy.com/concierge-services/article.cfm/view/how-to-throw-the-perfect-divorce-partyideas-tips-and-advice (accessed October 26, 2010).

42. Lisa Bower, "Throwing a Divorce Party," Life123.com, http://www.life123.com/relationships/divorce/divorce-advice/throwing-a-divorce-party.shtml (accessed June 17, 2010).

43. Alastair Taylor, "Man Stabs Ex-Wife to Death at Divorce Party," *The Sun* (London), April 7, 2010, http://www.news.com.au/world/man-stabs-ex-wife-to-death-at-divorce-party/story-e6frfkyi-1225850952964 (accessed June 17, 2010).

CHAPTER 7

1. Sheila Weller, "Call It Courage: Her Life after a Terrible Crime," *Redbook*, June 1, 1997, 116–123.

2. Lois Romano, "With Death, Hope That Life Goes On: On the Eve of an Execution, Victims Yearn for Peace at Last," *Washington Post*, August 8, 1996, A1.

3. Ibid.

4. Ibid.

5. Richard Jerome, "No Reprieve," *People*, August 26, 1996, 47.

6. *Ake v. State*, 778 P.2d 460 (Okla. Crim. App. 1989).

7. Ibid.

8. Closure has emerged as a powerful new framework for talking about social problems and a contemporary example of what scholars have identified as cultural resources, cultural narrations, moral vocabularies, emotional discourses, or cultural themes. See page 173n6 for a list of references that explain these concepts. In particular, closure has become a popular rhetorical resource in the cultural toolkit (e.g., Ann Swidler, "Culture in Action," *American Sociological Review* 51 [1986]: 273–286) of both death penalty advocates and abolitionists and has proved useful for doing social problems emotion work (e.g., Arlene Hochschild, "Emotion Work, Feeling Rules, and Social Structure," *American Journal of Sociology* 85 [1979]: 551–575; Loseke, "Ethos, Pathos, and Social Problems").

9. Bo Emerson, "Witnesses to the Execution: From Behind a One-Way Window, Victims' Families Find Redemption," *Atlanta Journal-Constitution*, May 13, 2001, 1M.

10. Romano, "With Death, Hope That Life Goes On," A1.

11. Emerson, "Witnesses to the Execution," 1M.

12. Romano, "With Death, Hope That Life Goes On," A1.

13. The victims' rights movement benefited from a growing interest in more punitive criminal justice policies and a conservative law and order administration. Within this political culture, it is not surprising that President Ronald Reagan ushered in several presidential and legislative events that elevated the growing crime victims' rights movement. In 1981, Reagan proclaimed the week of April 19 "National Victims' Rights Week." In 1982, Reagan appointed the President's Task Force on Victims of Crime to examine and recommend improvements in how victims of crime are treated. See Frank Carrington and George Nicholson, "Victims' Rights: An Idea Whose Time Has Come—Five Years Later: The Maturing of an Idea," *Pepperdine Law Review* 17 (1989): 1–18; David L. Roland, "Progress in the Victim Reform Movement: No Longer the 'Forgotten Victim,'" *Pepperdine Law Review* 17 (1989): 35–58. Also in 1982, Congress passed the Federal Victim and Witness Protection Act, which included victim restitution, use of victim impact statements at sentencing in federal cases, and victim protection (Roland, "Progress in the Victim Reform Movement"). Most states now have "victims' bill of rights" that focus on the rights of victims to participate in the criminal justice process (Roland, "Progress in the Victim Reform Movement";

Rachel King, "Why a Victims' Rights Constitutional Amendment Is a Bad Idea: Practical Experiences from Crime Victims," *University of Cincinnati Law Review* 68, no. 2 [2000]: 357–402; Robert P. Mosteller, "Victim Impact Evidence: Hard to Find the Real Rules," *Cornell Law Review* 88, no. 2 [2003]: 543–554). A victims' rights national constitutional amendment was first introduced in 1996 and continues to be pushed by victims' rights advocates (see Lynne Henderson, "Co-opting Compassion: The Federal Victims' Rights Amendment," *St. Thomas Law Review* 10, no. 3 [1998]: 579–606; King, "Why a Victims' Rights Constitutional Amendment Is a Bad Idea").

14. In *Booth v. Maryland* (1987), the Supreme Court considered for the first time whether or not the Eighth Amendment prohibits a capital sentencing jury from considering victim impact evidence. In the *Booth* decision, the Supreme Court argued that evidence from victim impact statements was prejudicial. When deciding sentencing, the jury should only consider (1) the defendant's background and record and (2) the circumstances of the crime (see Jennifer Culbert, "The Sacred Name of Pain: The Role of Victim Impact Evidence in Death Penalty Sentencing Decisions," in *Pain, Death, and the Law*, ed. Austin Sarat, Ann Arbor: University of Michigan Press, 2001, 103–135). Two years later, in *South Carolina v. Gathers* (1989), the Court ruled on whether or not the prosecutor should have argued that the defendant deserved the death penalty because of the victim's character. The Supreme Court ruled that characteristics about the victim that the defendant did not know ahead of time had no bearing on the crime and should not be allowed for sentencing consideration (Culbert, "The Sacred Name of Pain"; John H. Blume, "Ten Years of *Payne*: Victim Impact Evidence in Capital Cases," *Cornell Law Review* 88 [2003]: 257, 268).

15. The U.S. Supreme Court has identified three types of victim impact information: (1) evidence of the victim's unique personal characteristics, (2) evidence of the crime's impact on the victim's family and community, and (3) the victim's sentencing opinion (see Douglas E. Beloof, "Constitutional Implications of Crime Victims as Participants," *Cornell Law Review* 88 [2003]: 282–298). For homicide cases, the "victim" who is providing testimony is actually a family member of the victim or often described as a survivor. The *Payne* decision allowed the first two types of statements and left unclear the admissibility of victim or survivor sentencing opinions (Beloof, "Constitutional Implications of Crime Victims as Participants").

16. Jennifer Culbert argues that it was a combination of the change in personnel on the Court between 1989 and 1991 along with growing public pressure from the victims' rights movement that led to the Court's reversal on victim impact statements. See Culbert, "The Sacred Name of Pain."

17. Philip Talbert identifies four types of victim impact evidence: (1) victim's statements about the crime, (2) statements by relatives or close friends of the victim about the victim, (3) statements by family members of victim about the emotional impact on themselves, and (4) statements made by relatives and close friends about their opinions of the crime and defendant, and what punishment is deserved. See Philip Talbert, "The Relevance of Victim Impact Statements to the Criminal Sentencing Decision," *U.C.L.A. Law Review* 36 (1988): 199–232.

18. "Crime Victim Wrote State's Tough Law," *Deseret News*, August 8, 1996, http://archive.deseretnews.com/archive/print/506293/CRIME-VICTIM-WROTE-STATES-TOUGH-LAW.html (accessed February 27, 2009).

19. Personal interview with Brooks Douglass, November 18, 2010.

20. In April of that year, the first family members to witness an execution under Brooks Douglass' sponsored legislation did so by closed-circuit television.

21. Victoria Loe, "Oklahoma Siblings Could Be First to Witness Execution: Victims' Rights Law Author Is Crime Survivor," *Dallas Morning News* (republished in *Seattle Times*), http://community.seattletimes.nwsource.com/archive/?date=19960808&slug=2343211 (accessed October 14, 2008).

22. Weller, "Call It Courage," 123.

23. Loe, "Oklahoma Siblings Could Be First to Witness Execution."

24. Brooks Douglass, "Why I Want to Watch a Killer Die," *USA Today*, April 15, 1996, A19.

25. Romano, "With Death, Hope That Life Goes On," A1.

26. Jerome, "No Reprieve," 49.

27. Lois Romano, "Execution Closes a Tragic Circle: Douglass Children Watch Their Parents' Killer Die," *Washington Post*, August 10, 1996, A3.

28. Ibid.

29. Jerome, "No Reprieve," 49.

30. Romano, "Execution Closes a Tragic Circle," A3.

31. Ibid.

32. Personal interview with Brooks Douglass.

33. "Does Revenge Bring Closure?" *San Francisco Examiner*, February 7, 1999, available at http://www.fdp.dk/uk/closure.htm (accessed February 24, 2011).

34. Personal interview with Brooks Douglass.

35. "Does Revenge Bring Closure?"

36. Jody Burgin, "Anger Antidote," Lifeline, www.menslife.org/downloads/hmml_life_fal04.pdf (accessed November 13, 2006).

37. Phil Boatwright, "*Heaven's Rain* Depicts Murder, Forgiveness," *Baptist Press*, September 29, 2010, http://www.bpnews.net/BPFirstPerson.asp?ID=33775 (accessed November 22, 2010).

38. Ibid.

39. "Does Revenge Bring Closure?"

40. Tanya Connor, "Committee Hears Death Penalty," *Catholic Free Press*, March 26, 1999, http://www.macathconf.org/DP%20hearing.htm (accessed January 27, 2007).

41. For a fascinating discussion of McVeigh's case, the spectacle of executions, and consumerism, read Marita Sturken's *Tourists of History: Memory, Kitsch, and Consumerism from Oklahoma City to Ground Zero*, Durham, NC: Duke University Press, 2007.

42. Emerson, "Witnesses to the Execution," 1M.

43. Ibid.

44. "Brooks Douglass Recounts His Experience as a Witness at the Execution of the Man Who Murdered His Parents," *Today*, June 11, 2001.

45. Darrell Giles, "Grief Will Continue, Bombing Survivors Warned," *Herald Sun*, April 20, 2001, 17.

46. Dante Chinni and Peter Grier, "For Survivors, Execution Isn't the End," *Christian Science Monitor*, June 11, 2001, 1.

47. These objections fly in the face of the legal challenges, such as those found in *Baze v. Rees*, that claim poorly executed lethal injections can lead to needless pain and suffering. A main difference in these views is that some victims' family members object to what *appears* to be a serene death while the legal challenges question whether or not offenders are at times improperly anesthetized and thus able to feel pain but paralyzed to the point where they cannot respond.

48. Kerry Lauerman, "Killing as 'Closure,'" Salon.com, http://archive.salon.com (accessed June 7, 2005).

49. Marilyn Peterson Armour, "Journey of Family Members of Homicide Victims," *American Journal of Orthopsychiatry* 72, no. 3 (2002): 372–382; Marla Domino and Marcus T. Boccaccini, "Doubting Thomas: Should Family Members of Victims Watch Executions?" *Law and Psychology Review* 24 (2000): 59–75; Robert Mosteller, "Victim Impact Evidence: Hard to Find the Real Rules," *Cornell Law Review* 88, no. 2 (2003): 543–554.

50. Michael L. Goodwin, "An Eyeful for an Eye—An Argument against Allowing the Families of Murder Victims to View Executions," *Brandeis Journal of Family Law* 36 (1997): 585.

51. Marilyn Peterson Armour and Mark S. Umbreit, "The Ultimate Penal Sanction and Closure for Survivors of Homicide Victims," *Marquette Law Review* 91 (2007): 381, 398.

52. Susannah Sheffer, Kate Lowenstein, and Renny Cushing, *Not in Our Name: Murder Victims' Families Speak Out Against the Death Penalty*, Cambridge, MA: Murder Victims' Families for Reconciliation, 2003, 26.

53. Jeanne Bishop, "Grief, Closure, and Forgiveness," Pew Forum, http://pewforum.org/deathpenalty/resources/reader/27.php3 (accessed January 25, 2007).

54. Claudia Dreifus, "Forgiving the Unforgivable," http://www.willsworld.com/~mvfhr/forgivingunforgivable.htm (accessed February 24, 2009).

55. Ibid.

56. Renny Cushing, "Not In Our Name: Homicide Survivors Speak Out against the Death Penalty," joint presentation by Renny Cushing and Bud Welch to the Human Rights Initiative, Kennedy School of Government, Harvard University, March 16, 1999, http://www.willsworld.com/~mvfhr/budrenny.htm (accessed February 24, 2009).

57. Sheffer, Lowenstein, and Cushing, *Not in Our Name*, 30.

58. "Frequently Asked Questions," Daniel Mauser memorial web page, http://www.danielmauser.com/FAQs.html (accessed August 15, 2007).

59. "Women at the Top," Law.com, http://www.law.com/special/professionals/nlj/women_on_top/40_litigators.html#Siegler (accessed January 27, 2009).

60. Miya Shay, "Candidate for DA Explains Her Comments," ABC News, http://abclocal.go.com/ktrk/story?section=news/local&id=5886140 (accessed January 27, 2009).

61. Kelly Siegler, "There's No Such Thing as 'Closure,'" Women in Crime Ink, http://womenincrimeink.blogspot.com/2008/06/theres-no-such-thing-as-closure.html (accessed September 23, 2008).

62. Mark Bennett, "Is Only Kelly Siegler Man Enough to Tell the Truth?" Defending People, http://bennettandbennett.com/blog/2008/06/is-only-kelly-siegler-man-enough-to-tell-the-truth.html (accessed January 27, 2009).

63. There have been many studies on death penalty rhetoric. See, for example, Hugo Bedau, *Death Is Different: Studies in the Morality, Law, and Politics of Capital Punishment*, Boston: Northeastern University Press, 1987; Hugo Bedau, "The Present Situation of the Death Penalty in the United States," in *Death Penalty: Beyond Abolition*, ed. Roger G. Hood and Robert Badinter, Strasbourg, France: Council of Europe Publishing, 2004, 205–214; John F. Galliher, Larry W. Koch, David Patrick Keys, and Teresa J. Guess, *America without the Death Penalty: States Leading the Way*, Boston: Northeastern University Press, 2002; Herbert Haines, "Flawed Executions, the Anti–Death Penalty Movement, and the Politics of Capital Punishment," *Social Problems* 39 (1992): 301–314; Herbert Haines, *Against Capital Punishment: The Anti–Death Penalty Movement in America, 1972–1994*, New York: Oxford University Press, 1996; Craig Haney and Susan Greene, "Capital Constructions: Newspaper Reporting in Death Penalty Cases," *Analyses of Social Issues and Public Policy* 4, no. 1 (2004): 129–151; Jeffrey L. Kirchmeier, "Another Place beyond Here: The Death Penalty Moratorium Movement in the United States," *University of Colorado Law Review* 73 (2002): 1; Mona Lynch, "Capital Punishment as Moral Imperative: Pro-Death-Penalty Discourse on the Internet," *Punishment and Society* 4, no. 2 (2002): 213–236; Austin Sarat, "Innocence, Error, and the 'New Abolitionism': A Commentary," *Criminology and Public Policy* 4, no. 1 (February 4, 2005): 45–54. However, only a few have included the role of closure in the debate; most notable are Susan Bandes, "When Victims Seek Closure: Forgiveness, Vengeance and the Role of Government," *Fordham Urban Law Journal* 27, no. 5 (2000): 1599–1606; Vik Kanwar, "Capital Punishment as 'Closure': The Limits of a Victim-Centered Jurisprudence," *New York University Review of Law and Social Change* 27, no. 2–3 (2001): 215–255; Franklin Zimring, *The Contradictions of American Capital Punishment*, New York: Oxford University Press, 2003. All three of these scholars criticize the use of closure as a justification for the death penalty. Franklin Zimring shows that prior to 1989 closure did not appear in death penalty stories in the United States, but by 2001 there were more than 500 stories per year mentioning closure and capital punishment; see Zimring, *The Contradictions of American Capital Punishment*, 60. Vik Kanwar argues that "the cultural production of a feeling of closure" for victims has become an independent justification for the death penalty; see Kanwar, "Capital Punishment as 'Closure,'" 216. Kanwar and Bandes both discuss how victims seek closure in different ways: some through mercy and others through vengeance.

64. Stuart Banner, *The Death Penalty: An American History*, Cambridge, MA: Harvard University Press, 2002.

65. Hugo Bedau, *Killing as Punishment: Reflections on the Death Penalty in America*, Evanston, IL: Northwestern University Press, 2004, 160.

66. Michael L. Radelet and Hugo Adam Bedau, "The Execution of the Innocent," *Law and Contemporary Problems* 61 (1998): 105–124.

67. *Callins v. Collins*, 510 U.S. 1141 (1994).

68. James D. Unnever and Francis T. Cullin, "Executing the Innocent and Support for Capital Punishment: Implications for Public Policy," *Criminology and Public Policy* 4, no. 1 (2005): 3–32.

69. James R. Acker, "The Death Penalty: An American History," *Contemporary Justice Review* 6, no. 2 (2003): 169–186; Robert M. Bohm, *Deathquest II*, 2nd ed., Cincinnati: Anderson, 2003.

70. Michel Foucault, *The History of Sexuality*, vol. 1, London: Penguin, 1978; Ann Swidler, "Cultural Power and Social Movements," in *Social Movements and Culture*, ed. Hank Johnston and Bert Klandermans, Minneapolis: University of Minnesota Press, 1995, 25–40.

71. For participants in the criminal justice system, the closure story poses another problem: many people are unwilling or unable to fit their experience to the story. Participants may be forced to adapt themselves to institutional expectations, to develop a "legal self." They have to fit a particular story in order to gain access. Just as for stalking victims seeking legal protection and divorce clients seeking to demonstrate their morality, participants in death penalty cases need to follow feeling rules to gain the assistance of other actors in the legal process.

72. Judith W. Kay, "Murder Victims' Families for Reconciliation," in *Handbook of Restorative Justice*, ed. Dennis Sullivan and Larry Tifft, London: Routledge, 2006, 231.

73. Susan Bandes, "Victim Standing," *Utah Law Review* 2 (1999): 331–347; Richard Burr, "Litigating with Victim Impact Testimony: The Serendipity That Has Come from *Payne v. Tennessee*," *Cornell Law Review* 88 (2003): 517–529; Kanwar, "Capital Punishment as 'Closure'"; Bruce Shapiro, "Victims' Rights—and Wrongs," Salon.com, http://www.salon.com/june97/news/news970613.html.

74. Bandes, "Victim Standing"; Shapiro, "Victims' Rights—and Wrongs."

75. R. R. Cushing and S. Shaffer, *Dignity Denied: The Experience of Murder Victims' Family Members Who Oppose the Death Penalty*, Cambridge, MA: Murder Victims' Families for Reconciliation, 2002, 6.

76. Ibid., 7. This concern broadens when prosecutors are also given the discretion to deny opportunity to victims who do not fit the ideal image of a victim and thus would not be convincing enough.

77. Personal interview with Brooks Douglass.

78. Ibid.

79. Ibid.

80. "*Heaven's Rain* Feature Film," http://www.freihofercasting.com/index .php?pageID=6231&print_view=true& (accessed October 28, 2010).

81. Carla Hinton, "Feeling 'Heaven's Rain,'" NewsOK, http://iphone.newsok .com/s?a=3444152&f=life&p=1&s=16 (accessed October 28, 2010).

82. Carla Hinton, "Former State Senator Shares and Bares His Soul in 'Heaven's Rain,'" NewsOK, http://www.newsok.com/former-state-senator-shares-and-bares-his-soul-in-heavens-rain/article/3494559?custom_click=pod_headline_ae (accessed November 2, 2010).

CHAPTER 8

1. Fred W. Baker III, "Pentagon 9/11 Memorial Ensures a Nation Will Not Forget," U.S. Department of Defense, http://www.defense.gov/news/newsarticle .aspx?id=51134 (accessed February 3, 2010).

2. "Pentagon Memorial Remembers 9/11 Attacks," ABC News, http://abcnews .go.com/Politics/story?id=5777731&page=2 (accessed February 3, 2010).

3. Mike Mount, "Pentagon 9/11 Memorial Honors Victims in Symbols, Concrete," CNN.com, http://www.cnn.com/2008/US/09/11/pentagon.memorial/index.html (accessed February 3, 2010).

4. Lise Fisher, "State Maintains Hundreds of Memorials on Roadsides," TheLedger.com, November 30, 2004, http://www.theledger.com/apps/pbcs.dll/article?AID=/2004 (accessed March 5, 2009).

5. Tony Walter, *On Bereavement: The Culture of Grief*, Maidenhead, UK: Open University Press, 1999.

6. Dennis Klass, Phyllis R. Silverman, and Steven L. Nickman, *Continuing Bonds: New Understandings of Grief*, Washington, DC: Taylor and Francis, 1996.

7. I'm not saying that all grief scholars *use* closure; in fact, many of them do not like the term as discussed in chapter 3.

8. Gail Burwa, Chaplain, WTC Families for a Proper Burial, http://www.wtcfamiliesforproperburial.com/index_files/Page580.htm (accessed April 9, 2010).

9. Anthony Gardner and Diane Horning, "9/11 Victims Should Not Be Left in the Fresh Kills Dump, Families Say," NYDailyNews.com, http://www.nydailynews.com/opinions/2008/02/24/2008–02-24_911_victims_should_not_be_left_in_the_fr.html (accessed April 9, 2010).

10. Joe Pompeo, "The Remains of Fresh Kills," *New York Press*, http://www.nypress.com/article-16316-the-remains-of-fresh-kills.html (accessed April 9, 2010).

11. Anemona Hartocollis, "Landfill Has 9/11 Remains, Medical Examiner Wrote," *New York Times*, http://query.nytimes.com/gst/fullpage.html?res=950CEEDA1530F937A15750C0A9619C8B63 (accessed April 10, 2010).

12. "9/11 Families Argue to Remove Ashes from Fresh Kills Landfill," Silive.com, http://www.silive.com/westshore/index.ssf/2009/12/911_families_argue_to_remove_a.html (accessed April 10, 2010).

13. Martha Neil, "9/11 Rubble Can Stay in Landfill, Federal Judge Says," *ABA Journal*, http://www.abajournal.com/news/article/9_11_rubble_can_stay_in_landfill_federal_judge_says/ (accessed April 10, 2010).

14. Edward Skyler, "Memorandum: WTC Human Remains Recovery Update," http://www.where-to-turn.org/phpBB2/viewtopic.php?t=50493&sid=c53315a065b50d38b6a90e6369d3aa47 (accessed February 25, 2011).

15. "Forensic Identification of 9/11 Victims Ends," ABC News, http://abcnews.go.com/WNT/story?id=525937&page=1 (accessed April 10, 2010).

16. Sabrina Jaszi, "City's Still Looking for WTC Remains," Gothamist.com, http://gothamist.com/2010/02/01/were_still_not_done_looking_for_wtc.php (accessed April 9, 2010).

17. Scott Sarvay, "New Search for 9/11 Remains," Indiana News Center, http://www.indianasnewscenter.com/news/local/89395447.html (accessed April 10, 2010).

18. Eric Fiegel and Kate Bolduan, "An Emotional Fight over Land for Flight 93 Memorial," CNN.com, http://www.cnn.com/2009/POLITICS/05/29/flight.dispute/index.html (accessed February 3, 2010).

19. Vicki Rock, "Law Change Allows Eminent Domain at Flight 93 Crash Site," *Daily American*, http://www.dailyamerican.com/articles/2008/10/15/news/news/news115.txt (accessed February 3, 2010).

20. Ibid.

21. Sean Hamill, "Land Deal Is Reached for a 9/11 Memorial," *New York Times*, http://www.nytimes.com/2009/01/18/us/18memorial.html?_r=1&hp (accessed February 3, 2010).

22. Charles O. Collins and Charles D. Rhine, "Roadside Memorials," *Omega* 47, no. 3 (2003): 221–244.

23. Ibid.

24. C. H. Paquette, "Roadside Memorials," Flickr, http://www.flickr.com/photos/chpaquette/sets/72157600170462825 (accessed March 5, 2009).

25. "Roadside Memorials Become Touchy Issue Because They're Illegal," Vindy .com, http://www4.vindy.com/content/national_world (accessed March 5, 2009).

26. Erika Doss, "Spontaneous Memorials and Contemporary Modes of Mourning in America," *Material Religion: The Journal of Objects, Art and Belief* 2, no. 3 (2006): 294–319.

27. "Roadside Memorials Become Touchy Issue Because They're Illegal."

28. John P. Ferre, "Last Words: Death and Public Self-Expression," in *Quoting God*, ed. Claire Badaracco, Waco, TX: Baylor University Press, 2005, 136.

29. Dave Downey, "Caltrans Apologizes, Says Highways Wrong Place for Memorials," *North County Times*, September 13, 2007, http://www.nctimes .com/articles/2007/09/13/news/sandiego/22_28_089_12_07.txt (accessed February 5, 2009).

30. Erika Doss, *Memorial Mania: Public Feeling in America*, Chicago: University of Chicago Press, 2010, 87.

31. Ibid.

32. Brooks Jarosz, "Roadside Memorials Standardized in West Virginia," WSAZ Channel 3, http://www.wsaz.com/home/headlines/81614972.html (accessed February 4, 2010).

33. "Roadside Memorials Not Catching On," http://www.wsaz.com/home/headlines/95261524.html (accessed June 2, 2010).

34. Doss, "Spontaneous Memorials and Contemporary Modes of Mourning in America," 303.

35. Erin Madigan, "Safety Concerns Fail to Curb Roadside Memorials," Stateline.org, http://www.stateline.org/live/ViewPage.action?siteNodeId=136&languageId=1&contentId=15276 (accessed February 4, 2010).

36. "Remove Roadside Memorials," *Atheist Activist*, http://mcgowanbarry.com/AtheistActivist/Roadside.html (accessed February 25, 2011).

37. Paul Hammel, "Memorials Now under Scrutiny," World-Herald News Service, http://www.nptelegraph.com/articles/2010/01/30/news/state/60005384.txt (accessed February 4, 2010).

38. UnbornMemorials.com, http://www.unbornmemorials.com (accessed October 29, 2008).

39. National Memorial for the Unborn, http://www.memorialfortheunborn.org/history.htm (accessed January 8, 2009).

40. Ibid.

41. "Welcome," Kentucky Memorial for the Unborn, http://www.kymemorialfortheunborn.org/ (accessed January 8, 2009).

42. "A Place for Healing," Florida Memorial for the Unborn, http://www.floridababymemorial.com/ (accessed January 9, 2009).

43. UnbornMemorials.com.

44. In 1998, Jonathan Dube wrote an article for *Washington Monthly* discussing postabortion counseling politics. His description of what he calls pro-life counseling groups reflects much of the rhetoric on web pages and in news stories about memorials for the unborn.

45. Dana Goldstein, "The Abortion Counseling Conundrum," *American Prospect* online edition, June 30, 2008, http://www.prospect.org/cs/articles?article=the_abortion_counseling_conundrum (accessed January 10, 2009).

46. Julie Redman, "Letter from Planned Parenthood," http://www.ppaction.org/plannedparenthoodlam/noticedescription.tcl?newsletter_id=2902061 (accessed January 9, 2009).

47. Pro-Choice Resources, Emerge, http://www.prochoiceresources.org/emerge.php (accessed January 9, 2009).

48. William Saletan, "'Safe, Legal, and Never': Hillary Clinton's Anti-Abortion Strategy," *Slate*, January 26, 2005.

49. Naomi Wolf, "Our Bodies, Our Souls: Rethinking Pro-Choice Rhetoric," *New Republic*, October 16, 1995.

50. Katharyne Mitchell, "Monuments, Memorials, and the Politics of Memory," *Urban Geography* 24 (2003): 443.

51. Ibid.

52. Kirk Savage, *Monument Wars: Washington D.C., the National Mall, and the Transformation of the Memorial Landscape*, Berkeley: University of California Press, 2009, 267.

53. Erika Doss, "Death, Art and Memory in the Public Sphere: The Visual and Material Culture of Grief in Contemporary America," *Mortality* 7, no. 1 (2002): 63–82.

54. Savage, *Monument Wars*, 277.

55. Doss, "Death, Art and Memory in the Public Sphere," 66.

56. For an in-depth discussion on how material objects at memorials are treated as sacred objects in need of preservation, see Doss, *Memorial Mania*. Also, for more information on terrorism, memorials, and consumerism, see Marita Sturken, *Tourists of History: Memory, Kitsch, and Consumerism from Oklahoma City to Ground Zero*, Durham, NC: Duke University Press, 2007.

57. Catesby Leigh, "The Unbearable Lightness of the Pentagon Memorial," *Weekly Standard*, May 29, 2006, http://hnn.us/roundup/entries/26166.html (accessed September 13, 2008).

58. David Dunlap, "Display of Names at Trade Center Memorial Is a Painstaking Process," *New York Times*, March 23, 2009, http://www.nytimes.com/2009/03/24/nyregion/24names.html?_r=2 (accessed February 21, 2010).

59. "Names Arrangement," National 9/11 Memorial, http://www.national911memorial.org/site/PageServer?pagename=New_Memorial_NA (accessed November 2, 2010).

60. Andrew Goldstein, "The Victims: Never Again," Time.com, http://www.time.com/time/magazine/article/0,9171,992874,00.html?promoid=googlep (accessed June 21, 2008).

61. Doss, "Spontaneous Memorials and Contemporary Modes of Mourning in America," 311.

62. Bud Hunt, "Tearing Down Memorials Will Never Bring Closure," Rocky Mountain Collegian online, http://media.www.collegian.com/media/storage/paper 864/news/1999/09/30/UndefinedSection/Tearing.Down.Memorials.Will.Never .Bring.Closure-1691004.shtml (accessed February 5, 2009).

63. Valerie Richardson, "Columbine 'Memorial' Languishes as Parents Sue over Artwork," Insight on the News, http://findarticles.com/p/articles/mi_m1571/ is_48_17/ai_81392000/ (accessed February 5, 2010).

64. Charles Haynes, "School's Handling of Memorial Tiles Adds Sadness to Columbine Tragedy," FreedomForum.org, http://www.freedomforum.org/templates/ document.asp?documentID=17470 (accessed February 5, 2009).

65. "High Court Refuses to Consider Fight over Columbine Memorial," FreedomForum.org, http://www.freedomforum.org/templates/document.asp?docu mentID=17453 (accessed February 5, 2009).

66. "Four Months Later, Columbine Re-Opens," USA Today, http://www .usatoday.com/news/index/colo/colo177.htm (accessed June 21, 2008).

67. Columbine Memorial, http://www.columbinememorial.org/ (accessed June 10, 2009).

68. Dave Maddox, "Virginia Tech Tragedy Echoes in Columbine Community as Judge Orders 20-Year Wait for Killer Information," http://www.associatedcon tent.com/article/219293/virginia_tech_tragedy_echoes_in_columbine.html?cat=8 (accessed June 21, 2008).

69. Ann Schrader, "Columbine Dedication Today," Denver Post, http://www .denverpost.com/ci_6953472 (accessed June 21, 2008).

70. Associated Press, "Columbine School Shooting Memorial Opens," FoxNews .com, http://www.foxnews.com/story/0,2933,297676,00.html (accessed January 8, 2008).

71. Tim Chase, "Columbine Memorial Opens," Denverpost.com, September 22, 2007, http://www.denverpostphotoblog.com/2007/09/22/columbine-memorial-opens (accessed June 21, 2008).

72. "Brian Rohrbough's Inscription on the Columbine Memorial," Rocky Mountain News, September 21, 2007, http://www.rockymountainnews.com/news/ 2007/sep/21/brian-rohrboughs-inscription-on-the-columbine/ (accessed February 5, 2009).

73. "Columbine School Shooting Memorial Opens," FoxNews.com, http://www .foxnews.com/story/0,2933,297676,00.html (accessed February 5, 2009).

74. Cassie Hewlings, "Quiet Blooms after Memorial's Opening," Denverpost .com, September 23, 2007, http://www.denverpost.com/coloradocorporatestatements/ ci_6972640 (accessed February 5, 2009).

75. Robert Weller, "Foundation Hopes to Build Memorial to Columbine Dead," Oakland Tribune, April 20, 2003, http://findarticles.com/p/articles/mi_qn4176/ is_20030420/ai_n14550066 (accessed February 5, 2009).

76. For in-depth coverage of how the media covered the attacks of 9/11, see Brian Monahan, The Shock of the News: Media Coverage and the Making of 9/11, New York: New York University Press, 2010.

77. Doss, "Death, Art and Memory in the Public Sphere," 71.

78. Again, I refer you to Doss, *Memorial Mania*, for a longer discussion on which tragedies received memorials and which ones were publicly forgotten.

CHAPTER 9

1. The name has been changed.

Bibliography

Acker, James R. "The Death Penalty: An American History." *Contemporary Justice Review* 6, no. 2 (2003): 169–186.

Adler, Jonathan M., and Michael J. Poulin. "The Political Is Personal: Narrating 9/11 and Psychological Well-Being." *Journal of Personality* 77, no. 4 (2009): 903–932.

Armour, Marilyn Peterson, and Mark S. Umbreit. "The Ultimate Penal Sanction and Closure for Survivors of Homicide Victims." *Marquette Law Review* 91 (2007): 381, 398.

Bandes, Susan. "Victim Standing." *Utah Law Review* 2 (1999): 331–347.

———. "When Victims Seek Closure: Forgiveness, Vengeance and the Role of Government." *Fordham Urban Law Journal* 27, no. 5 (2000): 1599–1606.

Banner, Stuart. *The Death Penalty: An American History.* Cambridge, MA: Harvard University Press, 2002.

Bedau, Hugo. *Death Is Different: Studies in the Morality, Law, and Politics of Capital Punishment.* Boston: Northeastern University Press, 1987.

———. *Killing as Punishment: Reflections on the Death Penalty in America.* Evanston, IL: Northwestern University Press, 2004.

———. "The Present Situation of the Death Penalty in the United States." In *Death Penalty: Beyond Abolition*, ed. Roger G. Hood and Robert Badinter, 205–214. Strasbourg, France: Council of Europe Publishing, 2004.

Beike, Denise, and Erin Wirth-Beaumont. "Psychological Closure as a Memory Phenomenon." *Memory* 13, no. 6 (2005): 574–593.

Beloof, Douglas E. "Constitutional Implications of Crime Victims as Participants." *Cornell Law Review* 88 (2003): 282–298.

Berkowitz, L. "Frustration-Aggression Hypothesis: Examination and Reformulation." *Psychological Bulletin* 106 (1989): 59–73.

Berns, Nancy. *Framing the Victim: Domestic Violence, Media and Social Problems.* Hawthorne, NY: Aldine de Gruyter, 2004.

Best, Joel. "Rhetoric in Claims-Making." *Social Problems* 34 (1987): 101–121.

———. *Threatened Children: Rhetoric and Concern about Child-Victims.* Chicago: University of Chicago Press, 1990.

———. *Random Violence: How We Talk about New Crimes and New Victims.* Berkeley: University of California Press, 1999.

Blume, John H. "Ten Years of *Payne*: Victim Impact Evidence in Capital Cases." *Cornell Law Review* 88 (2003): 257, 268.

Bohm, Robert M. *Deathquest II.* 2nd ed. Cincinnati: Anderson, 2003.

Bonanno, George. *The Other Side of Sadness: What the New Science of Bereavement Tells Us about Life after a Loss.* New York: Basic Books, 2009.

Boon, Susan D., Vicki L. Deveau, and Alishia M. Alibhai. "Payback: The Parameters of Revenge in Romantic Relationships." *Journal of Social and Personal Relationships* 26, no. 6–7 (2009): 747–768.

Boss, Pauline. "Ambiguous Loss Research, Theory, and Practice: Reflections after 9/11." *Journal of Marriage and Family* 66, no. 3 (2004): 551–566.

———. *Loss, Trauma, and Resilience: Therapeutic Work with Ambiguous Loss.* New York: Norton, 2006.

Breen, Lauren, and Moira O'Conner. "The Fundamental Paradox in the Grief Literature: A Critical Reflection." *Omega* 55, no. 3 (2007): 199–218.

Burr, Richard. "Litigating with Victim Impact Testimony: The Serendipity That Has Come from *Payne v. Tennessee*." *Cornell Law Review* 88 (2003): 517–529.

Bushman, B. J. "Does Venting Anger Feed or Extinguish the Flame? Catharsis, Rumination, Distraction, Anger, and Aggressive Responding." *Personality and Social Psychology Bulletin* 28 (2002): 724–731.

Carlsmith, Kevin M., Timothy D. Wilson, and Daniel T. Gilbert. "What Do We Know about Revenge?" *Journal of Personality and Social Psychology* 95, no. 6 (2008): 1316–1324.

Carrington, Frank, and George Nicholson. "Victims' Rights: An Idea Whose Time Has Come—Five Years Later: The Maturing of an Idea." *Pepperdine Law Review* 17 (1989): 1–18.

Conrad, Peter. *The Medicalization of Society: On the Transformation of Human Conditions into Treatable Disorders.* Baltimore: Johns Hopkins University Press, 2007.

Conrad, Peter, and Joseph W. Schneider. *Deviance and Medicalization: From Badness to Sickness.* Philadelphia: Temple University Press, 1992.

Culbert, Jennifer L. "The Sacred Name of Pain: The Role of Victim Impact Evidence in Death Penalty Sentencing Decisions." In *Pain, Death, and the Law,* ed. Austin Sarat, 103–135. Ann Arbor: University of Michigan Press, 2001.

Cushing, R. R., and S. Shaffer. *Dignity Denied: The Experience of Murder Victims' Family Members Who Oppose the Death Penalty.* Cambridge, MA: Murder Victims' Families for Reconciliation, 2002.

Doss, Erika. "Death, Art and Memory in the Public Sphere: The Visual and Material Culture of Grief in Contemporary America." *Mortality* 7, no. 1 (2002): 63–82.

————. "Spontaneous Memorials and Contemporary Modes of Mourning in America." *Material Religion: The Journal of Objects, Art and Belief* 2, no. 3 (2006): 294–319.

————. *Memorial Mania: Public Feeling in America.* Chicago: University of Chicago Press, 2010.

Dunn, Jennifer L. "Vocabularies of Victimization: Toward Explaining the Deviant Victim." *Deviant Behavior* 31, no. 2 (2010): 159–183.

Foote, C., and A. Frank. "Foucault and Therapy: The Discipline of Grief." In *Reading Foucault for Social Work*, ed. A. Chambon, A. Irving, and L. Epstein, 157–187. New York: Columbia University Press, 1999.

Foucault, Michel. *The History of Sexuality.* Vol. 1. London: Penguin, 1978.

Galliher, John F., Larry W. Koch, David Patrick Keys, and Teresa J. Guess. *America without the Death Penalty: States Leading the Way.* Boston: Northeastern University Press, 2002.

Gamson, William A. *Talking Politics.* Cambridge: Cambridge University Press, 1992.

Goodwin, Michael L. "An Eyeful for an Eye—An Argument against Allowing the Families of Murder Victims to View Executions." *Brandeis Journal of Family Law* 36 (1997): 585.

Haines, Herbert. "Flawed Executions, the Anti–Death Penalty Movement, and the Politics of Capital Punishment." *Social Problems* 39 (1992): 301–314.

————. *Against Capital Punishment: The Anti–Death Penalty Movement in America, 1972–1994.* New York: Oxford University Press, 1996.

Haney, Craig, and Susan Greene. "Capital Constructions: Newspaper Reporting in Death Penalty Cases." *Analyses of Social Issues and Public Policy* 4, no. 1 (2004): 129–151.

Henderson, Lynne. "Co-opting Compassion: The Federal Victims' Rights Amendment." *St. Thomas Law Review* 10, no. 3 (1998): 579–606.

Hilgartner, Stephen, and Charles L. Bosk. "The Rise and Fall of Social Problems." *American Journal of Sociology* 94 (1988): 53–78.

Hochschild, Arlene. "Emotion Work, Feeling Rules, and Social Structure." *American Journal of Sociology* 85 (1979): 551–575.

————. *The Managed Heart: The Commercialization of Human Feeling.* Berkeley: University of California Press, 1983.

Holstein, James A., and Gale Miller. *Reconsidering Social Constructionism.* Hawthorne, NY: Aldine de Gruyter, 1993.

Horowitz, M. J., B. Siegel, A. Holen, G. Bonanno, C. Milbrath, and C. Stinson. "Diagnostic Criteria for Complicated Grief Disorders." *American Journal of Psychiatry* 154, no. 7 (1997): 904–911.

Horwitz, A. V. "Transforming Normality into Pathology: The DSM and the Outcomes of Stressful Social Arrangements." *Journal of Health and Social Behavior* 48 (2007): 211–222.

Ibarra, Peter R., and John I. Kitsuse. "Vernacular Constituents of Moral Discourse." In *Reconsidering Social Constructionism*, ed. James A. Holstein and Gale Miller, 25–58. Hawthorne, NY: Aldine de Gruyter, 1993.

Illouz, Eva. *Saving the Modern Soul: Therapy, Emotions, and the Culture of Self-Help.* Berkeley: University of California Press, 2008.

Jost, J. T., J. Glaser, A. W. Kruglanski, and F. Sulloway. "Political Conservatism as Motivated Social Cognition." *Psychological Bulletin* 129 (2003): 339–375.

Kanwar, Vik. "Capital Punishment as 'Closure': The Limits of a Victim-Centered Jurisprudence." *New York University Review of Law and Social Change* 27, no. 2–3 (2001): 215–255.

Kay, Judith W. "Murder Victims' Families for Reconciliation." In *Handbook of Restorative Justice*, ed. Dennis Sullivan and Larry Tifft, 230–245. London: Routledge, 2006.

King, L. A., and K. N. Miner. "Writing about the Perceived Benefits of Traumatic Events: Implications for Physical Health." *Personality and Social Psychology Bulletin* 26 (2000): 220–230.

King, Rachael. "Why a Victims' Rights Constitutional Amendment Is a Bad Idea: Practical Experiences from Crime Victims." *University of Cincinnati Law Review* 68, no. 2 (2000): 357–402.

Kirchmeier, Jeffrey L. "Another Place beyond Here: The Death Penalty Moratorium Movement in the United States." *University of Colorado Law Review* 73 (2002): 1.

Klass, Dennis, Phyllis R. Silverman, and Steven L. Nickman. *Continuing Bonds: New Understandings of Grief.* Washington, DC: Taylor and Francis, 1996.

Kruglanski, A., and D. Webster. "Motivated Closing of the Mind: Seizing and Freezing." *Psychological Review* 103 (1996): 263–283.

Kübler-Ross, Elisabeth. *On Death and Dying.* London: Routledge, 1973.

Kutchins, Herb, and Stuart Kirk. *Making Us Crazy: DSM: The Psychiatric Bible and the Creation of Mental Disorder.* New York: Simon and Schuster, 1997.

Laderman, Gary M. *Rest in Peace: A Cultural History of Death and the Funeral Home in Twentieth-Century America.* New York: Oxford University Press, 2003.

———. "Funeral Industry." *Encyclopedia of Death and Dying.* Deathreference.com. http://www.deathreference.com/En-Gh/Funeral-Industry.html.

Lifton, Robert Jay, and Greg Mitchell. *Who Owns Death? Capital Punishment, the American Conscience, and the End of Executions.* New York: William Morrow, 2000.

Loseke, Donileen R. "Constructing Conditions, People, Morality, and Emotion: Expanding the Agenda of Constructionism." In *Constructionist Controversies: Issues in Social Problems Theory*, ed. Gale Miller and James A. Holstein, 207–216. Hawthorne, NY: Aldine de Gruyter, 1993.

———. "Ethos, Pathos, and Social Problems: Reflections on Formula Narratives." In *Perspectives on Social Problems*, ed. James A. Holstein and Gale Miller, 12:41–54. Greenwich, CT: JAI, 2000.

Lowney, Kathleen S. *Baring Our Souls: TV Talk Shows and the Religion of Recovery.* Hawthorne, NY: Aldine de Gruyter, 1999.

Lynch, Mona. "Capital Punishment as Moral Imperative: Pro-Death-Penalty Discourse on the Internet." *Punishment and Society* 4, no. 2 (2002): 213–236.

Madeira, Jody Lynee. "'Why Rebottle the Genie?' Capitalizing on Closure in Death Penalty Proceedings." Indiana Legal Studies Research Paper 127 (2009). http://ssrn.com/abstract=1347844.

Mann, Michael. "The 'CSI Effect': Better Jurors through Television and Science?" *Buffalo Public Interest Law Journal* 24 (2005): 211–237.

Mendonca, Kylie. "The Business of the Beyond." *San Luis Obispo County's News and Entertainment Weekly,* October 24, 2007. http://www.newtimesslo.com/archives/.

Mitchell, Katharyne. "Monuments, Memorials, and the Politics of Memory." *Urban Geography* 24 (2003): 442–459.

Monahan, Brian. *The Shock of the News: Media Coverage and the Making of 9/11.* New York: New York University Press, 2010.

Mosteller, Robert P. "Victim Impact Evidence: Hard to Find the Real Rules." *Cornell Law Review* 88, no. 2 (2003): 543–554.

Nemetz, P. N., E. Tanglos, L. P. Sands, W. P. Fisher Jr., W. P. Newman III, and E. C. Burton. "Attitudes toward the Autopsy—An 8-State Survey." *Medscape General Medicine* 8, no. 3 (2006): 80.

Pals, J. L. "Narrative Identity Processing of Difficult Life Experiences: Pathways of Personality Development and Positive Self-Transformation in Adulthood." *Journal of Personality* 74 (2006): 1079–1110.

Papke, David Ray. "The American Courtroom Trial: Pop Culture, Courthouse Realities, and the Dream World of Justice." *South Texas Law Review* 40, no. 4 (1999): 919–933.

Pearl, Matthew. "Dante and the Death Penalty: How Capital Punishment Fails Its Audience." *Legal Affairs* (January 2003). http://www.legalaffairs.org/issues/January-February-2003/review_pearl_janfeb2003.msp.

Radelet, Michael L., and Hugo Adam Bedau. "The Execution of the Innocent." *Law and Contemporary Problems* 61 (1998): 105–124.

Rapping, Elayne. "Television, Melodrama, and the Rise of the Victims' Rights Movement." *New York Law School Legal Review* 43 (2000): 665.

Roland, David L. "Progress in the Victim Reform Movement: No Longer the 'Forgotten Victim.'" *Pepperdine Law Review* 17 (1989): 35–58.

Sarat, Austin. "Innocence, Error, and the 'New Abolitionism': A Commentary." *Criminology and Public Policy* 4, no. 1 (2005): 45–54.

Savage, Kirk. *Monument Wars: Washington D.C., the National Mall, and the Transformation of the Memorial Landscape.* Berkeley: University of California Press, 2009.

Shapiro, Bruce. "Victims' Rights—and Wrongs." Salon.com. http://www.salon.com/june97/news/news970613.html.

Sheffer, Susannah, Kate Lowenstein, and Renny Cushing. *Not in Our Name: Murder Victims' Families Speak Out against the Death Penalty.* Cambridge, MA: Murder Victims' Families for Reconciliation, 2003.

Shojania, K. G., and E. C. Burton. "The Vanishing Nonforensic Autopsy." *New England Journal of Medicine* 358, no. 9 (2008): 873–875.

Skitka, Linda J., Christopher W. Bauman, and Elizabeth Mullen. "Political Tolerance and Coming to Psychological Closure Following the September 11, 2001, Terrorist Attacks: An Integrative Approach." *Personality and Social Psychology Bulletin* 30, no. 6 (2004): 743–756.

Snow, David A., and Robert D. Benford. "Ideology, Frame Resonance, and Participant Mobilization." In *From Structure to Action: Social Movement Participation across Cultures,* ed. Bert Klandermans, Hanspeter Kriesi, and Sidney Tarrow, 197–217. Greenwich, CT: JAI, 1988.

Spector, Malcolm, and John I. Kitsuse. *Constructing Social Problems*. Hawthorne, NY: Aldine de Gruyter, 1987.

Strauss, Anselm, and Juliet Corbin. *Basics of Qualitative Research*. 2nd ed. Thousand Oaks, CA: Sage, 1998.

Sturken, Marita. *Tourists of History: Memory, Kitsch, and Consumerism from Oklahoma City to Ground Zero*. Durham, NC: Duke University Press, 2007.

Swidler, Ann. "Culture in Action." *American Sociological Review* 51 (1986): 273–286.

———. "Cultural Power and Social Movements." In *Social Movements and Culture*, ed. Hank Johnston and Bert Klandermans, 25–40. Minneapolis: University of Minnesota Press, 1995.

Talbert, Philip. "The Relevance of Victim Impact Statements to the Criminal Sentencing Decision." *U.C.L.A. Law Review* 36 (1988): 199–232.

Tenenboim Weinblatt, Keren. "Fighting for the Story's Life: Nonclosure in Journalistic Narrative." Paper presented at the annual meeting of the International Communication Association, Dresden, Germany, June 16, 2006.

Tice, D. M., and R. F. Baumeister. "Controlling Anger: Self-Induced Emotion Change." In *Handbook of Mental Control*, ed. D. M. Wegner and J. Pennebaker, 393–409. Englewood Cliffs, NJ: Prentice Hall, 1993.

Timmermans, Stefan. *Postmortem*. Chicago: University of Chicago Press, 2007.

Tyler, Tom R. "Viewing CSI and the Threshold of Guilt: Managing Truth and Justice in Reality and Fiction," *Yale Law Journal* 115 (2006): 1051–1085.

Unnever, James D., and Francis T. Cullin. "Executing the Innocent and Support for Capital Punishment: Implications for Public Policy." *Criminology and Public Policy* 4, no. 1 (2005): 3–32.

Walter, Tony. *On Bereavement: The Culture of Grief*. Maidenhead, UK: Open University Press, 1999.

———. "What Is Complicated Grief? A Social Constructionist Perspective." *Omega* 52, no.1 (2006): 71–79.

Webster, Donna M., and Arie W. Kruglanski. "Individual Differences in Need for Cognitive Closure." *Journal of Personality and Social Psychology* 67, no. 6 (1994): 1049–1062.

Winick, Bruce J. "The Jurisprudence of Therapeutic Jurisprudence." *Psychology, Public Policy, and Law* 3, no. 1 (1997): 184–206.

Worden, William. *Grief Counseling and Grief Therapy*. 3rd ed. New York: Spring, 1983.

Yoshimura, Stephen. "Goals and Emotional Outcomes of Revenge Activities in Interpersonal Relationships." *Journal of Social and Personal Relationships* 24, no. 1 (2007): 87–98.

Zimring, Franklin. *The Contradictions of American Capital Punishment*. New York: Oxford University Press, 2003.

Zunno, Kathryn. "*United States v. Kincade* and the Constitutionality of the Federal DNA Act: Why We'll Need a New Pair of Genes to Wear Down the Slippery Slope." *St. John's Law Review* 79 (2005): 769–821.

Index

Nancy Berns is an Associate Professor of Sociology at Drake University in Des Moines. Her teaching and research interests are in areas of grief, death, violence, justice, and social constructionism. She is the author of *Framing the Victim: Domestic Violence, Media and Social Problems*. Visit her online at www.nancyberns.com.